The White Masai

Corinne Hofmann

The White Masai

My Exotic Tale of Love and Adventure

Translated from the German
by Peter Millar

Amistad
An Imprint of HarperCollins*Publishers*

First Amistad paperback edition published 2007.

The Library of Congress has cataloged the hardcover edition as follows:

Hofmann, Corinne.
[Die Weisse Massai. English]
The white Masai / by Corinne Hofmann ; translated from the German by
Peter Millar.—4th ed.
p. cm.
This translation originally published: London: Bliss, 2005.
ISBN-13: 978-0-06-113152-3
ISBN-10: 0-06-113152-0
1. Hofmann, Corinne. 2. Women, White—Kenya—Biography.
3. Masai (African people)—Biography. I. Title.

DT433.545.M33H59 2006
305.896'5—dc22

2006042747

ISBN: 978-0-06-113153-0 (pbk.)
ISBN-10: 0-06-113153-9

07 08 09 10 11 BVG/RRD 10 9 8 7 6 5 4 3 2 1

For Napirai

I would like to thank all my friends who helped me while I was writing this, in particular: Hanny Stark, who got me writing the book in the first place, and Anneliese Dubacher, who took great pains to type up my handwritten manuscript on her computer.

Translator's Note

Corinne and Lketinga communicated with each other in what she calls their "special language," essentially a form of broken English, which neither spoke fluently, augmented by sign language and a very few phrases in the Samburu language, Maa. Throughout the book Corinne occasionally includes a few snatches of conversation in this basic rather stilted English. Rather than improve these I have left them in the original. When she reverts to normal, idiomatic German, I have, however, of course, used normal, idiomatic English.

The White Masai

Touchdown

Wonderful warm tropical air embraces us the minute we land at Mombasa Airport, and already I feel in my bones that this is my country: I'm going to be at home here. The extraordinary atmosphere works its magic only on me, however. My boyfriend Marco's comment is more succinct: "This place stinks!"

After customs control a safari bus takes us to our hotel. Mombasa is on a peninsula, and we have to take a ferry across a river to the southern bank. It's hot. We sit in the bus, gawking. Right now I have no idea that in three days' time this ferry will change my entire life, turn it upside down.

On the other side of the river we drive for another hour along rural roads through little settlements. Most women sitting outside their simple huts seem to be Muslims, wrapped up in black robes. At long last we reach our hotel, the Africana Sea Lodge. It's a modern but traditional African-style development, our accommodation a little round house, cute and cozy. Our first visit to the beach only amplifies my overwhelming impression: this is the most beautiful country I have ever visited. I could live here.

Two days later we've settled in and are ready to set off on the public bus to Mombasa, taking the Likoni ferry over for a spot of sightseeing. A Rasta runs past us, and I hear the whispered words: "Hashish, marijuana." Marco nods and says in English: "Yes, yes, where we can make a deal?" After a quick conversation we're supposed to follow him. "Leave it, Marco, it's too dangerous!" I say, but he pays no attention. When we find ourselves in a deserted, dilapidated district, I want to call it off, but the man tells us to wait for him and disappears. I'm uneasy, and eventually

Marco agrees we should go. We get out just in time before the Rasta turns up with a policeman. I'm furious and lose it with Marco: "Now do you see what might have happened?"

By now it's late afternoon, time to go home. But which way is home? I have no idea how to get to the ferry, and Marco is no better. Our first big disagreement, and it takes forever until we eventually catch a glimpse of the ferry. Hundreds of people with crates and chickens and crammed-full cardboard boxes are packed between lines of waiting cars. And all of them want to board the two-story ferry.

At long last we get on board, and then the unimaginable happens. Marco says, "Corinne, look, over there, on the other side, that's a Masai!" "Where?" I ask, and look where he's pointing. And then it's as if I've been struck by lightning. A tall, dark brown, beautiful man lounging on the quayside looking at us, the only white people in this throng, with dark eyes. My God, he's beautiful, more beautiful than anyone I've ever seen.

He is wearing almost no clothes—just a short red loincloth—but lots of jewelry. On his forehead is a large mother-of-pearl button with lots of little bright pearls, the whole thing glittering. His long red hair has been braided into thin braids, and his face is painted with symbols that extend right down onto his chest beneath two long necklaces of colored pearls. On each wrist he wears several bracelets. His face is so elegantly proportioned that it could almost be that of a woman. But the way he holds himself, the proud look and wiry muscular build betray his un-doubted masculinity. I can't take my eyes off him; sitting there in the last rays of the sinking sun, he looks like a young god.

Five minutes from now, I think to myself, suddenly depressed, You'll never see him again. The ferry will dock and chaos will break loose, people piling off onto buses and disappearing in every conceivable direction. All of a sudden my heart feels like lead, and I find it hard to breathe. And next to me Marco, of all things, says: "We ought to watch out for that Masai, they steal from tourists." Right now I couldn't care less, all that's running through my mind is how I can make contact with this breathtakingly beautiful man. I don't speak any English, and just staring at him isn't going to get me anywhere.

The gangplank drops, and everybody starts squeezing between the cars already starting to drive off. All I can see of the Masai is his glistening back as he lithely vanishes amid the mass of ponderous heaving humanity. It's over, I think, on the brink of tears. Why I feel like that, I have no idea.

Once again terra firma is beneath our feet, and we push our way toward the buses. It's already dusk; in Kenya darkness falls within half an hour. In next to no time all the buses are jam-packed with people and parcels. We're standing there, clueless. Sure, we know the name of our hotel, but not which beach it is on. I prod Marco impatiently: "Go on, ask somebody!" Why don't I do it, he says, even though I've never been to Kenya before and don't speak English. I'm unhappy; my thoughts are with the Masai who has somehow lodged himself in my head.

In total darkness we stand there and argue. All the buses have gone, and then from behind us a deep voice says, "Hello!" We turn around simultaneously, and my heart skips a beat: it's "my" Masai! A full head taller than me, even though I'm almost six feet. He's looking at us and speaking a language that neither of us understands. My heart is palpitating, and I've gone weak at the knees. Marco meanwhile is trying to explain where we want to get to. "No problem," says the Masai, and he tells us to wait. For the next half hour I simply look at this beautiful human being. He hardly notices me, but Marco is getting annoyed: "What's got into you?" he wants to know. "I'm embarrassed the way you're staring so fixedly at this man. Pull yourself together, you're not yourself." The Masai stands beside us and doesn't say a word. I only know he's there by the silhouette of his long body and his smell, which is giving me an erotic charge.

All around the bus station there are little shops that look like a shanty town and all sell the same things: tea, sweets, vegetables, fruits, and lumps of meat hanging from hooks. People in ragged clothing stand around these little shacks, which are lit feebly by gas lamps. As the only white people, we stick out like sore thumbs.

"Let's go back to Mombasa and get a taxi. The Masai didn't understand what we wanted, and anyhow I don't trust him. Apart from anything else, I think you're bewitched by him," says Marco. But as far as I'm concerned, the fact that of all these black people he was the one to approach us is a happy omen.

A few minutes later a bus stops, and the Masai says, "Come, come!," swings on board, and saves us two seats. Is he going to get out again or come with us? I ask myself. To my relief, he sits himself down across the passageway, directly behind Marco. The bus sets off along a country road in complete darkness. Now and then, between the palms and shrubs, a fire glows, hinting at the presence of people. Night changes everything; we are completely disoriented. Marco thinks the journey is taking far too long and several times moves to get out. Only my imprecations and a few words from the Masai make him see that we have no alternative but to trust this stranger. I'm not in the least afraid; on the contrary, I could travel like this forever. It's the presence of my friend that's starting to annoy me. He sees everything so negatively, and on top of it all he's blocking my view! The thought occurs to me: What happens when we get to the hotel?

After an hour or more the moment I've been dreading arrives. The bus stops, and Marco says thank you and climbs out with obvious relief. I look at the Masai and, not finding any words to say, throw myself off the bus. It drives off, who knows where, maybe to Tanzania. For me the holiday is as good as over.

My thoughts return to me and Marco and the business. For nearly five years now I've been running an upmarket nearly new clothing shop in Biel with a special department for bridal wear. After a few teething problems the business is doing well, and I now employ three dressmakers. For twenty-seven years old, I've got myself an impressive standard of living.

I came to know Marco when there was carpentry work to be done in setting up the shop. He was polite, good fun; and since I had just arrived in Biel and didn't know anybody, I took him up on an invitation to dinner one night. Over time the relationship developed, and six months later we moved in together. Back in Biel people think of us as a "dream couple." We have lots of friends, and all of them are just waiting for a wedding date to be set. But I think of myself as a full-time businesswoman and am actively looking for a second shop, in Bern, twenty-five miles away. I hardly have time for thoughts of weddings or children. Anyway, Marco can't get very worked up about all my plans, probably because I earn a lot more than he does. That gets to him, and of late it's led to arguments.

And now, all of a sudden, this completely new experience! I try to understand exactly what's happening to me. My feelings for Marco have evaporated to the point that I hardly even notice him. The Masai has lodged himself in my brain. I can't eat. The hotel has excellent buffets, but I can't bring myself to force anything down. It's as if my intestines have tied themselves in knots. All day long I gaze along the beach or walk up and down it in the hope of catching a glimpse of him. Now and then I

see a few Masai, but they are all smaller and not nearly as beautiful. Marco
leaves me to it; he has no option. He's looking forward to going home and
thinks everything will return to normal then. But this country has turned
my life upside down, and nothing will ever be the same again.

Marco decides to go on a safari into the Masai-Mara. I'm not
particularly entranced by the idea because it means there's no chance of
finding my Masai again. But I agree to a two-day trip.

The safari is tiring, because it means taking buses far into the interior.
After several hours of traveling, Marco is already bored: "We didn't need
to go through all this just for a couple of elephants and lions we could
have seen at the zoo back home." I'm enjoying the journey. Soon we
reach the first Masai villages. The bus stops, and the driver asks if we want
to get out and see the huts and the people. "Of course," I say, and the other
safari fans look at me askance. The driver negotiates a price and we pile
out, clumping in white sneakers through the muddy clay, careful not to
tread in the cow pies that are everywhere. We have hardly reached the
huts, the *manyattas*, when we are surrounded by women with their throngs
of children pulling at our clothes and wanting to swap spears, cloth, or bits
of jewelry for almost any and everything we have.

The men meanwhile have been lured into the huts. I can't bring
myself to tramp through the mud another single step, so instead I pull
myself free from the pushy mob of women and storm off back to the
safari bus, followed by hundreds of flies. The other passengers hurry back
too and shout, "Let's go!" The driver smiles and says: "Now maybe you've
been warned about this tribe. They're the last uncivilized people in Kenya;
even the government has problems with them."

It stinks in the bus now, and the flies are an absolute plague. Marco
laughs and says: "Well, now you know where your pretty boy comes from
and how they live." Funnily enough, in those few minutes I hadn't even
thought of "my" Masai.

We drive on in silence, past great herds of elephants. In the afternoon
we arrive at a tourist hotel. It's almost incredible to be spending the night
in a luxury hotel in the middle of this semidesert. We get our rooms
straightaway and head for the shower. Hair, face, everything is sticky with
sweat. Then there's a lavish meal laid on, and after nearly five days fasting
I've almost got an appetite. The next morning, we're up at five to see the
lions and really do find three of the animals still asleep. Then it's time for

the long trek home. The closer we get to Mombasa, the more I feel strangely happy. One thing is clear to me now: with just one week left, I have to find my Masai again.

In the evening the hotel has a Masai-dance floor show with a jewelry sale afterward, and I am full of hope that I'll see him again. We're sitting in the front row as the warriors come in, some twenty men in all, small ones, tall ones, good-looking ones, ugly ones, but my Masai isn't among them. I am disappointed. Even so, I enjoy the show, and once again I smell this aroma they exude that distinguishes them from the other Africans.

Not far from the hotel there's supposed to be an open-air dance joint called the Bush Baby Disco, where the natives can go too. So I say to Marco: "Come on, let's find this disco place." He's not so keen because the hotel management warns that it might be risky, but I insist. We wander along the dark road for a bit until we spot a light and hear a few bars of rock music. We go in, and I like the place immediately. At last something that isn't just another sterile air-conditioned hotel disco, but a dance floor under the heavens with bars between palm trees. All around tourists and natives are leaning on the bars. There's a relaxed feel. We sit ourselves down at a table. Marco orders a beer, and I ask for a Coke. Then I get up and dance on my own, because Marco isn't keen on dancing.

Toward midnight a few Masai come in. I take a good look at them but recognize only a couple who were in the show at the hotel. Disappointed, I go back to the table. I make up my mind to come here every night for the rest of our stay, as it seems the only chance of finding my Masai again. Marco protests but doesn't want to sit in the hotel on his own, so every evening after dinner we set out for the Bush Baby Disco.

After the second evening, it's December 21 already; Marco has had enough of these little excursions. I promise him we'll go just one more time. As always we sit ourselves down at what has become our regular table under the palm trees. I decide to dance on my own in the middle of the couples, black and white. He has to come!

I'm already dripping with sweat when just after eleven the door opens, and it's him! My Masai! He leaves the heavy stick he's carrying with the doorman, walks quietly across to a table, and sits down with his back to me. My knees have gone weak; I can hardly stand. Sweat is flowing from every pore. I have to hold on to a pillar on the edge of the dance floor to stop myself from collapsing.

I'm wondering frantically what to do. I've waited days for this moment. As calmly as possible I go back to our table and say to Marco: "Oh, look, there's that Masai who helped us out. You should get him over to our table and buy him a beer to say thanks!" Marco turns around, and at the same time the Masai spots us. He waves and comes over to us of his own accord. "Hello, friends," he says, laughing and holding out his hand to us. It feels cool and supple.

He sits down next to Marco, directly opposite me. Why, oh why, can't I speak English! Marco tries a bit of conversation, but it soon becomes clear that the Masai doesn't speak much English either. We try to communicate with signs and gestures. He looks at Marco and then at me, and pointing at me says to him: "Your wife?" When Marcos goes "Yes, yes," I protest: "No, only boyfriend, no married!" The Masai doesn't understand. He asks if we have children. Again I tell him: "No, no! Not married!"

He's never been so close to me before. There's only the table between us, and I can ogle him to my heart's content. He is fascinatingly attractive with his jewelry and his long hair and his proud look! I would be happy for time to stand still. He asks Marco: "Why you not dance with your wife?" While Marco, turned toward the Masai, tries to tell him he prefers to drink beer, I seize the opportunity to make it clear to the Masai that I would like to dance with him. He looks at Marco and, seeing no reaction, agrees.

We dance, me European-style, him more sort of hopping up and down like in a tribal dance. Not a muscle moves in his face. I have no idea if I'm even remotely attractive to him. Strange and alien as this man is, he attracts me like a magnet. After two tracks there's a slow dance, and I want to press him to me. But instead I pull myself together and leave the floor in case I lose control.

Back at the table Marco's reaction is sharp: "Come along, Corinne, we're going back to the hotel. I'm tired." But I don't want to go. The Masai is gesticulating again to Marco. He wants to invite us, to take us tomorrow to where he lives and introduce us to his friends. I agree quickly before Marco can refuse. We agree to meet in front of the hotel.

I can't get to sleep all night, and by morning I know that it's all over between Marco and me. He looks at me quizzically, and all of a sudden it all comes out: "Marco, we can't go on. I don't know what's happened to me with this complete stranger, I only know that I feel something that's beyond reason." Marco puts his arm around me and says: "There, there, it'll all be all right, and when we get back to Switzerland everything will sort itself out." But I turn on him crossly: "I don't want to go back. I want to stay here in this beautiful country, with wonderful people and above all this mesmerizing Masai." Marco thinks I'm mad.

The next day, as agreed, we're standing in searing heat in front of the hotel. All of a sudden he appears on the other side of the street and comes over. He greets us briefly and says, "Come, come!," and we follow him. For some twenty minutes we plow through jungle and brushwood. Here and there monkeys, sometimes half as big as we are, spring through the trees. Once again I'm astounded by the Masai's way of walking; it's as if he hardly touches the earth, as if he hovers, although his feet are clad in heavy sandals with car-tire soles. In comparison, Marco and I are like elephants.

Then we see five round houses in a circle, just like at the hotel except much smaller, and instead of concrete they're made of piled-up stones plastered with clay. The roofs are of straw. In front of one little house sits a stocky woman with big breasts. The Masai introduces her as his friend Priscilla, and for the first time we find out the Masai's name: Lketinga.

Priscilla greets us warmly, and to our astonishment she speaks good English. "You like tea?" she asks. I thank her and accept. Marco says it's far too hot, he'd prefer a beer. But here that will have to remain just a wish. Priscilla fetches a little portable cookstove, sets it down by our feet, and we wait for the water to boil. We tell them about Switzerland, about our jobs, and we ask how long they've been living here. Priscilla has lived by the coast for ten years, but Lketinga is new; he arrived just a month ago, which is why he speaks hardly a word of English.

We take pictures, and every time I come close to Lketinga I feel physically drawn to him. I have to force myself not to touch him. We drink the tea, which is excellent but hot. Both of us almost burn our fingers on the enamel cups.

It begins to get dark quickly, and Marco says, "Come on. It's time for us to be making tracks." We say good-bye to Priscilla and exchange addresses, promising to write. With a heavy heart I trail behind Marco and Lketinga. Outside the hotel he asks, "Tomorrow Christmas, you come again to Bush Baby?" I beam and before Marco can answer, I say, "Yes!"

The next day is our second to last, and I've made up my mind to tell my Masai that, after the end of the holiday, I'm leaving Marco. Compared with what I feel for Lketinga, everything that I have felt up until now seems laughable. Somehow I have to make that clear to him tomorrow and tell him that soon I will be coming back on my own. Only for a moment does it cross my mind that I don't know what he might feel about me, but immediately I tell myself there is only one answer: he feels exactly the same!

Christmas Day. But with temperatures of 104 degrees in the shade, there is hardly much of a Christmasy atmosphere. I make myself as attractive as possible for the evening and put on my best holiday dress. At our table we order champagne as a celebration, but it's expensive and bad and served too warm. By ten o'clock Lketinga and his friends still haven't shown up. What if he just doesn't come today? Tomorrow is our last day, and the following one we're off to the airport at dawn. I stare at the door imploringly, willing him to come.

Then a Masai turns up. He looks around him and comes up to us hesitantly. "Hello," he says, and asks if we're the white people who've arranged to meet Lketinga. We nod, and I feel a lump in my throat and break out in perspiration. He tells us that during the afternoon Lketinga was on the beach, where natives are normally not allowed. Because of his hair and clothing, he was hassled by other blacks. As a proud warrior he defended himself and lashed out at his tormentors with his *rungu,* the heavy stick I had seen him carrying. The beach police had arrested him without listening to his side of the story because they couldn't speak his language, and now he is in jail somewhere, either on the southern or northern coast of Mombasa. This man is here to tell us that and to wish us from Lketinga a safe journey home.

Marco translates, and as I take in what has happened, my world falls apart. It takes a huge effort to hold back the tears of my disappointment. I plead with Marco: "Ask him what we can do, we've only got one more day here!" He replies coldly: "That's the way things are here. There's nothing we can do, and I'll be glad to get home." I'm not giving up. "Edy"—that is the Masai's name—"can we find him?" Yes, he will go around to the other Masai this evening and get some money together and tomorrow morning at ten he will set out to try to find him. It will be difficult because nobody knows which of the five jails he's been taken to.

I ask Marco if we can go too; the man had helped us, after all. After a lot of hemming and hawing he finally agrees, and we arrange to meet Edy at ten outside the hotel. I can't sleep all night. I still don't know what's the matter with me, but I know that I want to, have to see Lketinga again before I go back to Switzerland.

The Search Party

Marco changed his mind and decided to stay at the hotel. He keeps trying to persuade me not to go ahead with this, but no well-meant advice has a chance against the force that's driving me. So I leave him behind with a promise to be back by two P.M. Edy and I head for Mombasa in a *matatu;* it's the first time I've used this type of taxi. It's a small bus with about eight seats, but when it stops, there are already thirteen people on board, jammed between their luggage. The ticket inspector hangs on outside. I'm staring speechless into the crush. "Go, go in!" says Edy, and I climb over bags and legs, hanging on bent double for fear of falling on people at corners.

Thank God we get out after just nine miles. We're in Ukunda, the first big village that has a jail. We go in together. But before my foot has even crossed the threshold, a beefy character stops us. I throw Edy a questioning look. He negotiates. I'm told to stay where I am. After several minutes the big man opens a door behind him. Standing in the bright sunshine, looking into the darkness, I can make out next to nothing. But there's such a stink coming out that a wave of nausea hits me. The hefty guy shouts something into this dark hole, and a few seconds later a completely wild-looking individual emerges, apparently a Masai but without any of the usual tribal ornaments. I shake my head in horror and ask Edy, "Is he the only Masai here?" Apparently so. The prisoner is thrown back in with the others huddled on the floor. We turn and leave. Edy says: "Come on, we'll take a *matatu*—they're faster than the big buses—and look in Mombasa."

We take the Likoni ferry again and then the bus to the edge of the city, where there's another jail. It's much bigger than the last one. Here too

I get harsh looks because I'm white. The man behind the barrier pays no attention to us, just leafs uninterestedly through his newspaper, leaving us at a loss what to do. I nudge Edy: "Go on, ask!" But nothing happens until Edy tells me I should slip the man a few Kenyan shillings. He doesn't say how many. I've never had to bribe anybody in my life before. I set down a hundred Kenyan shillings, which is about ten Swiss francs. He trousers the cash almost without noticing it and at long last looks up at us. No, no Masai called Lketinga has been brought in recently. There are two Masai here, but both are much smaller than the man we're describing. I still want to see them; after all, he might be wrong, and he's already got his money. He gives me a stern look but gets up and opens a door.

I am shocked by what I see: a crowd of people crammed together in a room without windows, some sitting on cardboard boxes, others on newspapers or on the concrete floor. Blinded by the sudden light, they hold their hands up to their eyes. Only a narrow space to walk has been left between these cowering human beings and in a minute I see why; a prison worker appears and throws a bucket of "food" in, directly onto the concrete. Unbelievable: even pigs are treated better. At the word "Masai" two of them come forward, but neither is Lketinga. I'm losing hope. What on earth do I expect when I find him?

We drive into the city center, take another *matatu,* and rattle along for an hour toward the northern coast. Edy tries to calm me down, saying he must be here. But we don't even get as far as the door. An armed policeman asks what we want. Edy tells him, and he shakes his head, says they haven't had anyone new brought in for two days. We leave. By now, I'm despairing.

Edy says it's already late and if I want to be back by two, we have to hurry. But I don't want to go back to the hotel. I only have today left to find Lketinga. Edy suggests we try the first jail again because inmates sometimes get moved from place to place. So in the sweltering heat we drive back toward Mombasa.

Crossing the river, our ferryboat passes another and I notice there are almost no people on board, just vehicles. One in particular stands out: a bright green van with barred windows. Edy says it's the prison transport van. I feel sick at the thought of the poor people inside but think no more of it. I'm tired, thirsty, and sweaty all over. By two-thirty, we're back in Ukunda.

There's a new guard outside the jail now, and he's a lot friendlier. Edy explains once again who we're looking for, and there's a lively discussion of which I understand nothing. "Edy, what's going on?" He tells me that barely an hour ago Lketinga was taken off to the north coast, where we've just come from. He had been in Kwale, then was here for a short while, and now is on his way to the jail where he will be kept until standing trial.

I'm starting to go mad. All morning we've been charging around and not half an hour ago he went right past us in the green prison van. Edy looks at me helplessly. We ought to get back to the hotel, he says, and tomorrow he'll try again, now that he knows where Lketinga is. I can give him the money, and he'll bail him out.

I need only a second to decide: I ask Edy to go back to the north coast with me. He's not exactly delighted but agrees to come along. We travel the whole way back in silence, and the whole time I'm asking myself: Corinne, why are you doing this? What on earth do I want to say to Lketinga? I have no idea, there's just this force driving me.

Just before six we're back at the jail on the north side. The same armed man is still standing there. He recognizes us and tells us Lketinga was brought in two and a half hours ago. I perk up immediately. Edy tells him we want to get the Masai out, but the guard shakes his head and says there's no way that's going to happen before New Year because the prisoner hasn't been processed yet and the jail's governor is on holiday until then.

I'd thought of everything except that. Even money won't get Lketinga out. By pleading and wheedling, I manage to get the guard to understand that I'm leaving tomorrow and to let me see Lketinga for just ten minutes. And the next thing he comes strolling into the courtyard with a beaming smile. I'm horrified. His jewelry is all gone, his hair is tied up under a dirty cloth, and he smells appallingly. Even so, he seems happy to see us and surprised only that I'm here without Marco. I could scream. He understands nothing. I tell him that we're flying home tomorrow but that I'll be back as soon as I can. I write my address down and ask him for his. Hesitantly and with some difficulty he writes his name and a PO box number. I manage to give him money, and then the warder takes him away again. As he's going, he turns around, says thank you, and sends his best wishes to Marco.

We head back, waiting for a bus as the darkness falls. Only now do I realize how exhausted I am and suddenly burst into uncontrollable sobbing. Everybody in the crammed *matatu* stares at the wailing white woman with the Masai, but I couldn't care less: I want to die.

While we're waiting for the ferry, Edy says: "No bus, no *matatu* to Diani Beach." At first I think I haven't heard him right. "After eight P.M. no more public buses to the hotel." I don't believe it! We're standing there in the dark, by the ferry, and the other side is as far as we can get. I wander between the waiting cars, looking for white people inside. There are two returning safari buses. I knock on the window and ask if they can give me a lift. The driver says no, he's not allowed to take any strangers. The occupants are Indian and in any case all the seats are full. At the last minute a car pulls onto the ramp, and I have a stroke of luck. Sitting in it are two Italian nuns. I explain my situation to them, and under the circumstances they agree to take Edy and me back to the hotel.

For the next three quarters of an hour, as we drive through the darkness, I start to worry about Marco: how he's going to react. I would understand if he gave me a clip around the ear; I deserve it. I almost hope he'll do something like that; that'll bring me to my senses. I still don't understand what's got into me, why I seem to have lost control of my capacity for reason. The only thing I know is that I'm more tired than I've ever been in my life, and for the first time I feel afraid, of Marco and of myself.

At the hotel I say good-bye to Edy, and a few minutes later I'm standing in front of Marco. He looks at me sadly. No shouting, no big words, just this look. I throw my arms around him and burst into tears again. Marco takes me into our little hut and tries to calm me down. I had been prepared for anything except such a loving welcome. He just says: "It's all okay, Corinne. I'm just glad you're still alive. I was about to go to the police and make a missing person report. I had almost given up hope of ever seeing you again. Can I get you something to eat?" Without waiting for an answer he goes out and comes back with a plate piled high. It looks delicious, and for his sake I eat as much as I can. He waits until we've finished before he asks: "Well, did you at least find him?" "Yes," I say, and tell him everything. He looks at me and says: "You're crazy but strong-willed. When you want something, you don't give up. Why can't I take the place of this Masai?" The answer is that I don't know. I can't explain, even to myself, what secret magic there is about this man. If anyone had told me two weeks ago I would fall in love with a Masai warrior, I would have laughed out loud. Now my life has been thrown into chaos.

On the flight home, Marco asks: "What's going to happen to us now, Corinne? It's up to you." It hurts to make Marco understand how confused I feel. "I'll find myself another apartment as soon as possible, even though it won't be for very long. I'm going back to Kenya. Maybe for good," I reply. Marco just shakes his head sadly.

A Long Six Months

It takes two months before I find a new apartment outside Biel. Moving is easy: I take only my clothes and a few personal items, the rest I leave to Marco. The hardest thing is leaving my two cats, but seeing as I'm leaving anyhow, it's the only solution. I keep working at the shop but with less enthusiasm because Kenya is on my mind all the time. I get hold of everything I can find about the country, including its music. All day long in the shop I listen to Swahili songs. My customers notice I'm not as attentive as I used to be, but I can't or won't explain.

Every day I wait for the post and then finally, after three months, I get a letter. Not from Lketinga, but from Priscilla. She tells me that Lketinga was let out of prison three days after we left. That same day I write to the address I got from Lketinga and tell him of my plan to return to Kenya in June or July, alone this time.

Another month crawls by, and finally I get a letter from Lketinga. He thanks me for my help and says he'd be happy if I were to visit his country again. That same day I charge into a travel agent's and book three weeks in July at the same hotel.

There's nothing to do now but wait. Time seems to stand still; days crawl one after another. Of the friends Marco and I had in common, there's only one left who still calls me from time to time, and we meet for a glass of wine. At least he seems to understand me. The departure day draws steadily closer, and I get restless because only Priscilla answers my letters. And then my resolve steels itself again, and I am as convinced as ever that this man is all I need to be happy.

In the meantime I have learned to make myself more or less understood in English. My friend Jelly gives me daily lessons. With three weeks still to go, my little brother Eric and Jelly, who's going out with him, decide to come with me. I've got through the longest six months of my life. We fly out.

The Reunion

July 1987. After more than nine hours' flying time we land in Mombasa. We plunge into the same heat, the same incredible atmosphere. Only this time, everything is familiar: Mombasa, the ferry, the long bus journey to the hotel.

I can hardly wait. Will he be there, or won't he? We're standing in reception, and immediately there's a "Hello!" behind me. We turn around, and there he is! He laughs and comes up to me, beaming. All at once the six months are swept away. I nudge him and say, "Jelly, Eric, here he is: Lketinga!" My brother fiddles embarrassedly in his pocket, but my friend Jelly smiles and gives him her hand. I introduce them, but for the moment I dare no more than a handshake myself.

In the general chaos we settle into our little beachside cabana while Lketinga waits at the bar. At last I can ask Jelly, "Well, what do you think of him?" She's searching for words and says, "He's certainly something special; perhaps I'll have to get used to him. Right now he seems a bit foreign and wild-looking." My brother has no opinion. The obsession is mine and mine alone, I think somewhat disappointedly.

I change and go to the bar. Lketinga's sitting there with Edy. I greet him happily too. And then we try to exchange stories. I learn from Lketinga that after he was released he went back to his tribe and only came back to Mombasa a week ago. He heard from Priscilla that I was coming back. A special allowance had been made so that he could greet us in the hotel because blacks who don't work there are normally not allowed in.

It occurs to me that without Edy's help I can say hardly anything to Lketinga. My English is still pretty basic, and Lketinga knows barely a dozen words. For a while we just sit on the beach beaming smiles at each other, while Eric and Jelly hang around the pool or in the room. Eventually it gets toward evening, and I'm wondering what we do next. We can't stay much longer in the hotel, and, apart from our initial handshake, nothing has happened between us. It's hard when you've waited six months to see a man; in my mind's eye I'd lain in this man's arms often, imagined kisses and the wildest of nights. Now when he's here next to me, I'm afraid even to touch his brown arm. I just give in to the happiness of having him next to me.

Eric and Jelly are off to bed, both tired from the long journey and the insane heat. Lketinga and I steal away to the Bush Baby Disco. I feel like a princess with my prince. We sit down at a table and watch the dancers. He laughs all the time. Even if we can hardly have a conversation, we sit there together and enjoy the music. The atmosphere and his presence give me goose bumps. I want to stroke his face and know what it's like to kiss him. When at long last a slow record comes on, I grab his hands and point to the dance floor. He gets up and stands there helplessly, doing nothing.

Then suddenly we take hold of each other and start moving to the rhythm of the music. All the tension in me drains away. My whole body is shivering, but this time I can hold him tight. It seems as if time is standing still, and my desire for this man, suppressed for six long months, comes back to life. I don't dare lift my head and look at him. What will he think of me? I know so little about him! Only when the tempo of the music changes do we go back to our seats, and I notice that we were the only ones on the floor. I imagine I can feel dozens of pairs of eyes following us.

We sit together a little longer, then get up to go. It's long past midnight when he brings me back to the hotel. At the entrance we look in each other's eyes, and I think I see a changed expression in his. In these wild eyes I think I recognize astonishment and excitement. At long last I dare to come close to his beautiful mouth and softly touch my lips to his. All of a sudden I feel his whole body go rigid, and he's staring at me in horror.

"What you do?" he asks and takes a step backward. Brought down to earth with a bang I stand there, understanding nothing; then, suddenly ashamed, I turn around and run into the hotel distraught. In bed I'm overcome by a fit of crying, as if the whole world's falling apart around me. There's only one thing going through my mind: that I desire him to the point of obsession and he obviously feels nothing for me. At some point, eventually, I fall asleep.

I wake late, long after breakfast. I don't care because I don't feel the slightest hunger. The way I look at the moment, I'm not fit to be seen, so I put on a pair of sunglasses and crawl down to the pool where my brother is romping around with Jelly like a dog with two tails.

I lie down on the beach, stare up at the blue sky, and ask myself: Was that it? Were my perceptions so totally wrong? No, something inside me screams. How could I have had the strength to break up with Marco, to shun sexual relations with any man for six months, if it weren't for that man?

Suddenly I sense a shadow fall over me and feel a soft touch on my arm. I open my eyes and look straight into that man's handsome face. He gives me his beaming smile and says, "Hello!" I'm glad I've got my sunglasses on. He spends ages looking at me as if he's studying my face. After a while he asks after Eric and Jelly and rather awkwardly tells me we're invited to tea with Priscilla this afternoon. Lying on my back I look up into two soft, hopeful-looking eyes. When I don't immediately reply, his expression changes, his eyes get darker and a proud glimmer shines in them. I struggle with myself and then ask what time we should come.

Eric and Jelly agree, so at the arranged time we're waiting at the hotel entrance. After about ten minutes an overfilled *matatu* stops and two long legs emerge, followed by Lketinga's long body. He's brought Edy with him. I know the way to Priscilla's from my first visit; my brother casts somewhat skeptical glances at the apes playing and eating along the route.

Seeing Priscilla again is great. She gets her little portable cookstove out and makes tea. While we're waiting, the three of them talk together, leaving us looking on, not understanding anything. Every now and then someone laughs, and I get the impression that I'm being talked about. We leave after about two hours, and Priscilla tells me I'm welcome to come with Lketinga anytime.

Although I've paid for two more weeks at the hotel, at Priscilla's invitation I decide to move out and lodge with her. I've had enough of eating without him and going to the disco. The hotel management warns me that I'll end up without any money or clothes. Even my brother is more than skeptical, but he still helps me to carry all my stuff into the bush. Lketinga carries my big traveling bag and seems happy.

Priscilla has cleared out her hut and moved in with a friend. When it gets dark and we can no longer hold off the moment of physical contact, I sit down on the narrow little cot and wait with pounding heart for the minute I have longed for. Lketinga sits down beside me, and all I can see is the mother-of-pearl button on his forehead, the ivory rings in his ears, and the whites of his eyes. All of a sudden everything happens at once. Lketinga presses me down onto the cot, and already I can feel his erection. Before I can even make up my mind whether or not my body is ready for this, I feel a pain, hear strange noises, and it's all over. I feel like bursting into tears of disappointment. This was not at all what I had expected. It's only now that I realize that this is someone from a completely alien culture. But my thoughts don't get any further than that when suddenly the whole thing happens again. It happens again several times during the night; and after the third or fourth time we "do it," I give up trying to use kisses or caresses to prolong the experience. Lketinga doesn't seem to like that.

At long last day breaks, and I wait for Priscilla to knock on the door. It's around seven before I hear noises outside. I peek out and find a basin full of water in front of the door. I bring it in and wash myself thoroughly; I'm covered in red marks from Lketinga's body paint.

He's still asleep when I go to see Priscilla. She's made tea and offers me some. When she asks me how my first night in a real African home was, it all comes tumbling out. Obviously embarrassed, she listens quietly and then says: "Corinne, we're not the same as white people. Go back to Marco. Come to Kenya for holidays, not to find a partner for life." She has learned that white men treat their women well, even at night. Masai men are different; what I have just experienced is normal. Masai don't kiss. The mouth is for eating, and kissing—she makes a face—is contemptible. A man never touches a woman below the stomach, and a woman is not supposed to touch a man's penis. A man's hair and face are also taboo.

I don't know whether to laugh or cry. I desire this wonderful man, but I'm not allowed to touch him. All of a sudden I remember the dreadful scene when I kissed him that first time, and I realize that what I'm hearing is the truth.

Priscilla hasn't looked at me while we've been talking, and I realize too that it must be hard for her to talk about things like this. Everything is rushing through my mind, and I'm not sure if I've understood it all properly. The night's experiences force themselves into the back of my mind, and the only thing I know is that I want this man and nobody else. I love him, and beyond that everything else can be dealt with, I tell myself.

Later on we take an overcrowded *matatu* to Ukunda, the next biggest village, where we meet more Masai sitting around in a native teahouse. It's nothing more than a few planks nailed together, a roof, a long table, and a few stools. The tea is brewed in a white pot hung over the fire. We sit down together, and people look me over with an eye that's partly critical, partly curious. And then they're all talking at once, obviously about me. I look each of them over in turn, and none of them looks as handsome or as peaceful as Lketinga.

We sit there for what seems like hours, but I don't mind not understanding anything. Lketinga is touchingly attentive, continuously getting me something to drink and then fetching a platter of meat: little pieces of goat that I can hardly bring myself to swallow, they're so bloody and tough. Three is as much as I can manage without choking, and I indicate to Lketinga that he should finish it, but neither he nor any of the other men will take anything from my plate, even though it's obvious that they're hungry.

After half an hour they get up, and Lketinga tries to explain something to me using his hands and feet. The only thing I understand is that they all want to go and eat but that I can't come with them. I'm determined, however, that I should. "No! Big problem! You wait here," I hear. I watch them disappear behind a wall, followed minutes later by mountains of meat. After a while one Masai comes back. He looks like a man with a full stomach, and I ask him why I had to stay behind, but all he says is: "You wife, no lucky meat." Something else I'll have to ask Priscilla about.

We leave the teahouse and take the *matatu* back to the beach. When we get to the Africana Sea Lodge, we decide to get out and visit Jelly and Eric. We're stopped at the entrance, however, and I have to explain to the doorman that we just want to visit my brother and his girlfriend before he lets us in without saying a word. At the reception desk the hotel manager greets me with a smile and says in English: "So you will now come back into the hotel?" I say no and tell him I like it just fine in the bush. He shrugs his shoulders and says: "We'll see how long it lasts!"

We find Eric and Jelly at the pool. Eric comes up to me and says irritably: "About time you showed yourself." He asks if I slept well, which makes me laugh, and I reply: "Well, I've spent more comfortable nights, but I'm happy." Lketinga's standing there, and he laughs and says: "Eric, what's the problem?" A few white people in swimsuits stare at us. A couple of women stroll past noticeably slowly and gape openly at my beautiful Masai in his finery and freshly applied body paint. He pointedly ignores them, rather embarrassed at the sight of so much flesh.

We don't stay long; I have shopping to do—kerosene, toilet paper, and above all a flashlight. Last night I didn't need to go out in the middle of the night to find the bush toilet, but I might not always be so lucky. The toilet is outside the village, reached by a rickety chicken ladder six feet above the ground—a little hut made out of woven-together palm leaves with two boards for your feet and a hole in the middle.

We get everything in one shop, obviously where the hotel employees do their shopping, and for the first time I notice how cheap everything here is. Compared to what I'm used to, all my purchases—apart from the batteries for the flashlight—cost next to nothing.

A bit farther along there's another shack with the word "Meat" painted in red. I follow Lketinga inside. A hunk of goat carcass is hanging from a big hook fixed to the ceiling. Lketinga looks at me questioningly and says: "Very fresh! You take two pounds for you and Priscilla!" I shiver at the very thought of having to eat this meat, but even so I do as he says. The butcher takes an axe and chops off a rear leg, then with another two or three blows he measures out our piece and hangs the rest back up on the hook. He wraps it all up in newspaper, and we head back to the village.

Priscilla is really pleased to get the meat. She puts tea on and goes to get another little cooker from a neighbor. She cuts the meat up, washes it, and boils it for two hours in salted water. In the meantime we drink our tea, which I've come to like. Priscilla and Lketinga talk nonstop. After a while Lketinga gets up and says he has to go but will be back soon. I try to find out where he's going, but he says only: "No problem, Corinne. I come back," smiles at me, and disappears. I ask Priscilla where he's gone, but she says she doesn't really know, it's not something you can ask a Masai, it's his business, but probably he's gone to Ukunda.

"For God's sake," I protest. "What does he want in Ukunda? We've just come from there."

"Maybe he wants something more to eat," replies Priscilla.

I stare at the simmering meat in the big iron pot: "Who's this for, then?"

"That's for us women," she tells me. "Lketinga can't eat this meat. No Masai warrior ever eats anything that a woman has touched or even looked at. They are not allowed to eat in the presence of women; they can only drink tea."

The curious business in Ukunda comes back to me, and suddenly my question for Priscilla about why all the men disappeared behind the wall is superfluous. So Lketinga can't even eat with me, and I can never cook anything for him. Funnily, this is something that shakes me even more than the idea of never having good sex. When I have collected myself, I try to find out more. What is married life like? Once again her answer is a disappointment. Basically the wife stays with the children while her husband associates with other men of the same status, warriors, at least one of whom must accompany him at mealtimes. Eating alone was not done either.

I'm speechless. All my romantic fantasies of cooking and eating together out in the bush or in a simple hut collapse. I can hardly hold back my tears, and Priscilla is looking at me in astonishment. Then she breaks out laughing, which makes me furious. Suddenly I feel quite alone and realize the obvious: Priscilla too is alien to me, someone who inhabits a completely different world.

But what has happened to Lketinga? It's night and Priscilla has served up the meat on two battered aluminum plates. I've got hungry by now, so I try the meat and am astonished at how tender it is. The taste is quite unique, salty like slow-braised pork. We eat with our hands, in silence.

When it gets late, I say good night and retreat into what was Priscilla's hut. I'm tired. I light the kerosene lamp and lie down on the cot. The sound of cicadas outside fills the air. My thoughts drift back to Switzerland, my mother, my little shop, and my everyday life in Biel. How totally different the world is here! Despite all the primitiveness of their lives, the people seem happier, maybe because they can get by with less expense, and that thought lingers and makes me feel better.

All of a sudden the wooden door squeaks open, and Lketinga is standing smiling in the doorway. He has to lower his head just to get in. He takes a look around and then sits down beside me on the bed. "Hello, how are you? You have eat meat?" he asks, and the way he asks about me and listens attentively makes me feel good, and I feel great desire for him again. He looks magnificent in the glow of the kerosene lamp. His jewelry gleams, his chest is naked, adorned with just the two strings of pearls. The knowledge that under his loincloth there is nothing but flesh excites me. I grab his long, slim, cool hand and press it against my face. At this moment I feel bound to this man whom I know to be wholly alien to me, and I know that I love him. I pull him toward me and feel the weight of his body on mine. I press my head against the side of his and inhale the savage perfume of his long red hair. We stay like that for what seems an eternity, and I notice that he too is excited. The only thing between us is my thin summer dress, and I pull it off. He forces himself inside me, and this time, if only briefly, I feel a whole new sense of joy, even without reaching a climax. I feel myself at one with this man, and now, this night, I know that despite all the barriers between us, I have already become a captive of his world.

During the night I feel stomach cramps and grab hold of my flashlight, which I have luckily left near my head. Apart from the never-ceasing cicadas it is quiet outside, and everyone must hear the creaking of the opening door. I make my way to the "chicken toilet," literally jumping the last step and reaching my destination only just in the nick of time. Because everything has to be done squatting, my knees are literally trembling. With the last of my strength I get back to my feet, grab my flashlight, clamber back down the chicken ladder, and make my way back to the hut. Lketinga is still sleeping peacefully. I squeeze myself onto the cot between him and the wall.

By the time I wake it is already eight A.M., and the sun is shining so strongly that even inside the hut there's a sticky heat. After the usual ritual of tea and washing I decide I want to wash my hair too. But how am I going to do it with no running water? Our water comes in five-gallon canisters, which Priscilla fills up each day from the nearby well. I try to explain to Lketinga what I want to do, and he's immediately ready to help: "No problem. I help you!" Using an empty tin, he pours water over my head, then laughing hilariously rubs the shampoo in for me and then professes amazement that with so much foam I've still got any hair left.

Then we decide to go and see my brother and Jelly at the hotel again. When we arrive, they're both sitting over a lavish breakfast. Looking at this magnificent spread, I realize just how frugal my breakfast is these days. This time I decide to tell them a bit, and Lketinga sits there listening but not understanding. When I get to my nighttime visit to the toilet and they both stare at me in horror, he goes: "What's the problem?" "No problem," I tell him with a smile. "Everything is okay!"

We invite the pair of them to come to have lunch at Priscilla's. I'd like to cook some spaghetti. They both agree, and Eric reckons he can find the way. We have two hours to find spaghetti, sauce, onions, and herbs. Lketinga hasn't a clue what sort of food I'm talking about but smiles and says, "Yes, yes, it's okay."

We take a *matatu* to the nearest supermarket, where they do indeed have everything we need. By the time we get back to the village I don't have much time left to prepare the "meal." I prepare everything sitting cross-legged on the ground. Priscilla and Lketinga watch the spaghetti boiling with amusement but say: "This is no food!" My Masai stares into the boiling water, watching with amazement as the brittle strands of spaghetti slowly soften. This is a mystery to him, and he doubts that a meal will emerge from it. While the pasta simmers I use a knife to open the tin of tomato purée and pour it into a beat-up saucepan. Lketinga looks on in horror and asks: "Is this blood?" Now it's my turn to laugh out loud: "Blood!? No, no, tomato sauce," I answer, giggling.

Jelly and Eric arrive, covered in sweat. "What's this? You're cooking sitting on the ground?" says Jelly in surprise. "Yes, did you think we had a kitchen?" I reply. As we start to extract the spaghetti, strand by strand, from the pot with forks, Lketinga and Priscilla vanish out of the hut. Priscilla's gone to get her neighbor, who looks at the white spaghetti, then the pot with the red sauce. She points at the pasta and, making a face, says: "Worms?" We have to laugh. All three of them think we're eating worms with blood and won't touch it. Somehow, though, I know how they feel because the more I look at the plate and think of worms and blood, the less appetite I have.

Washing up is the next problem. There is neither detergent nor a brush. Priscilla deals with the problem by using Omo washing powder and her fingernails. My brother addresses me soberly: "My dearest sister, somehow I don't see you staying here forever. In any case, your pretty long fingernails won't need a file any longer!" He's not wrong.

They have two more days left of their holiday, and then I'll be on my own with Lketinga. On their last evening in the hotel, there's a Masai dance, just like last time. Even though I've seen it before, Jelly and Eric haven't, and even Lketinga is going to be there. The three of us sit waiting in eager anticipation. The Masai gather outside the hotel and lay out spears, jewelry, cloth, and strings of pearls to sell afterward.

There are about twenty-five warriors who come in singing. I feel an affinity with these people and am as proud of them as if they were all my brothers. It's unbelievable how elegant they are in their movements, and what an aura they exude. Tears come to my eyes at this feeling of belonging, something I've never known before: as if I've found my family, my people. Jelly, a bit wary of so many crazily painted, decorated Masai, turns to me and says: "Corinne, are you sure that your future is here?" I can say only one word: "Yes."

The performance is over by midnight, and the Masai disappear. Lketinga comes and shows us proudly the money he has made selling pieces of jewelry. It doesn't look like much to us, but for him it means survival for another few days. We say our farewells emotionally because we won't see Eric and Jelly before they leave the hotel early in the morning. My brother has to promise Lketinga he'll come back: "You are my friends now!" he says in English. Jelly holds me tight, sobbing, and tells me to look after myself, think things through carefully, and come back to Switzerland in ten days' time. I don't think she trusts me.

We set off home. The night sky is filled with thousands and thousands of stars, but there is no moon. Lketinga could find the way through the bush blindfolded, but I have to hold on to his arm for fear of losing him. A yapping dog comes toward us on the outskirts of the village, but Lketinga emits short sharp noises and the hound scampers off. In the hut I reach for my flashlight. When I finally find it, I look for matches to light the kerosene lamp. For a brief moment it occurs to me how simple everything is back in Switzerland. There are street lamps, electric lights; it seems as if everything works of its own accord. I'm tired and want to sleep, but Lketinga has been working and is hungry and says I should make him some tea. Up until now I've always left that to Priscilla! In the semidarkness I first have to fill up the cookstove with fuel, and then when I find the tea leaves, I ask him: "How much?" Lketinga laughs and shakes about a third of the packet into the boiling water. Then sugar, not two or three spoonfuls but a whole cup. I'm shocked and can't imagine such tea being drinkable, but it tastes almost as good as Priscilla's. Now I understand that a cup of tea can indeed replace a meal.

I spend the next day with Priscilla. We have washing to do, and

Lketinga decides to go up to the north coast to find out which hotels do native dance evenings. He doesn't think to ask if I'd like to come too.

I go to the well with Priscilla and try to bring back a five-gallon water canister as she does, but it's not that simple. First of all a half-gallon bucket has to be dropped fifteen feet down and drawn back up again. Then you have to use an empty tin to transfer it via the narrow opening of the canister until the latter is full. It's all done extremely carefully to make sure not a drop of the precious liquid is lost.

When my canister is full, I try to drag it the two hundred yards to the huts. I had always considered myself to be sturdy, but I can't manage it. Priscilla, on the other hand, takes two or three swings with her canister to get it up onto her head, then she walks calmly and unhurriedly back to the huts. She comes back to meet me halfway and takes my canister back for me. My fingers are already aching. We do the whole thing several times because the Omo here is very frothy. Doing washing by hand in cold water, to Swiss standards of cleanliness, soon takes its toll on my knuckles. After a while they're red raw, and the Omo water burns them. My fingernails are ruined. Exhausted and with an aching back, I give up; Priscilla finishes the rest for me.

It's past lunchtime by now, but we haven't eaten anything. How could we? We don't keep supplies in the house or we'd be infested with mice and beetles. We buy what we need each day in the shop. So despite the incredible heat we set off on what is at least a half-hour walk as long as Priscilla doesn't stop to gossip with every single person we meet on the way. It seems to be the local custom to hail everyone we meet with *"Jambo"* and then stop to exchange half the family history.

At last we get there and buy rice and meat, tomatoes, milk, and even some soft bread. Now we have to go all the way back and then start cooking. By evening Lketinga still hasn't turned up. I ask Priscilla if she knows when he'll be back, but she just laughs and says: "No, I can't ask this a Masai man!" Exhausted by all this unfamiliar exertion in the heat, I go to lie down in the cool of the hut while Priscilla gets on with the cooking. It's probably just the lack of food that's made me so listless.

But I miss my Masai. Without him this world is only half as interesting and worth living in. Then at long last, just before darkness falls, he strolls up to the huts with his familiar, "Hello, how are you?" I answer somewhat crossly, "Oh, not so good," which shocks him, and he asks: "Why?" A bit disconcerted by the expression on his face, I decide not to nag him for being away so long; with both of us struggling to makes ourselves understood in English there are too many opportunities for misunderstanding. Instead I point to my belly and say: "Stomach!" He beams at me and says: "Maybe baby?" I laugh and say no. The idea frankly never occurred to me, because I'm on the Pill, which is something he doesn't know and has probably never heard of.

Red Tape

We're looking for a hotel in which a Masai with a white wife is apparently staying. I can hardly imagine it, but I'm eager to ask her a few questions. When we meet them, my initial reaction is disappointment. This Masai looks just like a "normal black" who doesn't wear jewelry or traditional clothing but a red made-to-measure suit. He's a few years older than Lketinga, and even his wife is already in her late forties. Everyone starts talking at once, but Ursula, who's German, says: "What? You want to come and live here with this Masai?" I say yes and ask shyly why not. "Do you know," she says, "my husband and I have been together for fifteen years. He is a lawyer, but he still has enormous difficulty with the German way of thinking. Now look at Lketinga: he's never been to school, can't read or write and barely speaks English. He has absolutely no idea of European customs and manners, let alone the Swiss obsession with perfection. That's doomed from the outset!" But for her there was simply no question of living in Kenya: women here have no rights. Holidays, on the other hand, are another thing entirely. But I ought to buy Lketinga some clothes; I can't go around with him like that.

She goes on and on, and my heart sinks with her endless list of problems. Even her husband agrees it would be better if Lketinga came to visit me in Switzerland. But that's something I can't imagine, and all my feelings would be wrong. All the same, we accept their offer of help and the next day set off to Mombasa to see about getting Lketinga a passport. When I mention my doubts, Lketinga asks if I have a husband back in Switzerland, because if not I can just take him with me. Only ten minutes ago he said he had no intention of leaving Kenya because he had no idea where Switzerland even is or what my family is like.

On the way to the passport office I have doubts that later turn out to have been justified. Our peaceful days in Kenya are over from this moment on, and the stress of dealing with bureaucracy has just begun. All four of us go into the passport office together and stand in a line for an hour before we're allowed into the right room. The official who deals with applications is sitting behind a huge mahogany desk. He and Ursula's husband have a discussion of which neither Lketinga or I understand a word. I just notice how every now and then they glance over at Lketinga in his exotic apparel. After five minutes it's "Let's go," and we leave the office. I'm confused and annoyed: standing in line for an hour only to have a five-minute interview appalls me.

But that is just the beginning. Ursula's husband says a few things have to be cleared up straightaway. There's no way that Lketinga can simply get on the plane with me. The earliest opportunity, if there are no problems, would be in a month's time. First of all we have to get photographs taken, then come back and fill in forms, which at the moment they've run out of and will be available again only in five days' time. I can hardly believe it: "What, are you telling me that in a big city like this they have no passport application forms?" But then it takes us ages to find a photographer, and he tells us that it will take several days before the pictures will be ready. Exhausted by the heat and the perpetual lining up and waiting, we decide to return to the coast. The other couple disappear back into their luxurious hotel, telling us that now we know where the passport office is and if there are problems we also know where to find them.

Because time is running out, we go back to the office three days later with the pictures. Again we have to line up, for longer than the first time. The closer we come to the door, the more nervous I get, because Lketinga doesn't feel at all comfortable and I'm self-conscious about my poor English. When finally we get to see the passport officer, I explain our case painstakingly. Eventually he looks up from his newspaper and asks what I want to take someone like that—with a dismissive gesture toward Lketinga—to Switzerland for? "Holidays," I reply. The passport officer laughs and says that until this Masai learns how to put on proper civilized clothes he won't be getting a passport. And because he has no education and no idea of Europe, I will have to pay a guarantee of one thousand Swiss francs and at the same time buy Lketinga a return ticket. Only when I have done all of that will he even consider giving me an application form.

Annoyed by the arrogance of this lump of lard, I ask him how long it would then take to get the passport, after I'd done all he asked. "About two weeks," he replies, waving us out of his office and reaching for his newspaper. Such barefaced nerve leaves me speechless, but instead of giving up all hope, his behavior makes me want to show him who's boss. Above all else, I won't have him denigrate Lketinga, who in any case I'm keen to introduce to my mother.

The whole thing becomes an idée fixe for me, and I make up my mind to take Lketinga, by now impatient and disappointed, into the nearest travel agent's to sort it all out. We find a friendly Indian who quickly understands the situation and warns me to be careful because a lot of white women have lost their money like this. I agree to deposit the money with him, and he agrees to give me a confirmation of the return ticket and a receipt and promises to return it all if the passport application is rejected.

Somehow or other I understand that this is all reckless, but I rely on my instincts for people. The important thing is that Lketinga should know where he has to go when he gets his passport to name the date for his flight. "One step further forward," I tell myself bravely.

At a nearby market we buy Lketinga trousers, a shirt, and shoes, which isn't easy because we have diametrically opposite tastes. He wants either white or red trousers. I reckon that white is impossible in the bush while red is not exactly a "manly" color in Western clothing. Fate comes to my aid: all the trousers are too short for my six-and-a-half-foot man. Eventually we find a pair of jeans that will do. When we get to shoes, it's the same thing again. Up until now he's only ever worn sandals made of old car tires. We agree on sneakers. Two hours later he's all dressed up in new clothes, but I don't like it any better. He, on the other hand, is very proud that for the first time in his life he's wearing trousers, a shirt, and sneakers.

Of course, by now it's too late to go back to the passport office, so Lketinga suggests we go over to the north bank. He wants me to meet friends and show me where he lived before he moved in with Priscilla. I'm not sure because it's already four P.M., and that will mean returning to the south bank in the dark. But once again he says, "No problem,

Corinne." So we wait for a *matatu* to the north, but it's not until the third bus that we find even a corner to squeeze into, and within seconds I'm dripping sweat.

Luckily we soon come to a big Masai village where for the first time I see women wearing jewelry. They welcome me cheerfully, and there's a great commotion between the huts. I'm not sure which amazes them more: me or Lketinga's new outfit. They all finger the material of the shirt and the trousers and are even amazed by the shoes. Slowly but surely the shirt gets darker. Two or three women try to talk to me at once, and I sit there smiling but speechless, understanding nothing.

In the meantime lots of children have come into the huts, and they all either stare at me or giggle. I notice how dirty they all are. Suddenly Lketinga says, "Wait here," and is gone. I'm not very comfortable. A woman offers me milk, but, looking at the flies, I decline. Another gives me a Masai armband, which I put on with glee. It would seem they all make jewelry of some sort.

A little later Lketinga comes back and says: "You hungry?" This time I honestly say yes because I am. We go into the nearest bush restaurant, a bit like the one in Ukunda, only bigger. Here there is one area reserved for women and, farther away, a separate one for men. Of course I have to go with the women, and Lketinga goes off with the other warriors. I'm not very happy with the situation; I would have preferred to be in Priscilla's little hut on the south bank. A plate, in which meat and even a few tomatoes swim in a liquid that could almost be a sauce, is put in front of me. On a second plate there is a type of flat bread. I watch another woman with the same "menu" breaking up the bread, dipping it into the sauce, taking a piece of meat, and putting the whole lot into her mouth with her hand. I copy her, although I need two hands. All of a sudden it goes quiet; everybody is watching me eat, which irritates me. There are even a dozen or so children gathered around me watching me with big eyes. Then everybody starts talking again all at once, but even so I have the feeling of being watched. I swallow it all down as quickly as possible and hope Lketinga turns up again soon. When there's nothing left but bones, I go to a sort of barrel from which people get water to run over their hands and wash the fat off, although it obviously doesn't work.

I wait and wait. At last Lketinga turns up. What I really want to do is throw my arms around his neck, but he gives me a funny look, almost angry, and I don't know what I'm supposed to have done. I can see he's eaten too, by the state of his shirt. "Come," he says to me. "Come." As we walk toward the road I ask him, "Lketinga, what's the problem?" The expression on his face scares me. It becomes clear that I'm the reason for his displeasure when he takes my left hand and says: "This hand no good for food! No eat with this one!" I understand the words, but why it makes him so angry I have no idea. I ask him why, but he doesn't answer.

Tired out by all our efforts and disconcerted by this new puzzle, I feel nobody understands me and wish we were back home in our little house on the south bank. I try to tell Lketinga this, saying, "Let's go home." He gives me a look, but of what sort I have no idea because once again all I can see is the gleaming mother-of-pearl button and the whites of his eyes. "No," he says. "All Masai go to Malindi tonight." My heart skips a beat. If I've understood him properly, he really intends to go to Malindi tonight for a tourist dance. "It's good business in Malindi," I hear him say. He notices that I am less than enthusiastic and in a concerned voice asks me: "You are tired?" Yes, I'm tired. I don't even know exactly where Malindi is, and I've no clean clothes. He says it's no problem, I can sleep here with the "Masai ladies" and he'll be back tomorrow. To stay here, alone without him, without being able to talk to anyone, just the idea fills me with panic. "No, we go to Malindi together," I decide. Lketinga laughs again—at long last—and once again there's the familiar "No problem." Along with some other Masai, we get into a public bus, which is a lot more comfortable than the dangerously overcrowded *matatus*. I fall asleep and when I wake we're in Malindi.

The first thing we do is find a Native Lodging House, because after the show it's likely everything will be booked up. There's not much choice. We find one where other Masai have already booked space and get the last empty room. It's barely ten feet by twelve. In each corner between two concrete walls stands an iron bed with thin sagging mattresses and two wool blankets. A naked bulb hangs from the ceiling, and there are two chairs sitting as if they were lost in the middle of the room. At least it costs next to nothing, about four Swiss francs a night, roughly. We still have half an hour before the Masai dancers' performance begins. I go to get a Coke.

When I come back into the room a few minutes later, I can hardly believe my eyes. Lketinga is sitting on one of the mattresses, his jeans down to his knees, pulling and tearing at them. Clearly he's trying to get them off because we have to leave and he obviously can't go onstage in European clothes. It's all I can do to hold back the laughter. He can't get the jeans off because he still has his sneakers on, and he can't get the pants off over them. As a result, the trousers are halfway down his legs, and he can't get them either up or down. Laughing, I bend down to try to pull the shoes out of the jeans. But he shouts: "No, no, Corinne, out with this," pointing at the trousers. "Yes, yes," I reply, and try to make him understand that he has to get back into them and then take his shoes off before he can get out of the jeans.

The half hour is long gone, and we rush to the hotel. I like him a thousand times better in his usual outfit. He's already got huge blisters on his heels from the new shoes, which he obviously wears without socks. We get to the show just in time, and I take a place among the white audience, a few of whom give me dirty looks. I'm still wearing the same clothes that I put on this morning, and they certainly haven't got any cleaner or more attractive. Nor do I smell quite as fresh as these white people straight from their showers, and that's saying nothing about my long greasy hair. Even so, I am probably the proudest woman in the room. As I watch these men dance I am overcome once again by the familiar feeling of belonging.

It's almost midnight by the time the dance and show are over. The only thing I want to do is sleep. Back at the lodging I feel I really have to wash, but Lketinga comes into our room followed by another Masai and reckons his friend can sleep in the second bed. I'm not exactly overjoyed by the idea of sharing this ten-by-twelve room with a strange man, but I say nothing for fear of seeming impolite. So still in my clothes I squeeze into the small sagging bed next to Lketinga and, despite everything, fall asleep.

In the morning I get to shower at last, even if it's hardly luxurious with an intermittent water flow, and ice cold at that. Despite the dirty clothes I feel a bit better on the trip back to the south bank.

In Mombasa I buy a simple dress because we want to call by the passport office and see if we can get the forms. Today it works. After checking the provisional ticket and confirmation that the guarantee money has been lodged, we are finally given an application form. But as we start trying to answer the rows of questions, I realize that I hardly understand most of them and decide to get the help of Ursula and her husband.

After another five-hour journey we are at long last back at our little hut on the south bank. Priscilla has been very worried because she didn't know where we spent the night. Lketinga has to explain to her why he's wearing European clothing. I go to lie down for a bit because it's really hot outside. I'm sure I've already lost several pounds.

There are just six days left before I'm due to fly home, and I still haven't spoken to Lketinga about our future together in Kenya. All our efforts are directed toward getting this stupid passport. I start thinking about what I could work at here. Living on these modest means certainly doesn't require much money, but even so I need something to do and a bit of income. That's when I get the idea of looking for a shop in one of the hotels. I could employ one or two seamstresses, bring in a few patterns from Switzerland, and run a little dressmaker's. There are more than enough fine fabrics to be had, good seamstresses too who would work for three hundred francs a month or so, and selling is what I do best.

Excited by my idea, I call Lketinga into the hut to try to explain it to him, but I soon realize that he doesn't understand. But to me it's important, so I call Priscilla. She translates while Lketinga just nods now and again. Priscilla explains to me that, without our getting married or my obtaining a work permit, my idea is impossible. But the idea is good because she knows some people who make good money from made-to-measure clothing. I ask Lketinga if he might be interested in getting married. Contrary to my expectations, his reaction is restrained. With a certain degree of common sense, he says that if I have such a good business in Switzerland, I shouldn't sell it but instead come to Kenya two or three times a year for "holidays" and he would always be waiting for me.

Now I'm a bit up in the air. I've been ready and willing to give up everything back home for him, and he's talking about holidays! I'm disappointed. He notices immediately and says, correctly of course, that he doesn't really know me very well, or my family at all. He needs time to think. And I should take my time too, and anyway he might come to Switzerland. I say simply, "Lketinga, when I do something, I don't do it by halves!" Either he feels the way I do and wants me to come, or I'll try to forget everything that's happened between us.

The next day we go to the hotel to find Ursula and her husband to fill out the form. But we miss them because they've gone off on a safari for several days. Once again I curse my poor command of English. We look for someone else to translate for us. Lketinga will have only a Masai; he doesn't trust anyone else.

We go back to Ukunda and spend hours in the teahouse until a Masai turns up who can read, write, and speak English. His attitude of superiority annoys me, but he sits down with Lketinga and fills it all out. His opinion, however, is that nothing here works without bribery. Since he shows me his own passport and has apparently been to Germany twice, I have to believe him. He adds that my white skin will push the size of the bribe up at least fivefold. For a little compensation he will go to Mombasa with Lketinga the next day and fix everything. I agree with bad grace, but I'm gradually losing my patience and can't face arguing with that arrogant passport official anymore. For just fifty francs he will sort everything out: even go with Lketinga to the airport. I hand over a bit of extra cash for bribes, and the pair set off for Mombasa.

At long last I retire to the beach and spoil myself with a lie in the sun and good hotel food that of course costs ten times what you'd pay in a local restaurant. In the evening I go back to the hut and find a furious Lketinga waiting for me. I ask him excitedly what happened in Mombasa, but all he wants to know is where I've been. I answer with a laugh: "On the beach and at the hotel for a meal." He wants to know who I talked to. I think nothing of it and say Edy and a couple of other Masai with whom I exchanged a few words on the beach. Only slowly does the dark cloud disappear from his face, and he tells me matter-of-factly that the passport will take three to four weeks.

I'm pleased and try to tell him about Switzerland and my family. He lets me know he likes Eric but doesn't know about other people. I reflect that I'm not exactly sure how the people in Biel will react to him either. And he's going to be confused by the traffic in the streets, the exotic pubs and restaurants, and the general luxury.

My last few days in Kenya are spent somewhat more quietly. We stroll into the hotel from time to time, or along the beach, or we spend the whole day in the village with different people, drinking tea or cooking. When the last day dawns, I'm sad and try hard to keep my composure. Even Lketinga is nervous. Lots of people bring me little presents, mostly bits of Masai jewelry. My arms are draped in bangles almost up to my elbows.

Lketinga washes my hair for me once more, helps me pack, and keeps asking: "Corinne, really you will come back to me?" He doesn't seem to believe that I'll come back. He says lots of white women say that but never come back, or if they do, they go off with another man next time. "Lketinga, I don't want another man. Only you!" I repeat again and again. I'll write lots, send photos, and tell him when I've settled everything. I still have to find someone to buy the shop from me and take over my apartment and all the furniture.

He should let me know via Priscilla when he plans to come, if he gets his passport. "If it doesn't work out or you decide you don't want to come to Switzerland, just tell me," I say to him. I will need about three months to deal with everything. He asks me how long three months is: "How many full moons?" "Three full moons," I reply, laughing.

We spend every minute of the last day together and decide to go to the Bush Baby Disco until four in the morning and not sleep but make the most of our time. We talk in language, signs, and signals all night long, and it's always the same question: Will I really come back? I promise for the twentieth time and realize how genuinely worked up Lketinga is too.

Half an hour before my departure we turn up at the hotel, accompanied by two other Masai. The whites waiting for us, tired from the early start, look at us with obvious irritation. With my suitcase and the three Masai with their *rungu* clubs we must make a curious picture. Then it's time for me to get on board the bus. Lketinga and I fall into each other's arms one more time, and he says: "No problem, Corinne. I wait here, or I come to you!" And then—I can hardly believe it—he kisses me on the mouth. I'm moved. I climb on board and wave good-bye to the three figures vanishing in the darkness.

Burning Bridges

Back in Switzerland, I immediately begin looking for someone to take over the shop. A lot of people are interested, but only a few are suitable and they don't have the money. Obviously I want to make as much as possible on the deal because I don't know when I'm going to start earning again. You can live for two days in Kenya easily enough on ten francs. So I've become very stingy, putting aside every franc for my future in Africa.

A month passes quickly, and I hear nothing from Lketinga. I've already written three letters. Now, somewhat worried, I write to Priscilla. Two weeks later I get a letter from her that confuses me. Two weeks after I left Lketinga vanished and she hasn't seen him since; he's probably living back on the north bank again. Things aren't going well with his passport, and with good intentions she advises me that I'd be better off staying in Switzerland. I'm knocked sideways and write a letter right away, addressing it to the PO box on the north bank where my first letters reached Lketinga.

After two months back home a girlfriend decides to take over the shop at the end of October. I'm delighted that at least this big problem has been solved. Theoretically, therefore, I can take off in October, but unfortunately I still haven't heard a word from Lketinga. I reckon there's no point in his coming to Switzerland now that I'll be back in Mombasa soon, and I continue to believe in our great love. Another two confused letters arrive from Priscilla, but with my faith intact I go into the travel agent's and book a flight to Mombasa for October 5.

That leaves me with two weeks to get rid of the apartment and my cars. The apartment is no problem: I sell it, furnished, to a young student at a rock-bottom price. That way at least I can remain there until the last minute.

My friends, business colleagues, everyone who knows me thinks I'm crazy. It's particularly hard for my mother, although I have the impression that she understands me better than most. She hopes and prays that I will find what I am looking for and be happy.

I sell the car on the very last day and have the purchaser drive me to the station. Buying a "single" ticket to Zurich airport excites me. With a tiny piece of hand luggage but a huge suitcase packed with T-shirts, underwear, simple cotton skirts, and a few presents for Lketinga and Priscilla, I board the train and wait for departure.

When the train starts moving, I could jump for joy. I lean back glowing like a lantern and laugh to myself. I'm overcome with a wonderful feeling of freedom. I could shout aloud and share my happiness and plans with everybody on the train. I'm free, free, free! I don't know what's waiting for me in Kenya, whether Lketinga got my letters, and, if he did, whether anyone translated them properly for him. I know nothing except that I'm enjoying an ecstatic feeling of weightlessness.

I'll have three months to settle in before I need to apply for another visa. My God—three months! Time to work things out and get to know Lketinga better. I've worked on my English, and I've packed some good textbooks with lots of pictures. In fifteen hours' time I will be in my new home. With that thought in my mind I board the plane, lie back, and peer through the cabin window for a last look at Switzerland. Who knows when I'll be back? To celebrate my departure and a new beginning, I order champagne and don't know whether to laugh or cry.

A New Homeland

From Mombasa airport I can take a hotel bus as far as the Africana Sea Lodge, even though I haven't booked a room. Priscilla and Lketinga ought to know when I'll get there. I'm in a real tizzy. What if nobody turns up? But barely have I had time to think about it before I'm at the hotel, look around, and see there's nobody there to welcome me. All of a sudden, standing there with my heavy bag, all my excitement gives way to immense disappointment. Then out of nowhere I hear my name, and when I turn around to look up the path there's Priscilla charging toward me, her enormous bosom wobbling. Tears of joy and relief flood into my eyes.

We embrace, and of course I have to ask about Lketinga. A cloud passes over her face, and she turns away from me to say: "Corinne, please! I don't know where he is!" She hasn't seen him since shortly after I left, more than two months ago. She's heard stories but doesn't know what's true and what isn't. I want to hear everything, but Priscilla says we should go back to the village first. At her request, I pile my heavy bag on top of her head, and with me carrying just my little piece of hand luggage, off we go.

But my God, I'm thinking to myself, what happened to my dreams of great love and happiness? Where on earth is Lketinga? I can't believe he's simply forgotten everything. In the village I meet another woman, a Muslim. Priscilla introduces her as a friend and explains that for the moment at least the three of us have to share her accommodation because this woman doesn't want to return to her husband.

We drink tea, but I'm awash with unanswered questions. I ask about my Masai, and Priscilla with no little hesitation tells me what she's heard. One of his fellow warriors is supposed to have said he'd gone back home, sick and unhappy because he'd had no letter from me for such a long time. "What?" I explode. "I wrote at least five times." Now even Priscilla looks surprised: "Really? Where to?" she asks. I show her the PO box address on the north bank. Ah, she says, no wonder Lketinga didn't get any letters. This PO box apparently belongs to all the Masai on the north bank, and any of them can take whatever they want out of it. Given that Lketinga can't read, someone else has probably taken them.

I can hardly believe what Priscilla is telling me: "I thought all the Masai were friends, almost like brothers. Who'd do a thing like that?" That's when I find out for the first time about the jealousy among the warriors living here on the coast. When I left three months ago, some of the men who'd been on the coast a long time had teased and hassled Lketinga, saying things like: "A woman like her, young and pretty, with lots of money, isn't going to come back to Kenya for a black man with nothing." According to Priscilla, because he hadn't been living here long and hadn't received any letters, he'd probably believed them.

I ask Priscilla curiously where, then, is home for Lketinga. She's not certain, but somewhere in the Samburu District: a three-day journey away. I shouldn't even think of it. Now that I'm here, she'll find someone to go out there in the near future and get a message through. "Give it time, and we'll find out what's happened. *Pole, pole,*" she says, which means something like "slowly, slowly." "You're in Kenya now, you need time and patience."

The two women fuss over me like a child. We chat among ourselves a lot. Esther, the Muslim woman, tells me about the hard time she's been having with her husband and warns me never to marry an African. She says they're unfaithful and treat women badly. My Lketinga is different, I think to myself, but I say nothing.

After the first night we decide to buy a bed. I didn't get a wink of sleep. Priscilla and I shared a narrow bed, while Esther slept on another, but, given that there's a lot of Priscilla, I had hardly any room and had to hang on to the edge of the bed to stop myself from continuously rolling into her.

So it's off to Ukunda, where we trail from one dealer to another in temperatures of 104 degrees F in the shade. The first doesn't have a double bed but could produce one in three days. But I want one now. At the next place we find a magnificent carved bed for eighty francs, and I want to buy it immediately, but Priscilla is indignant: "Too much!" I can't believe my ears. Such a superb double bed, handmade, for that price! But Priscilla has stormed off: "Come, Corinne, too much!" That's the way it goes half the afternoon until at last I'm allowed to buy one for sixty francs. The carpenter takes it apart, and we carry it all to the main road. Priscilla gets hold of a foam mattress, and after an hour's wait in the boiling heat on the dusty street we take a *matatu* back to the hotel, where we unload it all. So there we are standing with the pieces, all of which are made of solid wood and very heavy.

We look around us helplessly until three Masai appear from the beach. Priscilla has a word with them and immediately these normally work-shy warriors give us a hand to carry my new double bed to the village. I have to bend double with laughter for the whole thing looks hilarious. When we finally get to the village, I want to set to work immediately, screwing the pieces of the bed together, but I don't get the chance because each of the Masai insists on doing it for me. By now there are six men working on my bed.

It's still late before we can all sit down tired out on the edge of the bed. There's tea for everyone who helped, and the conversation lapses once again into the Masai language I don't understand a word of. Every now and then one of the warriors gestures in my direction, and I hear the name "Lketinga." After an hour they all leave us, and we women get ready for bed. That means washing outside the house, which is fine because it's pitch black and no one can see us. Even a late-night pee has to be done in the open because it's too dark to cope with the chicken ladder. I fall back onto my new bed exhausted, and this time I don't come into contact with Priscilla because the bed's wide enough. That said, there's not much space left in the hut, and anyone who comes to visit now has to sit on the bed.

The days pass quickly, and Esther and Priscilla spoil me. One cooks while the other fetches water and even washes my clothes. When I protest, they say only that it's too hot for me to work. So I spend most of my time on the beach, waiting for some word from Lketinga. In the evenings Masai warriors often come around, and we play cards or try to tell stories. Gradually I notice that one or another of them is showing an interest in me, but I don't reciprocate because there's only one man for me. None of them is half as beautiful and elegant as the "demigod" for whom I've given up everything. When the warriors realize I'm not interested, I hear a few more rumors about Lketinga. It seems everyone knows I'm here waiting for him.

On one occasion when I politely but firmly turn down the offer of a "friendship"—read "love affair"—he says: "Why are you waiting for this one Masai when everyone knows that he took the money you gave him to get a passport and went off to Watamu Malindi and drank it all with African girls?" Then he gets up and says I should think again about his offer. I tell him angrily to get lost and not come back. Even so, I feel lonely and betrayed. What if it's true? All sorts of thoughts run through my head, and in the end all I know is that I don't want to believe it. I could go to the Indian in Mombasa, but I can't summon up the courage because I wouldn't be able to bear hearing what he might tell me. Every day I meet warriors on the beach, and I hear more stories. One even tells me that Lketinga is "crazy" and had to be taken home, where he married a young girl and won't be coming back to Mombasa. And if I need comforting, this guy'll always be there for me. My God, I think, will they ever leave me alone? I'm beginning to see myself as a deer lost among lions; they all want to eat me up.

In the evenings I tell Priscilla the latest rumors and calumnies, but she says it's just normal. I've been here three weeks now without a man, and these men's experience is that white women never live for long on their own. Then Priscilla tells me about two white women who've been living in Kenya for years and run after almost every single Masai. On the one hand, I'm shocked—on the other, astounded—to hear that there are other white women here and that they even speak German. The news awakens my curiosity. Priscilla points to another hut in the village and tells me: "That belongs to Jutta, a German. She's somewhere in the Samburu District working in a tourist camp at present but will come back for a short while sometime in the next two or three weeks." I'm more than curious about this mysterious Jutta.

In the meantime men continue to flirt with me, and I'm no longer comfortable. It seems that a woman on her own is considered fair game. Even Priscilla can't—or won't—do anything about it. When I say anything to her she laughs almost childishly, which I can't understand.

A Trip with Priscilla

One day Priscilla suggests that I go with her for a couple of weeks to her village to see her mother and her five children. "You have five children?" I gasp in astonishment. "Where do they live?" "With my mother or sometimes with my brother." Priscilla lives on the coast only to make money, selling jewelry, and twice a year she takes it home. She and her husband haven't lived together for years. Once again, Masai ways amaze me.

When we come back, I think, maybe Jutta will be here, and so I agree to go. The trip would be one way of getting away from the Masai men's attention. Priscilla is delighted, as she's never brought a white person home before.

With the decision made, we leave the next day. Esther will stay behind to look after the house. In Mombasa, Priscilla buys several school uniforms to take to her children. I take only my little backpack with some underwear, a pullover, three T-shirts, and a spare pair of jeans. We buy our tickets, but as there's lots of time before the bus leaves in the evening I go to a hairdresser to have my hair braided African-style. This takes nearly three hours and hurts immensely, but it seems a lot more practical for the journey.

Long before the bus is due to depart dozens of people are milling around it, loading every conceivable type of baggage onto the roof. By the time we leave it's pitch dark, and Priscilla suggests we get some sleep. It'll be at least nine hours to Nairobi; then we have to change and it's nearly another four and a half hours to Narok.

I can't get comfortable and the journey seems to last forever, so it's a great relief when we arrive. But even now there's a long trek on foot ahead. For nearly two hours we march, always slightly uphill, through fields, meadows, even a forest of pine trees. From the landscape alone, I could almost imagine myself back in Switzerland; there is not a human being to be seen.

At long last I see smoke rising in the distance and make out a few dilapidated wooden shacks. "Soon be there," says Priscilla and explains that she has to fetch a case of beer as a present for her father. I can hardly believe my eyes when she gets the case and plonks it on her head on top of everything else. I can't wait to see how these Masai live; Priscilla has told me they're more affluent than the Samburu tribes to which Lketinga belongs.

When we finally get up to our destination there's a huge "Hallo," and a crowd of people rushes toward Priscilla, then suddenly stops and stares in silence at me. Priscilla apparently tells them all that we're friends. First of all we have to go to her brother's house because he speaks a bit of English. The dwellings are all bigger than our village house, with three rooms, but everything is dirty and covered with soot because they cook on open wood fires. Chickens, puppies, and cats run around all over the place as do children, everywhere you look: kids of every age, bigger ones carrying the little ones piggyback. Priscilla hands out the first presents.

The people here don't dress as traditionally. They wear Western clothing and live as farmers. When the goats come back from the fields, it's my duty as guest to pick out the one we'll have for a welcome dinner. I can't bring myself to hand out a death sentence, but Priscilla tells me that it's traditional and considered a great honor. For all I know I'll have to do this daily and whenever we visit anyone else. So I point out a white goat, which is immediately rounded up. Two men cut the poor animal's throat, and I have to turn my eyes away from its death throes. Already it's got dark and cooled down. We go into the house and sit around the fire burning on the earth in one of the rooms.

Where the animal is being roasted or boiled, I have no idea. I'm all the more surprised, therefore, when I'm presented with a whole foreleg and a huge bush knife. The other leg is put down in front of Priscilla. "I can't eat all this," I tell her, "I'm not starving." She laughs and tells me we'll simply take the rest with us and eat it tomorrow. The idea of gnawing at this leg again for breakfast doesn't thrill me. But for form's sake I eat what I can, although I get laughed at for my lack of appetite.

Dog-tired and suffering from a backache, I ask where we're going to sleep. We're given a narrow couch that we're supposed to share. There's no sign of any water to wash with, and without a fire the room is terribly cold. I put on my pullover and a thin jacket to sleep in. I'm even glad to be squeezed next to Priscilla; at least it's warmer. In the middle of the night I feel an itch and wake up to find tiny creatures running all over me. My first instinct is to leap off the couch, but it's pitch black and freezing cold. There's nothing for it but to stick it out until morning. At first light I wake Priscilla and point to my legs. They're covered in red bites, probably from fleas. There's not much to be done since I haven't brought a change of clothes. I want to wash, but when I go outside, I'm taken aback: the whole area is covered in mist, and there's a frost on the lush meadows. I could almost be on a farm in the Swiss Jura Mountains.

Today we're off again to see Priscilla's mother and her children. We tramp across hills and fields, meeting children or old folk here and there. The children keep their distance from me, but the older people, women mostly, want to touch me; some hold my hand and mutter something I don't understand. Priscilla says most of them have never seen a white woman before, let alone touched one. That turns out to be why when our hands are together they spit on them: it's a particular honor.

After three hours' walk we finally reach the hut in which Priscilla's mother lives. Immediately children charge toward us and hang on to Priscilla. Her mother, who's even rounder than Priscilla, is sitting on the ground washing clothes. They obviously have a lot to talk about, and I try to get the gist of at least a bit of it.

This hut is the most modest of all those I've seen. It's round like the others and knocked together out of various planks, fabrics, and bits of plastic. I can hardly stand up indoors, the fire in the middle fills the entire room with choking smoke, and there's no window. I drink my tea outside because otherwise my eyes would be smarting and tears would be running down my cheeks. I ask Priscilla, somewhat worriedly, if we have to spend the night here. She laughs and says, "No, Corinne." Another brother with a bigger house lives a half hour away: we'll spend the night with him. There's no room here anyway, because all the children sleep here, and there's nothing to eat but milk and corn. I breathe a sigh of relief.

Just before dusk we set off for the other brother's. Once again we get a festive welcome. Apparently, they hadn't been told Priscilla was coming and bringing a white visitor. This brother is very friendly, and I can have a decent conversation with him. Even his wife speaks a little English, and they've both been to school.

But once again I have to select an animal. I don't know what to do because I don't want to eat the tough goat meat again, but on the other hand I really am hungry. So I steel myself and ask if there's anything else, explaining that we white people aren't used to so much meat. They all laugh, and his wife asks if I would prefer chicken with potatoes and vegetables. "Oh, yes!" is my immediate reaction to such a magnificent alternative menu, and his wife goes off and comes back with a plucked chicken, potatoes, and a sort of spinach. These Masai are proper farmers; some of them have been to school, and they work hard in the fields. We women and children eat a really good meal together, a sort of stew that tastes quite wonderful.

We stay here for almost a week, using it as a base to visit other people. They even provide hot water especially for me to wash in. Even so, our clothes are dirty and smell appallingly of smoke. I'm beginning to get tired of this life and wish I were back in Mombasa with the beach and my new bed. When I tell Priscilla I'd like to leave, she tells me we're invited to a wedding in two days' time. So we stay.

The wedding is a few miles away. One of the richest Masai there is marrying his third wife. I'm surprised to find out that the Masai apparently can have as many wives as they can feed. It reminds me of the rumors about Lketinga: Could it be that he really is married? The thought preys on me, but I tell myself he wouldn't have kept it a secret from me. There's some other reason behind his disappearance, and I have to find it out as soon as I get back to Mombasa.

The ceremony is impressive, with hundreds of men and women. The proud bridegroom is presented to me, and he informs me that if I want to get married he would take me as well. I'm speechless. He turns to Priscilla and actually asks her how many cows he'd have to pay for me. Priscilla manages to put him off, however, and he leaves.

Then, accompanied by the first two wives, the bride arrives: a stunningly beautiful girl painted from head to foot. I'm shocked by her age, for she can't be older than twelve or thirteen. The other two wives are probably no more than eighteen or twenty. The bridegroom isn't exactly an old man, but he's probably at least thirty-five. I ask Priscilla: "How can people get married when they're little more than children?"

That's just the way it is, she says; she was not much older herself. I feel a sort of pity for the girl, who looks proud but unhappy.

Once again my thoughts turn to Lketinga. Does he have any idea that I'm twenty-seven? All of a sudden I feel old, unsure of myself, and certainly not very attractive in these grubby clothes. The numerous offers directed to me via Priscilla do nothing to diminish the feeling. I don't fancy any of them, and in any case Lketinga is the only one I can imagine as a possible husband. I want to go home to Mombasa. Who knows, maybe he's turned up in the meantime. I've been back in Kenya a month now.

Jutta

We spend one more night in the hut and head back to Mombasa the next day. I stride toward the village with my heart in my mouth. Even at a distance I can hear unfamiliar voices, and Priscilla calls out: "*Jambo, Jutta!*" My heart takes a little leap of joy at her words: after nearly two weeks with barely any conversation the arrival of a white woman is welcome.

She greets me coolly, however, and speaks to Priscilla in Swahili. Once again I'm left understanding nothing! But then she turns to me with a smile and says in German, "So, how do you like life in the bush? If you weren't covered in dirt, I wouldn't have believed you were up to it," and she looks me up and down with a critical eye. I tell her that I'm glad to be back here because my hair itches and I've been bitten all over. Jutta laughs: "Fleas and lice, that's all that's wrong with you! But if you go into the hut with them you'll never get them out!"

She says the best way to deal with fleas is to take a dip in the sea and then a shower in one of the hotels, a luxury she makes the most of whenever she's in Mombasa. I ask doubtfully if that's possible, as I'm not staying in one of them, but she dismisses my fears: "There are so many white people that you can get away without being noticed." She even goes to get food at the hotel buffets, although not always the same one of course. I'm impressed by Jutta and amazed by all her little tricks. She promises to come with me later and disappears into her hut.

Priscilla tries to unbraid my hair. It hurts terribly. The hairs have all become matted and stuck together with smoke and dirt. I've never been so dirty in my life and feel as bad as I look. After more than an hour—

and hair falling out in clumps—we succeed: all the braids are undone. I look like I've been struck by lightning. Armed with soap, shampoo, and fresh clothes, I call for Jutta, and we go off together. She has pencils and a sketchpad with her. When I ask her why, she says, "To earn money. It's easy to make money in Mombasa; that's why I'm here for a couple of weeks."

"How?" I ask.

"I draw caricatures of tourists. It takes ten to fifteen minutes, and I make ten francs a picture. If I can do four or five people in a day, I can make a decent living."

For five years now she's been getting along like this; she knows every trick and comes across as hugely self-confident. I'm in awe of her.

When we get to the beach, I plunge straight into the refreshing brine and don't come out for an hour. When I do, Jutta shows me the money she has made in the meantime. "Okay, let's go shower," she says with a laugh. "You just have to relax and walk past the beach guard with an air of self-confidence, because we're white, you always have to remember that!" It works! I spend ages under the shower washing my hair maybe five times over until I finally feel clean. Then I put on a little light summer dress, and we go off for the traditional four o'clock tea. All for no charge.

That's when Jutta asks what I'm doing in the village. I tell her my story, and she listens attentively before giving me her advice: "If you really are determined to stay here and want your Masai, then there are a few things that are necessary. For a start you have to rent your own hut—that costs next to nothing, and you'll have peace. Secondly you should hang on to the money you've brought and start earning: for example, get customers for me to draw, and we'll share the proceeds. Thirdly, don't listen to any black on the coast. When you get down to it, all they want is money. To find out if your Lketinga is really worth it, tomorrow we'll go to the travel agent's and see if the money you left is still there. If it is, then the tourist industry hasn't totally corrupted him yet. I'm serious!" If I had a photo of him it would be easy to find him, she reckons.

Jutta is good. She speaks Swahili, knows her way around, and has the energy of a female Rambo. The next day we go into Mombasa, but not on the bus. Jutta has no intention of throwing away her hard-earned money. Instead she sticks her thumb out at the roadside, and, as it happens, the first private car to come along stops. They are Indians and will take us to the ferry. Virtually the only people to own private cars here are Asians or whites. Jutta laughs at me. "You see, Corinne, there's something else you've learned."

After much searching we eventually locate the travel agent's. I pray passionately that the money I left more than five months ago is still here, not so much because of the money itself but because I want confirmation that I haven't got it wrong about Lketinga and our love. Apart from anything else, Jutta will only help me find him if he hasn't taken the money. She obviously doesn't think that very likely.

My heart is pounding as I open the door and cross the threshold. The man behind the desk looks up, and I recognize him immediately. But before I can say a word he gets up and comes out to me holding out his hand, saying, "Hello, how are you after such a long time? And where is the Masai man? I haven't seen anything more of him." Those few words are enough to fill my heart with a warm glow, and after saying hello I explain to him that the passport didn't work out and I've come to get my money back.

Even now I don't quite dare believe it, but the Indian disappears behind a curtain, and I glance nervously at Jutta. She just rocks on her heels, but in a second he's back with bundles of notes in his hands. I could cry with happiness. The moment I take hold once again of this substantial sum of money I feel a new strength. My trust is restored, and I can shrug off all the rumors and other nonsense.

I thank the Indian for his honesty, and we go back out. Finally Jutta says: "Corinne, you really have to find this Masai. Now I believe your whole story, and I suspect there are other people involved." I throw my arms around her in happiness. "Come on," I say. "Let's go eat like tourists. My treat!"

Over lunch we plan what to do next. Jutta suggests we head out for the Samburu District in about a week's time. It's a long way to Maralal, the administrative center for the district, where she wants to look out for a Masai she knows from the coast. If she can show him the pictures of Lketinga, then he ought to be able to tell us where to find him: "Out there everybody knows everybody." My hopes are rising by the minute. We can stay with friends of hers whose house she helped to build. I agree to everything she says: at last I'll be doing something and not just sitting around waiting.

The week with Jutta passes pleasantly. I help her make appointments for sittings, and she does her caricatures. It works well, and I meet a lot of nice people. We spend most evenings in the Bush Baby Disco because Jutta needs a fix of music and entertainment. She has to watch the money, though, or else we'll spend it as fast as we earn it and in a month's time we'll still be here.

At last it's time to pack. I take about half my clothes in my bag and leave the rest in the house with Priscilla. She's not happy about my going and says it's all but impossible to find a Masai warrior. "They move about all the time. Unless they're married they don't have a home, and only their mothers at best have a clue where they might be." But I'm not going to be put off my plan; I'm certain it's the right thing to do.

We start by catching a bus to Nairobi. This time the eight-hour journey doesn't bother me at all. I can't wait to see where my Masai comes from, and every hour brings us nearer.

Jutta has things to do in Nairobi, so we spend three days at the Igbol, a backpacker hotel. Backpackers from all over the world come here, and they couldn't be more different from the tourists in Mombasa. Nairobi itself is completely different too. Everything is chaotic, and there are a lot of cripples and beggars. Because our hotel is right in the middle of the nightlife area, I also notice how much prostitution there is. In the evenings one bar after another tempts the customers in with Swahili music, and almost every woman in the bars can be bought, either for money or just a few beers. The main customers in places like this are locals. It's noisy but has a certain fascination. As two white women, we stick out like sore thumbs, and every few minutes someone's asking if we're looking for a "boyfriend." Luckily, Jutta can fend them off in Swahili. At night in Nairobi it's so dangerous she never goes out without a *rungu,* the traditional Masai club.

By the third day I'm hassling Jutta for us to move on. She agrees, and around lunchtime we get on a bus heading for Nyahururu. This bus is a lot more dilapidated than the one from Mombasa, and that was hardly a luxury coach. Jutta just laughs: "Wait until you see the next one! Then you'll have a shock. This one's fine." We sit in the bus for an hour because they won't leave until it's packed full and there's not a space to spare. Another six-hour journey lies ahead of us, gently uphill all the way. Every now and then the bus stops, a few people get off and a few more get on.

And naturally all of them have masses of household goods, which have to be loaded or unloaded.

At long last we reach today's destination: Nyahururu. We trail along to the nearest boardinghouse and rent a room, then we eat and get to bed. I can't spend any more time sitting down. Overjoyed to be able to stretch out at last and rest my weary bones, I'm asleep in a second. We have to be up by six A.M. because the only bus to Maralal leaves at seven. By the time we get there it's already nearly full. But I see a few Masai warriors on the bus and immediately feel more at home. Once again, however, everybody stares at us, as we're the only whites on the bus.

This bus really is a disaster. Springs stick out of the seats everywhere, dirty foam rubber protrudes from the upholstery, and several windows are broken. On top of all that, it's chaos inside. Getting on board requires climbing over all sorts of boxes with chickens in them. On the other hand, it's the first bus with a genuinely happy atmosphere. Everyone is talking or laughing. Jutta jumps out again to get something to drink from one of the numerous stands. She comes back and hands me a bottle of Coke. "Here, take this but don't drink it all at once. You'll get very thirsty, particularly on the last stretch, which is dusty because we'll be traveling along unpaved roads. There's nothing between here and Maralal except wasteland and bush." The bus starts, and it's barely ten minutes before we leave the tarmac road and start bumping along a red potholed track.

Now the entire bus is shrouded in a cloud of dust. Anyone who has a pane of glass in their window shuts it, the others pull caps or scarves over their faces. I cough and screw my eyes up. Now I know why the back seats were the only free ones. The bus is going slowly, but even so I have to hang on so as not to be thrown forward when it piles into one huge pothole or another. "Hey, Jutta, how long does this go on?" She laughs: "Oh, about four or five hours, unless we get a puncture, even though it's only seventy-five miles." I'm horrified, and only the thought of Lketinga allows me to imagine this part of the journey as even remotely romantic.

Every now and then we catch a distant glimpse of a *manyatta*, and then once again there's only scrub, red earth, and the very occasional tree. Sometimes a few children with goats or cows, out in search of what passes for pasture, appear and wave at the bus.

The bus makes its first stop after about an hour and a half. On either side of the road there are a few shacks, a couple of them offering bananas, tomatoes, and other bits and pieces of food. Women and children crowd up to the windows of the bus, trying to sell something in the few minutes we're stopped. A few of the passengers load up with food, and then the bus rattles off again. Nobody got off, but three more warriors, all brightly painted, got on. Each of them is carrying two long spears. Looking at the three of them, I feel sure that I'll soon find Lketinga again. "The next stop is Maralal," says an obviously tired Jutta. I'm exhausted too from the nonstop pitching and heaving on this bad joke of a road. But in fact we've been lucky: we've had neither a puncture nor a breakdown, both of which happen frequently. And the road is dry; when it rains, the red earth is nothing but mud.

After another hour and a half we at last arrive in Maralal. The bus hoots its way into town and does what appears to be a victory lap around its single street before stopping at the end. Immediately we're surrounded by dozens of curious bystanders. We climb out onto the dusty street, covered from head to foot with a fine powder. There's a regular melee around the bus as people of every age crowd around. We wait for our bags, which are buried under the boxes, baskets, and even mattresses. But just the sight of this village and its exotic inhabitants awakens a sense of adventure in me.

There's a little market just fifty yards from the bus stop, and everywhere there are sheets of colored cloth flapping in the wind. Mountains of clothing and shoes are laid out on plastic sheets, and behind them, almost exclusively, women sit trying to sell their wares.

At long last we get our bags. Jutta suggests we get a cup of tea and something to eat before we set out for her house, which is about an hour's walk away. Hundreds of pairs of eyes follow us. One of the locals—a Kikuyu woman—greets Jutta. People here know her because she has been working on a house nearby for three months and, as the only white in the area, is hardly inconspicuous.

The teahouse is like the one in Ukunda. We sit at a table, and the food is served—meat with sauce and chapatis, as usual—along with our tea. A bit farther along there's a group of Masai warriors. "Jutta, do you by any chance know one of that lot who keep looking over at us?" I ask. "You get stared at all the time here," says Jutta calmly. "We'll start looking for your Masai in the morning. We've still got a bit of a climb ahead of us today."

After a meal that, as far as I can see, costs next to nothing, we set off. It's a dusty, steadily rising trek in scorching heat. After barely a mile my bag seems unbearably heavy. Jutta has an idea. "Wait a minute. Let's take the shortcut to the Tourist Lodge. Maybe there'll be somebody there with a car!"

Suddenly, on the narrow path, there's a rustling in the thicket nearby. "Corinne, don't move!" calls Jutta. "If it's buffalo, stay perfectly still." In terror, I try to make some sort of mental image out of the word "buffalo." We stand there motionless, and I recognize something about fifty feet away: pale with black stripes. Jutta spots it too and laughs with relief: "Phew, just zebras!" They gallop away from us in fear. I give Jutta a questioning look. "You said 'buffalo.' Are there any that close to the village?" "Just wait!" she replies. "When we get to the lodge there's a watering hole, and with any luck you'll see buffalos, zebras, apes, and gnus." "Isn't it dangerous for people using this path?" I ask in surprise. "Of course it is, but normally the only people who use this path are armed Samburu warriors. The women have bodyguards, and other people stick to the main road. It's safer, but this path is half as long."

I feel more secure when we get to the lodge. It's really rather splendid, not as pompous as the one where Marco and I stayed on the Masai-Mara. This is more modest but fits in better with the surrounding countryside. Compared with the native dwellings in Maralal, it's like a mirage appearing in the desert. We stroll in, but it's as dead as a tomb. We sit on the veranda, and indeed there at the water hole, just a hundred yards away, are herds of zebra. Over to the right a group of female baboons are tumbling around with their little ones. In their midst I spot an occasional huge male. They're all trying to get at the water.

Eventually a waiter strolls up and asks what we want. Jutta chats to him in Swahili and orders a couple of Cokes. While we're waiting she tells me with some satisfaction: "The manager of the lodge will be back in an hour or so. He has a Land Rover and is sure to take us on up, so we may as well sit back and wait." Both of us retreat into our private thoughts. I look at the hills all around. I'd give a fortune to know on or behind which of them Lketinga was. And if he could feel my presence.

We end up waiting nearly two hours before the manager arrives. He's a pleasant, unassuming, dark black man with no pretensions. He tells us to climb in, and a fifteen-minute shuttle takes us to our destination. We thank him, and Jutta shows me her workplace with pride. The house is a long concrete box divided into different rooms, two of which are nearly finished. We can live in one of them. The room has just one bed and one chair. There are no windows, so if you want to see, the doors have to be left wide open all day. I'm amazed that Jutta can feel at home in such a gloomy room. We light candles in order to see anything in the gathering darkness. Then we lie down together on the bed and make ourselves as comfortable as possible. I soon fall asleep from exhaustion.

We are woken early next morning by people noisily beginning work. First of all we clean ourselves thoroughly at a basin filled with cold water, which takes some courage, but then I want to look pretty when I finally see my Masai again.

Ready and raring for action, I want to head down to Maralal and take a closer look at the town. Given how many Masai warriors were around when we arrived, the one Jutta knows has to be among them. I manage to infect Jutta with my enthusiasm, and after the ritual cup of tea we set off. Every now and then we overtake women or young girls heading in the same direction carrying milk in calabashes to sell in town.

"What we need now are patience and good luck," says Jutta. "The main thing is to keep wandering around until we're spotted, or I recognize someone." There's not a lot to wander around. The single street runs in a sort of square with shops on either side. They're all half empty, and most of them sell the same stuff. In between the shops there are a few boardinghouses where you can buy something to eat or drink in the front room. The sleeping quarters are at the back, little compartments next to one another, like rabbit hutches. Then there's the toilet: an earth closet, usually. If you're lucky there might be a shower with a dribble of water. The most impressive building is the Commercial Bank, all concrete and fresh paint. Next to the bus stop there's a gas pump, but up until now I've seen only three cars: two Land Rovers and one pickup.

Our first tour of the village is rather fun. I look into every shop, and one or other of the shopkeepers tries to talk to us in English. All the time a whole pack of children drags along behind us laughing and talking excitedly. I understand only one word: "*Mzungu, mzungu*—white people, white people."

About four o'clock in the afternoon we set off for home again. My initial high has evaporated, even though logically I know I was never likely to find Lketinga on the first day. Jutta humors me: "Tomorrow there'll be a whole new set of people in the village. Very few people actually live there, and they're not who we're looking for. New faces show up every day. Tomorrow a few more people will know that there are two white women here because the ones who were here today will tell others out there in the bush." Jutta thinks it will be three or four days at least before there's a real chance.

The days pass, and everything that was new and exciting about Maralal loses its appeal as I get to know every last corner of the place. Jutta showed my photos of Lketinga to a few warriors, but we got nothing more than suspicious looks. By the end of a week nothing's happened except that we start to feel stupid doing the same thing every day. Jutta says she'll come with me one more time, and then it's up to me to show the photos around on my own. I pray that night that something will happen and that the whole long journey won't have been wasted.

Next day we're on our third circuit of the village when a man comes up and speaks to Jutta. The big holes in his earlobes lead me to recognize him as a former Samburu warrior. A lively conversation ensues, and I get the happy impression that Jutta knows him. His name is Tom, and when Jutta shows him the photos of Lketinga he looks at them long and hard before saying: "Yes, I know him."

I feel as if I've had an electric shock. But because the two are mostly speaking Swahili, I understand next to nothing. I keep asking Jutta: "What is it? What does he know about Lketinga?" We go into a restaurant and sit down for Jutta to translate. Yes, he knows him, not very well, but he knows that this man lives at home with his mother and takes the cattle out every day. "Where does he live?" I ask in excitement. It's a long way, he says, about seven hours on foot for a fit man. There's thick jungle on the way, which can be dangerous because of elephants and buffalo. Even then, he can't be absolutely sure that the mother still lives at the same place— Barsaloi—because people move about with their animals, depending on the water supply.

Hearing this makes Lketinga seem as distant as ever once again, and I'm at my wits' end. "Jutta, ask him if there's any way to get a message to him. I'm ready to pay." Tom thinks and then says he can take a letter from me tomorrow evening, but first he'd have to tell his new wife, who's still new to Maralal and doesn't know anyone. We settle on a fee, giving him half now and the other half when he comes back with some news. I dictate a letter for Jutta to write in Swahili. The Samburu says we should be back in Maralal in four days' time because if he finds Lketinga and he wants to come with him, they would be back during that day.

Four long days, during which I pray every evening. By the last day my nerves are at a breaking point. On the one hand, I'm really excited; but on the other, I know that if it hasn't worked, I'll have to go back to Mombasa and try to forget the love of my life. I take my bag with me because I've decided to spend the night in the village rather than at Jutta's house. One way or the other, with or without Lketinga, I'm leaving Maralal tomorrow.

Jutta and I traipse around the town like before. After three hours we split up and go in opposite directions to give ourselves more chance of being spotted. On one circuit I fail to bump into Jutta at the usual halfway point. I stroll on, however, until all of a sudden a little boy runs up to me calling, "*Mzungu, mzungu,* come, come." He's grabbing at my arm and pulling my skirt. At first I think something's happened to Jutta. The boy pulls me toward the first set of boardinghouses, where I've left my bag, speaking in Swahili all the time. Then he points behind the house.

Magical Maralal

With my heart hammering, I follow the direction he's pointing and peer around the corner of the houses. And there he is! My Masai! Standing there next to Tom and laughing at me. I'm speechless. Still laughing, he holds out his arms and says: "Hey, Corinne, no kiss for me?" Only then do I shake myself out of a stupor and rush toward him. We fall into each other's arms, and it is as if the world stops turning. Then he holds me at arm's length and says: "No problem, Corinne." The same old words that right now make me want to weep with happiness.

Then Jutta appears from behind me to share our delight. "There you are, then, together again! I recognized him straightaway and brought him here so that the two of you could greet each other without the whole village looking on." I thank Tom with all my heart and tell him we're all going for tea, and then the two men can eat as much meat as they want, all on my tab. We go into the room I've taken, sit on the bed, and take a look at the menu. Jutta has spoken to Lketinga and told him that there's no problem for him to eat with us because we're not Samburu women. He consults with Tom and in the end agrees.

There he is at last. I can't take my eyes off him, and he keeps his big beautiful eyes on me. I want to know why he didn't come to Mombasa. It turns out he really didn't get any of my letters. Twice he went to see about the passport, but the official just laughed at him and teased him. The other warriors took against him too and wouldn't let him join in their dances for the tourists. If he couldn't dance, he couldn't make any money, so he saw no reason to stay any longer down by the coast. After about a month he decided to go home. He didn't believe anymore that I was coming back. Once he tried to telephone me from the Africana Sea Lodge, but nobody would help him, and the manager told him the phone was for tourists only.

On the one hand I'm touched by all the effort he made: on the other, I'm absolutely furious at his so-called friends who only caused problems instead of helping him. When I tell him that I want to stay in Kenya now and not go back to Switzerland, he says, "It's okay. You stay now with me!" Jutta and Tom the messenger leave us to get on with our happy attempts at conversation. Lketinga says it's a shame that we can't go back to his home but there's a drought and not enough food. Apart from milk there's nothing to eat, and in any case there isn't a spare house. I tell him I don't mind as long as we're together. So he suggests that first we go back to Mombasa. There will be time enough for me to get to know his home and his mother, but he wants to introduce me to his brother James, who goes to school in Maralal. James is the only one of the family to have been to school. He can tell James he's gone back to Mombasa with me, and when he goes home in the school holidays he can tell their mother.

The school is about a mile from the village. They have strict rules. Boys and girls play in separate playgrounds. But they all dress alike: the girls in simple blue dresses, the boys in blue trousers and white shirts. I wait to one side while Lketinga goes over to the boys. Soon they're all staring at him and then at me. He chats with them, and then one of them runs off and comes back with another boy, who goes up to Lketinga and greets him respectfully. They talk for a bit, and then both come over to me. James holds out his hand with a friendly smile and shakes mine. I put him at about sixteen. He speaks very good English and says he sorry he can't come into the village with us but they have just a short break and they aren't allowed out in the evenings. The headmaster is very strict, he says. Then the bell rings and in the blink of an eye they've all gone, including James.

We go back into the village, and I suggest we might retire to the room in the boardinghouse, but Lketinga laughs and says: "This is Maralal, not Mombasa!" It seems that a man and woman don't go into a room together until it's dark and then as inconspicuously as possible. It's not that I'm desperate for sex—after all, I know what it's like—but after all these months I could do with some physical contact.

We stroll around Maralal, and I keep a respectable distance, as this seems the thing to do. Every now and then he talks to other warriors or a few girls. The girls are all young and with pretty jewelry and quickly cast a curious glance in my direction and then giggle, whereas the warriors look me over in more detail. I seem to be the subject of most of the conversations, which makes me uncomfortable, because I don't know what anyone's saying. I can hardly wait for it to get dark.

At the market Lketinga buys a little plastic bag with red powder, pointing at his hair and his war paint. On one of the other stalls someone is selling little stalks with leaves, tied together in bundles about eight inches long. There's a real argument going on between the five or six men examining them.

Lketinga heads for this stall too. The salesman takes some newspaper and wraps up two bundles. Lketinga pays a fat price for them and quickly sticks them under the kanga cloth wrapped around him. On the way back to the boardinghouse he buys at least ten sticks of chewing gum. When we get to the room I ask him about the plant. He beams at me and says: "*Miraa*, it's very good. You eat this, no sleeping!" He gets everything out, pops a bit of chewing gum in his mouth, and separates the leaves from the stalks. He uses his teeth to strip the bark from the stalks and chews it along with the gum. I watch in fascination how elegantly his beautiful, long, thin hands move. I have a go, but it's far too bitter for me, and I spit it out immediately. I lie down on the bed and feel happy just watching him and holding his hand. I feel as if I could hug the entire world. I've attained my goal. I've found my one great love again, and tomorrow we'll go back to Mombasa and start our wonderful life together.

I must have fallen asleep only to wake up and find Lketinga still sitting there, chewing away. The floor looks like a trash can or worse with leaves, stripped stalks, and spat-out green lumps all over the place. He looks at me with a steady gaze, strokes my hair, and says: "No problem, Corinne, you tired, you sleep, tomorrow safari." "And you?" I ask him. "You not tired?" No, he says, before a long journey he can't sleep, that's why he's eating *miraa*.

The way he says it, I get the impression that this *miraa* is the equivalent of Dutch courage, for Masai warriors are not allowed to touch alcohol. I can understand that he needs courage because he doesn't know what lies ahead of us, and his experience of Mombasa was not exactly the best. This is his world. Mombasa may be in Kenya, but it's not where his tribe comes from. I'll help him, I tell myself, and go back to sleep.

The next morning we have to get up early to get seats on the only bus that goes to Nyahururu. But as Lketinga hasn't been to bed, that's not a problem. I'm amazed by how fit he is and the way he can just set out on such a long journey spontaneously with no luggage, wearing just jewelry and some cloth and carrying his stick.

This is just the first stage. Lketinga has secreted the rest of the *miraa* somewhere and chews on the same piece. He's quiet, and somehow there isn't the same atmosphere as on the bus Jutta and I arrived on.

Once again the bus lurches through thousands of potholes. Lketinga has pulled his second kanga cloth over his head so that only his eyes can be seen, and his beautiful hair is protected from the dust. I hold a handkerchief against my nose and mouth so that I can at least partly breathe. About halfway Lketinga nudges me and points to a long gray hill. It's only when I take a longer look that I realize that I'm looking at hundreds of elephants. It's a phenomenal sight: these giant creatures as far as the eye can see with their little ones among them. The bus comes alive with chatter as everyone stares at the vast herd; from what I can gather, it's a rare sight.

At last the first stage is behind us, and by midday we're in Nyahururu. We go for tea, or chai, and a lump of bread. The next bus to Nairobi's in just half an hour, and we'll get there by nightfall. I suggest to Lketinga that we spend the night there and get the bus to Mombasa in the morning. He doesn't want to stay in Nairobi because the boardinghouses charge too much. Given that I'm paying for everything, I find that touching and reassure him, but he still reckons Nairobi is dangerous and there are too many police. Despite the fact that we've been on a bus since seven this morning, he wants to do the longest stretch of the journey all at once. And when I notice how unsure of himself he seems in Nairobi, I agree.

We get something to eat and drink quickly, and I'm happy that at least he's eating with me, even if he pulls the kanga across his face so that no one will recognize him. The bus station isn't far, and we walk the few hundred yards. Here in Nairobi even the natives give Lketinga strange looks: some laughing, some respectful. He doesn't fit into this hectic modern city. When I realize that, I'm relieved the passport didn't work out.

Eventually we get ourselves onto one of the sought-after night buses and wait for it to set off. Lketinga gets more *miraa* out and starts chewing again. I try to relax, but my whole body hurts. Only my heart is at peace.

After four hours, during which I've dozed on and off, the bus stops in Voi. Most people, including me, climb out to answer the call of nature. But when I see the fouled state of the hole in the ground that serves as a toilet, I decide to hold on for another four hours. I get back on the bus with two bottles of Coke. Half an hour later we set off again. Now I can't get back to sleep at all. We hurtle through the night on dead-straight roads. Every now and then we pass a bus going the opposite way. There are almost no cars.

Twice we go through police checkpoints. The bus has to stop because they have laid wooden planks with long nails across the road. Then a policeman, armed with an automatic weapon, walks along each side of the bus and shines his flashlight in every face. After five minutes we're allowed to continue again. I'm still trying to get comfortable when I see a sign that says "157 miles to Mombasa." Thank God, not too far now to home. Lketinga still hasn't slept a wink. This *miraa* obviously really does keep you awake. The only thing is that his eyes stare more than usual, and he doesn't seem to want to talk. It disquiets me a bit. But then there's the smell of salt in the air, and the temperature starts to rise. Nairobi's cold and damp are just memories.

Back to Mombasa

We finally arrive in Mombasa just after five A.M. A few people get out at the bus station. I go to get off too, but Lketinga holds me back, saying that there are no buses along the coast before six, and it's less dangerous to wait on the bus. We've arrived at last, but we still can't get off the bus. I'm bursting. I try to tell Lketinga this, and he says, "Come!," and gets up. We get out, and between two empty buses, with no one to be seen save a few roaming cats and dogs, I finally empty my bladder. Lketinga laughs as he watches my "river."

The air on the coast is wonderful, and I ask him if we can't just go to the nearest *matatu* stand. He grabs my bag, and we set out in the pale dawn light. A night watchman brewing chai on a charcoal brazier outside a shop even offers us our breakfast cup. In return, Lketinga gives him some *miraa*. From time to time huddled figures pass by: some babbling to themselves, others silent. Here and there people are sleeping on newspapers or cardboard boxes on the ground. This time, before the shops open, is given over to ghosts. But with my warrior at my side I feel totally safe.

The first *matatus* start hooting just before six, and within ten minutes or so the whole area is alive. We get on board a bus to the ferry, and once again a feeling of great happiness comes over me. Then there is the last hour on a bus to the south coast. Lketinga seems nervous. I ask him: "Darling, are you okay?" "Yes," he says, and then starts talking to me. I don't understand everything he says, but I gather he intends to find out who stole my letters to him and which of the Masai told me he was married. He looks so grim that it almost scares me. I try to calm him down, tell him that none of it matters anymore, but he doesn't answer and just looks out of the window.

We go straight to the village, where Priscilla is astounded to see the two of us. She greets us warmly and makes chai. Esther has gone. All my stuff is hanging neatly folded over a string behind the door. Lketinga and Priscilla talk, amicably at first, but then the discussion takes a serious tone. I try to find out what's going on, and Priscilla tells me he's accusing her of knowing that I'd written. Eventually Lketinga calms down and goes off to sleep on our big bed.

Priscilla and I remain outside to try to find a solution to our sleeping arrangements: the three of us together, particularly with a Masai woman, is not an option. Then another Masai who's planning to move to the northern coast offers us his hut. So in the end we clean my new home, drag my big bed across, and when I've sorted things out as best I can, I'm happy with the arrangement and a rent that costs the equivalent of ten Swiss francs a month.

The next two weeks are an idyll. I start teaching Lketinga to read and write. He's delighted and shows real enthusiasm for learning. The English picture books are a great help, and he takes pride in every letter he learns to recognize. In the evenings we sometimes go to watch Masai dances for the tourists and sell Masai trinkets that we make ourselves. Lketinga and I make pretty armbands, and Priscilla embroiders belts.

On one occasion there's a daylong sale of paintings, trinkets, and spears at the Robinson Club. A lot of people from the north bank come over for it, including Masai women. Lketinga has gone into Mombasa and bought some things from local traders to give us more to display. Business is brilliant. The white people swarm around our stand and swamp me with questions. When we've sold nearly all our stuff, I join some of the other sellers to help them. Lketinga doesn't like that because some of these Masai are still to blame for keeping us apart for so long. On the other hand, I don't want any ill feeling because they have generously allowed us to join in.

Time and again one or other group of tourists at the bar invites us to join them for a drink. I join a few of them, but once or twice is enough. It's more fun selling. Lketinga hangs around the bar with a couple of Germans. From time to time I glance across but see only their backs. After a while I go over to join them briefly and am horrified to see Lketinga drinking beer. For a warrior alcohol is forbidden. Even if the Masai on the coast drink occasionally, Lketinga is from the Samburu District and certainly not used to alcohol. I ask him worriedly: "Darling, why you drink beer?" But he just laughs: "These friends invited me." I tell the Germans to stop buying him beer immediately because he's not used to alcohol. They apologize and try to calm me down, saying he's only had three! I just hope it's okay.

Eventually the sale comes to an end, and we pack up what remains. Outside the hotel the Masai are splitting up the money. I'm hungry, tired from the heat and standing all day, and want to go home. Lketinga, a bit tipsy but still in a good mood, decides to go to Ukunda to eat with a couple of the others. I pass and go back disappointed, alone.

That is my biggest mistake as I learn later. In five days' time my visa is due to run out, I realize on the way back to the village. Lketinga and I intend to go to Nairobi, although I can't bear the thought of the long journey, let alone the Kenyan authorities! It'll be okay, I tell myself as I open the door to our hut. I cook some rice and tomatoes for myself, which is all there is in the kitchen. The village is quiet.

A little earlier it had occurred to me that since my return with Lketinga, hardly anyone comes to visit anymore. I miss that a bit now because the evenings spent playing cards were fun. Priscilla isn't there either, and so I lie down on the bed and start writing a letter to my mother. I tell her what a peaceful life we're leading and how happy I am.

It's already ten P.M., and Lketinga isn't back yet. I'm starting to get worried, but the clicking of the cicadas calms my nerves. Just before midnight the door flies open with a bang, and Lketinga appears in it. First of all he stares at me, taking in the whole room. His face is hard, and there's no trace of his former merriness. He's chewing *miraa*, and when I say hello, he asks, "Who was here?" "Nobody," I reply. At the same time my pulse is racing. Never before has he asked who else has been in the house. Angrily I repeat that there's been no one here while he, still standing in the doorway, insists that he knows I have a boyfriend. Of all things! I sit up in bed and give him a frosty glare. "Where did you get such a stupid idea from?" He knows, because they told him in Ukunda that I had a different Masai in the house every evening, and they stayed with me and Priscilla until late. All women are the same, he says, I've had someone all the time!

His harsh words shatter my little world. At long last I've found him
again, we've had two wonderful weeks together, and now this! The beer
and the *miraa* have completely addled his wits. To stop myself bursting into
tears, I pull myself together and ask him if he'd like some chai. Eventually,
he comes away from the door and sits down on the bed. With trembling
hands I light a fire and try to be as calm as possible. He asks where Priscilla
is, but I don't know; her house is in darkness. He gives a nasty laugh and
says: "Maybe she's down the Bush Baby Disco trying to score with a
whitey!" I have to keep from laughing at his wild imagination. Instead I
stay silent.

We drink our chai, and I ask cautiously if he's okay. He says he's fine,
except that his heart is pounding and his blood rushing. I try to work out
exactly what he's trying to tell me, but I'm not sure I know. He keeps
walking around the hut or going out and roaming around the village and
then he's back, chewing his weed. He looks nervous, restless. I wonder
what I can do to help. Obviously, he's had too much *miraa*, but I can't just
take it away from him.

After two hours he's finished it all, and I hope he'll come to bed and
tomorrow it'll all be forgotten. He lies down, but he can't sleep. I daren't
touch him, so instead I squeeze up against the wall, glad that the bed's so
big. After a while he jumps up and says he can't sleep in the same bed as
me. His blood's rushing like mad, and he thinks his head's going to burst.
I'm wracked by confusion: "Darling, where will you go?" He says he'll go
and sleep with the other Masai and disappears. I'm dejected and furious
all at once. What on earth have they done to him in Ukunda? I ask myself.
The night goes on forever. Lketinga doesn't come back. I don't know
where he's sleeping.

Sick in the Head

At the crack of dawn I'm straight up and washing my puffy, tearstained face. Then I go over to Priscilla's. It's not locked up, which means she must be there. I knock and call softly: "It's me, Corinne, please open the door. I have a big problem." Still more than half asleep, Priscilla comes out and stares at me in shock. "Where is Lketinga?" she asks. With immense difficulty I hold back my tears and tell her everything. She listens attentively while she's getting dressed and tells me to wait while she goes to the Masai to find out what's going on. Ten minutes later she's back and says we'll have to wait, he's not there, didn't sleep with them, and must have run off into the bush. He'll be back for sure and if not we'll go and find him. "What would he be doing in the bush?" I ask, confused. Probably the beer and the *miraa* were doing things to his head, says Priscilla. I should just wait a bit.

But he doesn't turn up. I go back into our little house and wait. Then, at about ten A.M., two warriors turn up carrying a completely exhausted Lketinga. They drag him into the house and lay him down on the bed. I'm angry that I don't understand any of what's being said. He lies there apathetically staring at the ceiling. I speak to him, but he just looks through me as if he doesn't recognize me. He's sweating all over. I'm close to panic because I don't understand what's happening. The others don't have a clue either: they found him in the bush under a tree and say he ran amok. That's why he's so exhausted. I ask Priscilla if I should fetch a doctor, but she says there's only one here at Diani Beach and he won't come out to the village. We'd have to go to him, and in the circumstances that's out of the question.

Lketinga falls asleep again and has weird dreams about lions attacking him. He throws his arms about wildly, and the two warriors have to hold him down. It breaks my heart to look at him. What has happened to my brave, good-humored Masai? I can't stop myself crying, which annoys Priscilla: "That's no good. You only cry when someone dies."

It's the middle of the afternoon before Lketinga comes to and stares at me, befuddled. I smile happily at him and say: "Hello, darling, you remember me?" "Why not, Corinne?" he answers weakly, then looks over at Priscilla and asks what's going on. They talk to each other, and he shakes his head and can hardly believe his ears. I stay with him while the others all go off to work. He's hungry and has a stomachache. When I ask if I should get some meat, he says: "Oh, yes, it's okay." I hurry to the meat stand and back. Lketinga's still in bed, asleep again. An hour later, when the food is ready, I try to wake him. He opens his eyes and stares at me in confusion again. Who am I, what do I want with him? "I'm Corinne, your girlfriend," I reply. But he keeps asking me who I am. I don't know what to do, and Priscilla hasn't returned from selling her kangas on the beach. I tell him he should eat something, but he laughs scornfully. He's not going to touch any of this so-called food; I'm obviously trying to poison him.

Now I can no longer hold back the tears. He looks at me and asks who's died. To keep myself in check, I pray aloud. At last Priscilla comes back, and I bring her in immediately. She tries to talk to him too but doesn't get any further. After a while she says: "He's crazy!" A lot of the *morans*, the warriors who come along the coast, get Mombasa madness, she says, and his is a bad case: maybe someone made him crazy. "What, how, and who?" I stammer, adding that I don't believe in superstitious things. But Priscilla tells me that I've a lot to learn in Africa. "We have to help him," I implore her. "Okay!" she says, she'll send someone up to the north bank to get help. That's the big center for the coastal Masai, and their chief is acknowledged as the leader of all the warriors. He will have to decide what is to be done.

Around nine o'clock in the evening two warriors from the north bank come to see us. Although they aren't very pleasant toward me, I'm pleased that something's being done. They talk to Lketinga and massage his forehead with a pungent flower. When they talk to him, he gives completely normal answers. I can hardly believe it. Before he was so confused, and now he's talking calmly. I can't understand a word and feel helpless and redundant. So to have something to do I make chai for everyone.

There is such trust between the three men that they are barely aware of my presence. Nonetheless, they accept the tea gladly, and I ask what the matter is. One of them speaks some English and tells me Lketinga is not well: he is sick in the head. He needs rest and space, which is why the three of them are going to go off to sleep out in the bush. Tomorrow they will take him to the north bank to see to things. "But why can't he sleep here with me?" I ask, flustered and unwilling to believe anybody anymore, even though he's obviously feeling better. No, they say, my proximity now would be bad for his blood. Even Lketinga apparently agrees that, as he's never been ill like this before, it must be to do with me. I'm shocked, but I've no choice other than to let him go with them.

The next morning they do indeed come back and have tea. Lketinga seems well, almost his old self, but the other two insist that he must come with them to the north bank. He laughs and agrees: "Now I'm okay!" When I mention that tonight I have to go to Nairobi to get my visa extension, he says, "No problem. We'll go to the north bank and then on together to Nairobi."

When we get to the north bank, there's a lot of chattering and gossiping before we're brought to the "chief's" hut. He's not as old as I had anticipated and greets us warmly, although he can't see us because he's blind. He talks patiently with Lketinga. I sit there and watch, not understanding a word. In any case I wouldn't dare to interrupt the conversation. Time is getting short, however, and although I'm getting the night bus I need to get the ticket about three or four hours earlier if I want to get a place.

After an hour, the chief tells me I have to go without Lketinga because Nairobi would not be good for his condition and his sensitive disposition. They will look after him and I should come back as soon as possible. I agree because I would be completely useless if the same thing were to happen again in Nairobi. So I promise Lketinga that I'll catch the bus back tomorrow night as long as everything goes okay. He looks very sad as I climb on board the bus, holding my hand and asking me if I really will come back. I reassure him and tell him not to worry, I'll be back and we'll see what to do then. If he is still not well, we'd find a doctor. He promises me he'll wait and do everything possible to avoid a recurrence. The *matatu* leaves, and my heart sinks. As long as everything goes okay!

In Mombasa I get my ticket, but now I have to wait five hours before the bus goes. Eight hours after that I arrive in Nairobi in the early morning. Once again I have to wait in the bus until just before seven, before getting out. I have a cup of tea and take a taxi to the Nyayo Building, the only way I know to find it. When I arrive, the place is in chaos. Whites and blacks alike are pushing and shoving at the various windows. I suffer through all the forms that I have to fill in, all in English of course. Then I hand them all in and wait. Three whole hours pass before my name is called. I hope fervently that I get the necessary stamp. The woman at the window looks me up and down and asks why I want to stay another three months. As relaxed as I can, I answer: "Because I've seen nothing like enough of this magnificent country, and I've got enough money to stay another three months." She opens my passport, flicks through it, and then thumps down a huge stamp on the relevant page. I've got my visa: one step further! I pay the fee happily and leave the dreadful building. Right now I cannot imagine that I will eventually see so much of this building that I will hate it with a vengeance.

With a ticket for that night's bus securely in my pocket I head off for something to eat. It's still early afternoon, and I wander around Nairobi to stop myself from falling asleep. I haven't slept properly in more than thirty hours. In order not to get lost I restrict my wanderings to two streets. By seven o'clock it's dark, and as the shops close the nightlife slowly begins in the bars. The figures on the streets become more sinister with every passing minute, and I decide not to linger there any longer. A bar is out of the question, so I opt to pass the next two hours in a nearby McDonald's.

Eventually I'm on the bus back to Mombasa. The driver is chewing *miraa*. He drives like a madman but gets us back in record time, arriving at just four in the morning. Once again I have to wait for the first *matatu* to the north bank. I can't wait to see how Lketinga is.

Just before seven I'm already back in the Masai village. Everyone's still asleep, and the teahouse isn't open yet, so I wait outside it, as I don't know which hut Lketinga is staying in. Around seven-thirty the teahouse owner arrives and opens up. I go in, sit down, and wait for the day's first cup of chai. He brings it to me, then disappears back into the kitchen.

Soon after a few warriors come in and sit down at other tables. The atmosphere is very quiet, suppressed, but I put that down to the fact that it's still early morning.

After half an hour I can no longer contain myself and ask the owner if he knows where Lketinga is. He shakes his head and disappears again. But after another half hour he sits down at my table and tells me I should go back to the south bank and not wait around any longer. I stare at him in astonishment and ask: "Why?" "He's not here anymore," the man says. "He went home last night." My heart misses a beat. "Home to the south bank?" I ask naively. "No, home to Samburu-Maralal."

"No, that's not true!" I shout, horrified. "He's here. Tell me where!" Two others come across from their table to try to calm me down. I beat back their hands, rage, and shout at them in German: "You pack of lying pigs, you planned all this!" Tears of anger run down my face, but I couldn't care less.

I'm so furious that I'm ready to lay into any of them. They put him on the bus knowing that I'd be getting the very same bus in the opposite direction. We must have passed in the night. I can't believe it. How mean could they get! As if these eight hours were all that mattered! More spectators have gathered, but I charge out of the place to get away from them. As far as I'm concerned they're all the same. Sad and bitter, I set off back to the south bank.

"You Come to My Home"

I no longer know what to do. I've got my visa, but Lketinga's gone. Priscilla and two warriors are sitting in her hut. I tell her what happened, and she translates for the others. Eventually Priscilla tells me that, although Lketinga is really nice, it's better that I forget him. Either he really is sick or the others threatened him with something that made him go back to his mother because he couldn't stay in Mombasa. He needed a medicine man. I couldn't help him, and in any case it would be dangerous for a white to set herself up against all the others.

I'm completely at a loss and don't know what or whom to believe anymore. Only my instinct tells me that Lketinga was sent off against his will before my return. That same evening the first warriors turn up to start paying court again. When the second one comes out with it and says I need him for a boyfriend because Lketinga was "crazy" and won't be back, I'm angered and throw them all out. When I tell Priscilla, she just laughs and says that's how it goes, I shouldn't be so uptight. She obviously hasn't grasped that I don't want just anybody and only gave up my whole life back in Switzerland for Lketinga.

The next day I write a letter to his brother James in Maralal. Maybe he'll know more. But it'll be two weeks before I get an answer. Two long weeks without knowing what's going on. I'll go mad. On the fourth day I can't take it any longer. In secrecy I plan to pack up and undertake the long route to Maralal alone. Then I'd see what I'd do, but I wasn't giving up. I'd show them. I don't tell even Priscilla what I'm planning because I no longer trust anybody. When she goes off to the beach to sell her kangas, I pack my bag and set off for Mombasa.

Once again I put another eight hundred miles behind me before I'm back in Maralal. I take the same boardinghouse room as last time, for four francs, though the landlady is astonished to see me again. I lie down on the cot in the spartanly furnished little room and think: What now? Tomorrow I will go to see Lketinga's brother.

First I have to persuade the headmaster to fetch James for me. I tell James everything that happened, and he says that if he's allowed he'll take me to his mother. After a lot of persuasion the headmaster agrees, as long as I can find a car to take James and me to Barsaloi. Pleased at having gotten so far with my modest English, I ask around Maralal for someone who has a car. The few who do are almost all Somalis, but when I tell them where I want to go, they just laugh at me or demand astronomical prices.

On the second day I bump into my savior from the time before, Tom, who went and found Lketinga. He too asks me where Lketinga is. When I explain, he understands, with some astonishment, and says he'll try to find a car, because my skin color just puts the price up fivefold. And indeed, by lunchtime we're both sitting in a Land Rover he has hired, including its driver, for five hundred Swiss francs. James stays behind, as Tom has agreed to come.

The Land Rover takes us out of Maralal along a desolate red clay road. After a while it leads into thick forest of giant trees covered in tropical vines. We can't see more than six or seven feet into the trees, and soon even our trail is recognizable only from car tracks. Everything else is overgrown. Sitting in the back of the Land Rover, I can hardly see anything. Only our shifting angle of incline hints that the path is steep and winding. When we emerge from the forest an hour later, we're faced with enormous lumps of rock. There's no way to pass. Until my two companions get out and manage to move a couple of them. Then we set off again, slowly, over the debris and scree in our way. Now I appreciate the price I paid, and from what I feel rather than see, I'd be ready to pay more. It seems miraculous that the vehicle can get over it at all in one piece, but the driver is a genius and we do it.

Now we pass occasional *manyattas* and see children with herds of goats or cattle. I'm getting excited. When will we be there? Is it somewhere out here where my darling lives? Or has the whole exercise been in vain? Is there still any hope? I say my prayers quietly. My savior, however, is calm.

Eventually we cross a wide riverbed, and a couple of bends away I spot a few blockhouses and above them, on a height, a huge building that rises out of the landscape like an oasis, green and welcoming. "Where are we?" I ask my companion. "This is Barsaloi town, and up there is the new Mission building. First we'll go to the *manyattas* and see if Lketinga is at his mother's," he tells me. We drive past the Mission, and I'm amazed by the amount of greenery because it's so dry, like a steppe or semidesert.

After three hundred yards we turn off the road and rattle over the steppe. Two minutes later the car stops, Tom gets out and tells me to come with him. He tells the driver to wait. A few adults and several children are sitting under a big, flat-topped tree. My companion goes up to them while I wait a little way back. They all glance over at me. After a long chat with an old woman, he comes back and says to me: "Come, Corinne, his mama tells me Lketinga is here." We walk through tall, prickly plants until we come to three very simple *manyatta* houses set about sixteen feet apart. There are two long spears stuck in the ground before the middle one. Tom points to it and says: "Here he is inside." I don't dare move, so he bends down and goes in. I'm so close to him, I can't see past his back, but I hear Tom speak and then Lketinga's voice. That's enough for me, I squeeze in past him. The happy, surprised, almost incredulous look on Lketinga's face when he sees me will remain with me all my life. Lying on a cowhide in a little room behind the fire in the smoky half darkness, he suddenly erupts with laughter. Tom makes way for me as well as he can, and I crawl into Lketinga's outstretched arms. We hold each other tight for ages, and he says: "I know always, if you love me, you come to my home."

Seeing each other again like this, I find this reunion is better than anything else so far. At this very moment I know that I will stay here even if we have nothing but each other. Lketinga speaks to me from his heart and says: "Now you are my wife, you stay with me like a Samburu wife." I'm overjoyed.

My traveling companion looks at me skeptically and asks if he should really go back to Maralal in the Land Rover alone. He says I'd find it hard here, there's not much to eat, and I'd have to sleep on the ground. And there's no way I'd make it back to Maralal on foot. I couldn't care less, and I tell him: "Wherever Lketinga lives, I can live too!"

For a second it goes dark in the hut. Lketinga's mother is pushing through the little entranceway. She sits down opposite the fire and looks at me gravely for a long time. I'm aware that this is a decisive moment, so I say nothing. We sit there, holding hands, our faces glowing. If we could radiate light, the hut would be bright as day.

Lketinga says only a couple of words to his mother, and I can make out *"mzungu"* or "Mombasa." His mother looks at me unblinkingly. She is very black. There is a pretty shape to her shaven head, and she wears colored pearls for earrings and around her neck. She is plumpish with two long, enormous naked breasts and a dirty skirt covering her legs.

Then all of a sudden she reaches out her hand and says: *"Jambo."* Then she breaks into a torrent of speech. I look at Lketinga. "Mother has given her blessing. We can stay with her in the hut." Then Tom takes his leave, and I go to fetch my bag from the Land Rover. When I come back, there is a whole crowd of people around the *manyatta*.

Toward evening I hear a tinkling of bells. We go out, and I see a huge herd of goats. Most just pass by, but some are driven into our wicker corral. There are about thirty in the pen, which is reinforced with thorny branches. Then his mother takes a calabash gourd and goes to milk the goats. There is just enough milk for the chai, I discover later. The herds are looked after by an eight-year-old boy. He sits down outside the *manyatta* and looks at me apprehensively as he swallows a couple of cups of water thirstily. He is the son of Lketinga's older brother.

An hour later it's dark. The four of us are sitting in the little *manyatta*, Mama in front near the entrance with Saguna, a frightened little girl of three who is the boy's little sister, next to her. She cuddles timidly up to her grandmother, who is now her mother. When the first girl of the eldest son is old enough, Lketinga explains, she will belong to his mother to help her in her old age with gathering wood and fetching water.

The two of us sit on the cowhide. Mama pokes around amid the lumps of flint in the ash until she gets a glow, then she blows slowly but continuously on the sparks. For a few minutes there is acrid smoke, which brings tears to my eyes. Everybody laughs. I get a fit of coughing and have to push my way out into the open air. Air is the only thing I can think of.

Outside the hut it's as black as pitch. But the millions of stars look so close you might pluck them from the sky. I enjoy the sensation of peace. Everywhere there's the glow of fires in the *manyattas*, including ours now, and Mama is cooking chai, our evening meal. After chai, my bladder begs for attention, but Lketinga laughs and says: "Here no toilet, only bush.

Come with me, Corinne!" Deftly he slips out, pushes a thornbush aside, and opens a way through. These thornbushes are the only protection against wild animals. We go some three hundred yards away from the corral, and he points with his *rungu* club to a bush that from now on is to be my toilet. At night I can pee closer to the *manyatta*, because the sand soaks everything up, but never the rest, or else we'd have to offer a goat to the neighbors and move away, which would bring great shame.

Back next to the *manyatta* the thornbush is moved into place again, and we sit back on the cowhide. Washing here is not done because there's only enough water for the chai. When I ask Lketinga how we're to keep ourselves clean, he says: "Tomorrow, at the river, no problem!" Inside the hut it is warm now, but outside it is cold. The little girl is already sound asleep naked next to her grandmother, and the three of us attempt a conversation. People here go to bed around eight or nine P.M., and we too snuggle down as the fire is gradually fading and it's getting hard to see one another. Lketinga and I cuddle together. Although we'd both like to do more, obviously nothing can happen in the presence of his mother and in this total silence.

The first night, unused to the hard earth, I sleep badly, tossing and turning from one side to the other and listening to every little sound. Now and then a goat's bell tinkles, ringing, it seems to me, like church bells in the silence. Some animal howls in the distance. Then there's a rustling at the thorn fence—quite clearly, someone's trying to come into the corral. My heart's pounding, and I'm straining to listen. I crawl flat on my stomach to the entrance and look out at two black girders—no, they're legs—and the tips of two spears. At that moment a man's voice rings out: *"Supa moran!"* I prod Lketinga in the side and whisper: "Darling, somebody is here." He makes strange noises, more like grunts, and for a split second stares at me almost angrily. "Somebody is outside," I tell him pointedly. Then there's the voice again: *"Moran supa!"* Then there's an exchange of words, and the legs suddenly move and disappear. "What's the problem?" I ask. The man, another warrior, wanted to spend the night with us, which normally wouldn't have been a problem, but because I'm here it isn't possible. He will try to find room in another *manyatta*. I should go back to sleep.

The sun rises at around six A.M., and men and animals rise with it. The goats bray loudly, wanting out from their pen. There are voices everywhere, and already Mama's place is empty. We get up an hour later and drink chai. This is almost torture because the flies wake up too with the morning sun, and if I put the cup on the ground dozens immediately cluster around it. They buzz continuously around my head. Saguna seems not to notice them, even though they settle around her eyes and in the corners of her mouth. I ask Lketinga where they all come from. He points to the pile of goat dung that's built up overnight. In the course of the day the dung dries out, and there are fewer flies. That was why I hadn't found them so persistent the night before. He laughs and says wait until the cows come back, then it'll be much worse; their milk attracts thousands of flies. The mosquitoes that appear after it rains are even nicer! After chai, I want to go down to the river to wash at last. We head off, me armed with soap, towels, and clean clothes, while all Lketinga carries is a yellow canister to fetch water for Mama's chai. We walk about a mile down a narrow path to the wide riverbed we crossed the day before in the Land Rover. Big, luxuriant trees border the river on both sides, but there's no sign of water. We wander along the dry riverbed until rocks appear round a bend, and here indeed a little stream emerges from the sand.

We aren't the only ones here. Next to the little stream a few girls have dug a hole in the sand and are patiently using beakers to fill their water canisters. When they see my warrior they drop their heads in embarrassment and giggle among themselves. Twenty yards farther along a group of warriors are standing next to the stream washing one another. Their loincloths are laid out on the warm stone to dry. They fall silent at the sight of me, although they are not obviously embarrassed by their nakedness. Lketinga stops and talks to a few of them. Some of them stare at me openly, and I don't know where to look. I've never seen so many naked men who don't seem to realize they are. Their slim elegant bodies shine magnificently in the morning sun.

Not knowing how I'm supposed to behave in an unfamiliar situation like this, I stroll on for a few yards and sit down by the sluggishly flowing stream. Lketinga comes up to me and says: "Corinne, come, here is not good for lady." We walk on around another bend in the riverbed to where we can't be seen, and here Lketinga takes his sparse clothing off and starts washing. When I go to do the same, he looks at me in horror: "No, Corinne, this is not good!" "Why not?" I ask. "How am I supposed to wash if I can't take my T-shirt and skirt off?" He tells me that to expose my legs would be indecent. We argue gently and in the end I kneel down naked and give myself a thorough wash. Lketinga rubs soap on my back and into my hair, all the while looking around to make sure there really is no one watching us.

The ritual of washing takes a couple of hours, and then we go back. There's lots going on by the river now: several women washing their head and feet, others digging holes to fill with water for the goats to drink. And still others are patiently filling water canisters. Lketinga sets his down too, and a girl immediately fills it for him.

Then we wander around the village because I want to see the shops. There are three square mud huts that are supposed to be shops. Lketinga talks to the owner of each, all of them Somalis. They each shake their head: there's nothing to buy except for some powdered tea and Kimbo brand tins of fat. The largest shop has a couple of pounds of rice. When we start to pack it up, I discover that the rice is full of little black beetles. "Oh, no," I say. "I don't want this." He says sorry and takes it back. We now have nothing to eat.

A few women sitting under a tree are selling cow's milk from calabashes. So at least we can buy milk. For a couple of coins we get two full calabashes, about a liter altogether, and take them home. Mama is delighted to see so much milk. We make chai, and Saguna gets a whole cup of milk, which makes her happy.

Lketinga and Mama discuss the situation, and I am genuinely left wondering how these people feed themselves. From time to time the Mission distributes a pound or two of maize meal to old women, but there's nothing to be had there for the moment. Lketinga decides to slaughter a goat that evening when the herds return. But in the midst of all this new experience I'm not really hungry.

We spend the rest of the afternoon in the *manyatta*, while his mother sits under the tree, chatting to the other women. At last we can make love. Cautiously I keep my clothes on, because it's still day and someone could come into the hut at any time. We perform the brief act of love several times that afternoon. I'm not used to it all being over so quickly and then almost immediately starting again, but I don't mind. I don't regret it, because I'm happy to be with Lketinga.

In the evening the goats come home, and Lketinga's older brother, Saguna's father, is with them. He and the mother have a long serious conversation, during which he every now and then fires wild looks in my direction. Later on I ask Lketinga what was going on, and he tries to explain his brother is just very worried about my health, saying it wouldn't be long before the district manager comes out and starts wanting to know why a white woman is living in a hut like this. It isn't normal.

Within two or three days everybody for miles around will know that I am here and come to see me. If anything happens to me, even the police will turn up, and in the whole history of the Leparmorijos—that's their family name—nothing of the kind has ever happened before. I reassure Lketinga and promise him that I'm fine and everything is in order with my passport if the district manager comes. So far I've never been seriously sick in my whole life, I tell him, so let's go and eat a goat, and I'll do my best to eat as much as I can.

As soon as it's dark the three of us head off: Lketinga, his brother, and me. Lketinga has a goat in tow, and we walk about a mile from the village into the bush, because Lketinga is not allowed to eat in Mama's hut if she is there. I'm accepted perforce because I'm white. I ask what Mama and Saguna will eat. Lketinga laughs and says certain bits of the animal are for women, and men don't eat them. When there was meat to be had, she'd be up late into the night, and they'd wake up Saguna too. I'm satisfied, although I'm never quite sure that I understand everything properly because our conversation in English mixed with Masai and gestures with hands and feet is not exactly fluent.

At last we reach the spot, and they fetch wood and cut from a bush green branches that are arranged together on the sandy earth to form a sort of bed. Then Lketinga grabs the complaining animal by a hind leg and a foreleg and lays it down on its side on the green wood. His brother holds the head, forcing its mouth closed, and stabs it. The animal jerks fiercely but briefly and then stares motionless into the starry sky. I have no choice but to watch it all close-up, because I'm not going to wander off in the dark. I ask why they don't cut its throat rather than stabbing it so gruesomely. The answer is brief: among the Samburus no blood must be allowed to flow until the animal is dead. That's the way it's always been.

Now it's my first time to watch an animal being butchered. They make an incision at the neck, and as the brother pulls at the fleece, it forms a sort of trough that immediately fills up with blood. I look on in horrified amazement as Lketinga actually bends over this pool of blood and takes a few slurps. His brother does the same thing. I'm grossed out but don't say anything. Lketinga points and says: "Corinne, you like blood, make very strong!" I shake my head. No.

After that everything goes quickly. The fleece is deftly removed, the head and the feet severed and laid on the bed of green branches. The stomach is opened carefully, and a horrid stinking green mass—the contents of the stomach—falls out onto the ground. My appetite has gone completely. The brother continues butchering while my Masai patiently blows on the fire. After an hour we're ready to pile the cut-up pieces of meat onto a sort of pyramid built of sticks. The ribs, all in one piece, go on first because they don't take as long as the rear legs. The head and feet go straight onto the fire.

The whole thing looks pretty vile, but I know that I have to get used to it. After a short time the ribs are hauled off the fire and bit by bit the rest of the goat is grilled. Lketinga uses his bush knife to cut off half the ribs and hands these to me. I grab them bravely and nibble at them, though it would probably be better with a bit of salt. I have difficulty biting the tough meat off the bones, but Lketinga and his brother eat noisily with accustomed speed. The gnawed bones are thrown over their heads into the bush, and soon there's a rustling noise. I have no idea who's making off with the remains, but with Lketinga next to me I'm not afraid.

The pair of them now cut slices off the hind leg, throwing them back on the fire to grill through. The brother asks me if I like it, and I reply "Oh, yes, it's very good!" and keep on chewing. After all, I'm going to end up skin and bones myself before long if I don't get something into my stomach. By the time I've finished my teeth ache. Lketinga reaches over to the fire and hands me a whole front leg. I look at him quizzically: "For me?" "Yes, this is only for you." But my stomach is full; I simply can't eat any more. They can't believe it and tell me I'm not a proper Samburu: "You take home and eat tomorrow," says Lketinga good-humoredly. So I sit there and watch as they swallow pound after pound of meat.

When they have finally had enough, they use the fleece to wrap up all the leftovers including the head, feet, and internal organs, and we walk back to the *manyatta*. I'm carrying my "breakfast" home with me. The corral is fast asleep. We crawl into our hut, and Mama immediately rises from her sleeping place. The men give her some of the leftover meat. I can see nothing but the red ashes in the hearth.

The brother goes off to take some meat to his wife's *manyatta*. Mama pokes around in the ashes and blows carefully to rekindle the fire. Of course that sends a cloud of smoke up again, and I start coughing. Then a flame flickers into life, and all at once the hut seems warm and cozy. Mama starts dealing with a piece of grilled meat and wakes Saguna. I'm amazed to see this little girl, plucked from a deep sleep, tackle the hunk of meat, cutting little pieces with a knife and putting them straight in her mouth.

While the two of them eat, the water for chai boils. Lketinga and I drink our chai with my leg of goat hanging from the ceiling above us. As soon as the pot is emptied of chai, Mama throws some little cut-up bits of meat into it and stir-fries them until they are crispy brown, then she tips them into empty calabashes. I wonder what she's doing, but Lketinga explains that this is a way of preserving the meat so that it lasts several days. Mama starts to cook all that's left; otherwise, tomorrow lots of other women will come and she'll have to share with them and we'd be left with nothing again. The goat's head, completely blackened by the ash, is supposed to be particularly good; she keeps that for tomorrow.

As the fire burns down Lketinga and I try to get some sleep. He lays his head on a three-legged, wooden stool about four inches high to stop his long red hair getting tangled and spreading the coloring everywhere. In Mombasa, where he didn't have such a stool, he used to tie his hair up in a cloth. It's a mystery to me how anyone can sleep with his neck stretched and his head on something so hard. But it's obviously not a problem for him because he's already fast asleep. I, however, am not having such an easy time; the ground is very hard, it's not easy to ignore the noises made by Mama, who is still eating, and mosquitoes buzz aggravatingly around my head.

In the morning I'm woken up by the pesky flies and a strange noise. All I can see through the doorway is Mama's skirt with a fast-flowing stream gushing between her legs. It seems the women pee standing up while the men, as I've noticed with Lketinga, prefer to crouch down. When the noise fades away, I climb out and make my way behind the hut to relieve myself in my own way. Then I wander across to watch Mama milk the goats. After the usual morning chai, we go down to the river again to fetch a gallon of water.

On our return there are three women sitting in the *manyatta*, but when they see Lketinga and me, they get up to leave. Mama is in a bad mood because apparently other women had already come to call and she had neither powdered tea nor sugar nor even a drop of water. Hospitality requires that every visitor be offered chai or at the very least a cup of water. They all want to know about the white woman, she says. Nobody has bothered with her before, but now they won't leave her alone. I suggest to Lketinga that we go and get some powdered tea at least from one of the shops. When we get back, there's a crowd of elderly people milling around in the shade near the *manyatta*. They have unbelievable patience and can wait around for hours, just chatting with one another, in the knowledge that sooner or later the *mzungu* will have to eat and the laws of hospitality demand that the old folks will get a share.

As a warrior, Lketinga feels uncomfortable among so many married women and old men and says he wants to show me the countryside. We head off into the bush, and he tells me the names of all the plants and animals we encounter. The whole area is bone dry, and the ground either rock-hard red earth or sand. The earth is cracked, and from time to time we come across what look like craters. It's hot and I'm thirsty, but Lketinga reckons the more water I drink the thirstier I'll get. He cuts a couple of twigs from a bush, sticks one in his mouth, and gives me one, and says it's good for cleaning the teeth and at the same time takes away the thirst.

My full cotton skirt keeps getting caught on thorns, and after another hour I'm really sweating and insist on drinking something, so we head down toward the river, which is identifiable from a distance because the trees next to it are greener and taller. But I search the dried-up riverbed in vain for any trace of water. We walk along the riverbed for a bit until we catch sight of a group of apes near some rocks. They scamper away from us, and Lketinga goes over to the rocks and digs a hole in the sand. Gradually the sand grows darker, slowly a little pool of water appears, which eventually clears. I satisfy my thirst, and we head back home.

My meal that evening is the rest of the goat leg. Sitting around in the twilight we converse as well as we can. Mama wants to know about my country and my family. From time to time the difficulties in understanding one another make us laugh. As ever, Saguna is asleep, snuggled up close to Mama. She has more or less grown used to my presence, although she still won't let me touch her. By nine o'clock we're ready for bed. I keep my T-shirt on but fold up my skirt beneath my head as a pillow and use a thin kanga as a blanket, though it's little protection from the early-morning cold.

On the fourth day Lketinga and I go off to look after the goats for the whole day together. I am very proud at being allowed to go with him. It's not easy to keep all the animals together. When we come across other herds, I'm amazed at how even the children know exactly which are their animals, although there are only about fifty goats at most. We stroll casually for mile upon mile, the goats nibbling at the almost bare bushes. Around lunch we drive them down to the river to drink before moving on. We drink the same water, and that is all we consume all day. We return to the house toward evening, exhausted and sunburned, and I think: Once, but never again! I am amazed that people can do this, day in and day out, all their lives. Mama, the brother, and his wife are at the *manyatta* to welcome us back, and I glean from their conversation that I have won some respect, and they are proud that I could do it. For the first time I sleep soundly the whole night through.

The next morning I clamber out in a fresh new cotton frock. Mama is amazed and wants to know how many I have. I hold up four fingers, and she suggests that I might care to give her one, as she has only one and has been wearing it for years. That's not hard to believe, looking at how dirty it is and the holes in it. But mine are far too long and too tight at the waist. I promise to bring her one back on my next expedition. Compared to the average Swiss woman, I have very few clothes, but here four skirts and ten T-shirts are an almost shameful excess.

Today I plan to do my washing in the meager waters of the river. So we go into a shop and buy Omo. This is the only washing powder to be bought in Kenya and is used not just for clothes but for the body and hair as well. It's not easy washing clothes with little water and a lot of sand. Lketinga even helps me, although the other women and girls watch and giggle. The fact that he'll do that for me makes me love him even more. The men here do almost no work at all, certainly not "women's work," like fetching water, finding firewood, or washing clothes, although they usually will wash their own kanga.

In the afternoon I decide to go up to the grandiose-looking Mission and introduce myself. A grumpy but astonished-looking missionary opens the door and says, "Yes?" I muster my best English to tell him that I'm intending to stay here in Barsaloi and live with a Samburu man. He looks at me somewhat dismissively and with an Italian accent says, "Yes, and now?" I ask him if it would be possible to go with him to Maralal from time to time to get foodstuffs. He replies coldly that he never knows in advance when he has to go to Maralal and in any case has to transport sick people rather than help with shopping expeditions. He holds out his hand and bids me a cool good-bye with the words "I'm Father Giuliani, *arrivederci*."

I'm left standing in front of the closed door, trying to come to terms with my first encounter with a missionary. I'm angry and ashamed to be white. Slowly I make my way back to the *manyatta* and my own poor folk, who are ready to share with me even though I'm a total stranger.

I tell Lketinga about my experience, and he laughs and says those two missionaries are no good. The other one, Father Roberto, is a bit more approachable, though. Their predecessors had helped the local community more and always distributed maize meal when there was a famine. This pair would wait until it was too late. I'm sad not to be able to count on the priest for a ride, and I've no intention of begging.

The days pass by at the same tempo, varied only by the different groups of visitors in the *manyatta*. Sometimes it's old people, sometimes warriors all the same age, and then I'm usually left sitting for hours without understanding more than the occasional word.

The Land Rover

After a fortnight it's clear that I can't continue to survive on this unbalanced diet, even though I take a European vitamin tablet every day. My skirts are getting too big for me, which only goes to show that I've already lost several pounds. I want to stay, there's no doubt about that, but I don't want to starve. Also, I've no toilet paper left, and I'm running out of paper handkerchiefs too. With the best will in the world, there's no way I can clean myself with a stone the way the Samburu do, even if it is more environmentally friendly than my bits of white paper left behind the bush.

Eventually I make up my mind: I need a car. Obviously it'll have to be a Land Rover because nothing else is any use out here. I talk about it to Lketinga, who talks in turn to Mama, who considers the idea absurd. A car is something that belongs to someone from another planet with enormous sums of money. And then, what would people say? No, Mama is not happy with the idea, although she understands my problem, which is the same as everyone else's: a lack of food.

The idea of having a Land Rover and becoming independent inspires me, however. But because my money is in Mombasa it means undertaking the whole long journey again. I'd have to get my mother to transfer money from my Swiss bank account to Barclays Bank in Mombasa. I dither in the hope that Lketinga will come with me because I haven't a clue how to get hold of a car. I haven't seen any car dealerships like we have in Switzerland, and I've no idea how to get a license plate or papers, but I know one thing: I'm going to come back in a car.

I force myself to go back to the Mission again. This time it's Father

Roberto who opens the door. I tell him my plans and ask for a ride on the next trip to Maralal. He replies politely that I should come back in two days as he might be going down then.

Just before I leave, Lketinga says he won't be coming with me. He doesn't want to go back to Mombasa. I'm disappointed, but after everything that's happened I understand. We spend half the night talking, and I feel he's afraid I won't come back. Mama thinks so too. Again and again I promise them I'll be back in a week at most, but the atmosphere in the morning is somber, and I find it hard to be cheerful.

An hour later I'm sitting beside Roberto traveling a route that's new to me—to Baragoi in the Turkana District—before we go on to Maralal. The road is not so rocky, and we hardly need the four-wheel drive. On the other hand, it's littered with small sharp stones that could cause a puncture, and the route is twice as long; it will take four hours to get to Maralal. We arrive after two in the afternoon, and I say thanks politely and go to the boardinghouse to drop off my bag. I'll be spending the night there because the bus doesn't leave until six the next morning. I'm wandering around Maralal to kill time when suddenly I hear my name. I turn around in astonishment and recognize with delight my erstwhile savior, Tom. It's nice to find a familiar face among all the strange ones staring at me.

I tell him my plan, and he tells me it won't be easy because there are never many secondhand cars on the market in Kenya. Two months ago there was someone in Maralal trying to sell a Land Rover. Maybe it is still available. We agree to meet up at the boardinghouse at seven.

That would be the best thing that could happen for me. And indeed Tom turns up half an hour earlier than planned and says we ought to go to take a look at the Land Rover straightaway. I go with him full of anticipation and find that the Land Rover is very old but exactly what I have been looking for. I negotiate with its owner, a fat man from the Kikuyu tribe. After a lot of haggling we settle on a price of twenty-five hundred Swiss francs. I can hardly believe my luck but try to play it cool as we shake on the deal. I tell him the money's in Mombasa, and I'll be back with it in four days, but he's not to sell it at any price because I'm relying on him. I don't, however, want to put down a deposit because the seller doesn't look like the most trustworthy type. He promises me with a grin he'll wait four days. My savior and I leave the Kikuyu and go for dinner. Happy to have one worry less, I promise to take him and his wife on a safari sometime.

The journey to Mombasa passes off without problems. Once there, I get the money from the bank, which is not easy. Business like that takes time. After nearly two hours I'm in possession of a huge amount of paper currency that I now have to conceal on my person. The banker warns me to take care because so much money is a fortune here and people have been murdered for less. Leaving the bank I feel uneasy, imagining that people are outside watching and waiting for me. Over one shoulder I have my travel bag with the rest of my clothes from Mombasa and in the other a sturdy stick, a lesson learned from Jutta-in-Rambo mode. If I have to, I won't hesitate to use it.

I keep crossing the street to try to ascertain if anyone's been following me from the bank, and it's an hour before I feel secure enough to go to the bus station to get my ticket for the night bus to Nairobi. Then I go back to find a seat in the Hotel Castel, the most expensive in Mombasa, and under Swiss management. At long last I can eat a European meal again, even if it costs a fortune, but what the hell: no telling when I'll next see a salad or chips.

When it's time to go, the bus departs punctually, and I look forward to getting home again and proving to Lketinga that he can trust me. But after barely an hour and a half, the bus suddenly swerves and comes to a dead stop. All of a sudden everybody starts talking at once. The driver announces that we've got a puncture on the right rear tire. Everybody gets out. A few sit down by the edge of the road and get out sheets or woolen blankets. It's pitch black, and there's no sign of life for miles around. I say something in English to a man with glasses, assuming that someone with gold glasses will speak the language. He does indeed and tells me that it's likely to take a long time before a vehicle passes in the opposite direction to take someone to Mombasa who can ask them to send out a spare tire.

I don't believe what I'm hearing! A bus packed full of people sent out at night without a spare tire on board! Nobody else seems to be bothered; they just sit there or lie down on the edge of the road. It's cold, and I'm freezing. After three-quarters of an hour a vehicle going in the opposite direction finally appears. The car stops, and a man gets in. Now we have to wait again for at least three hours, since it took us an hour and a half to get here.

The thought of the long journey home starts me panicking. I take my bag and march out into the middle of the road, determined to stop the next passing car. Before long I spot two bright headlights in the distance. I wave like mad. A man hands me a flashlight, saying they'll knock me over and kill me otherwise. He recognizes from the lights that it's a bus, and indeed, when screeching tires bring it to a halt in front of me, it turns out to be a Maraika safari company bus. I tell them I have to get to Nairobi as quickly as possible and ask for a lift. It appears to be an Indian company, as most of the occupants are Asian. They agree to take me, but only if I pay.

But thank God my money and I are off the dark empty road. I nod off and must have actually been asleep when suddenly a commotion breaks out in the hitherto quiet bus. I peer sleepily out into the darkness and realize that our bus too has come to a halt on the roadside. A lot of the passengers have already gotten out and are standing around. I clamber out and inspect the tires, which all seem okay. Only then do I notice the hood is up and someone tells me the drive belt has snapped. "What do we do now?" I ask. It's a problem: we're two hours from Nairobi and the garages, which are the only places we'll find a replacement, don't open until seven in the morning. I turn away to hide my welling tears.

Twice in the same night with two separate buses I've ended up stranded on this same god-awful road. This is the third day I've been traveling, and tomorrow I have to get the seven A.M. bus from Nairobi to Nyahururu in order to catch the only bus to Maralal the following morning; otherwise, my Kikuyu's likely to have sold my car. I despair at so much bad luck when every hour counts. The thought that I must be in Nairobi by morning is hammering in my head.

Two cars pass, but I'm wary of asking for a ride from a small group. After two and a half hours once again I spot the large headlights of a bus. With a lit cigarette lighter in each hand I park myself in the middle of the road and hope the driver sees me. He stops. It's the first bus I was on. Laughing, the driver opens the door, and I climb on board in embarrassment.

When we reach Nairobi, I have just enough time to down some chai and a piece of cake before getting on the next bus to Nyahururu. My back, neck, and arms all ache. But I'm consoled by the fact that with all this money on me, I'm still alive and still on time.

Back in Maralal I hurry into the Kikuyu's shop with my heart pounding. There's a woman behind the counter who doesn't speak any

English. From her Swahili I gather that her husband isn't there and I should come back tomorrow. The stress and uncertainty aren't over yet.

It's nearly noon the next day before I finally see his fat face again. And the Land Rover too, standing fully laden outside the shop. He gives me a brusque welcome and empties the car. I stand there like something ordered but not collected. When he finally takes out the last package, I suggest we get down to business. With a show of embarrassment he rubs his hands together and says he has to ask for another one thousand Swiss francs or he could sell the car to someone else.

I just about manage to hold myself back and tell him I have the amount of money we agreed with me but no more. He shrugs his shoulders and says he can wait until I get the rest. It's impossible, I tell myself: it will take days for the money to get here from Switzerland and I'm not repeating the journey to Mombasa. He leaves me standing there and goes off to serve other people. I charge off to the boardinghouse. The stinking bastard! I could murder him!

The Land Rover belonging to the manager of the Tourist Lodge is standing in front of the boardinghouse. I have to go through the bar to get to the bedrooms at the rear of the house, and the manager recognizes me and invites me to have a beer with him. He introduces me to his companion, who works in their Maralal office. We make small talk for a bit. I'm obviously interested to know whether or not Jutta is still around, but unfortunately she's not; she's gone to Nairobi for a bit to make some more money painting.

Eventually I get around to mentioning the episode with my Land Rover. The manager laughs and says that car isn't worth even two thousand Swiss francs; if it were, it would have been sold long ago. There are so few vehicles here everybody knows each one of them. I'm still prepared to pay my twenty-five hundred providing I get it. He promises to help me, and we drive back to the Kikuyu's place in his car. They argue back and forth until in the end I get the car.

The manager tells me that I have to get the registration from the Kikuyu and go to the local government office to do the transfer because here the license plate and insurance are transferred along with the vehicle. The manager insists that we do the deal on paper with him as a witness. We find the office just before it closes and at last, with another hundred francs less in my pocket, I finally have the registration in my name. The Kikuyu hands me the keys and wishes me luck.

As I've never driven a car like this before, I let him explain everything to me and drive him back to his shop. The street is full of potholes, and before I've gone five yards I discover there's a lot of play in the steering. Changing gears is hard work, and the brakes kick in late. So of course I immediately go into the first pothole. My passenger grabs the dashboard in terror and turns to me in doubt: "You have a driver's license?" "Yes," I snap, struggling again to change gear and eventually managing it. He breaks my concentration again to insist I'm driving on the wrong side of the road. Oh, shit! They drive on the left here! When we reach his shop, the Kikuyu gets out with relief. I drive on down to the school to get used to the Land Rover where he can't see me, and after a few bends I've got the hang of it, more or less.

Next I head for the gas station because the indicator shows only a quarter of a tank. The Somali who runs it says he's sorry there's no fuel at the moment. "Well, when will it arrive?" I ask optimistically. This evening or tomorrow, it's been promised for ages, but nobody's quite certain when it's coming. Already I've run into my next problem: now I've got a car but no fuel.

It's the supreme irony! I go back to the Kikuyu and ask him to sell me some. He says he hasn't got any but gives me a tip as to where there's always some to be had on the black market. In the end I get four gallons at four Swiss francs per gallon, but that isn't enough to get to Barsaloi and back. I drive out to the Tourist Lodge, and the manager comes up with another four gallons. At last I'm happy and plan to head off directly to Barsaloi after doing some shopping the next morning.

Braving the Bush

Early the next morning I go to the nearest bank and open an account in Maralal, which is not easy, given that I can provide neither a street nor postal address. When I tell them I live in one of the *manyattas* in Barsaloi, they simply don't believe it. How on earth do I get there? they ask. I tell them about the car, and in the end they let me open an account. I write to my mother, telling her now to send any money to Maralal.

I load up with food and set off. Obviously I take the shortest route, through the bush; otherwise, I wouldn't have enough fuel to get there and come back later. I can't wait to see Lketinga's face when I arrive at the village in the car.

The Land Rover copes with the steep dusty track, although I have to engage the four-wheel drive just before I get to the forest to avoid getting stuck. I'm proud of myself for having come to grips with the car so well. The trees are enormous, and I can tell from the overgrown path that the route has not been used for a long time. Then it goes downhill again, and I'm motoring along happily until suddenly I see a great herd of animals across the path. I break sharply. Didn't Lketinga tell me there were no herds of cows around here? But one hundred and fifty feet closer to the herd I realize that what I thought were cows are in fact fully grown buffalo.

What was it Lketinga said? The most dangerous animal in the bush isn't the lion but the buffalo. And here are at least thirty of them, with young ones, great giants with broad noses and sharp horns. A few of them continue to graze peacefully, but some others have turned to look at my car. There's steam coming from the herd, or is it rising dust? I stare frozen at them. Should I honk or not? Do they recognize a car? I wait and wait, but they don't move from the track, and eventually I honk at them. At once they all raise their heads in my direction. Gingerly I engage reverse and honk again at short intervals. That is the end of their peaceful grazing. A few of the huge beasts start to lower their horns and cast around them. I watch in frozen terror, hoping they'll disappear into the thick forest rather than come up the path toward me. But before I can take in exactly what's happening, the track is suddenly clear. The ghosts have vanished, leaving only a cloud of dust behind.

Even so, I wait cautiously for a few minutes before putting my foot down. The Land Rover rattles like it's falling apart, but the only thought in my head is to get out of here as fast as possible. When I reach the spot where the animals were, I risk a quick glance into the forest but can see nothing, even though I can smell their freshly dropped dung. I have to hold on tight to the steering wheel to stop it from being wrenched from my hands. After five minutes at top speed I slow down a bit, because the track is getting steeper and steeper. I stop and engage the four-wheel drive. I hope that will get me across this patch without tipping over because everywhere I look now I can see huge potholes and ravines. Feverishly I pray that the car will keep all four wheels on the ground. I don't dare use the clutch for fear of falling out of gear! I make progress yard by yard with every imaginable disaster going through my head. Sweat is dripping into my eyes, but I don't dare wipe it away because I need both hands to hang on to the steering wheel. After two or three hundred yards the worst of it is behind me, the forest is thinning out, and I'm happy to have a bit more light and air around me. Shortly afterward I reach the scree slope. Even that looks different now. The last time I was sitting in the back, thinking only about Lketinga.

I stop and get out to see if the track really does keep going. In some places the stones are nearly half as big as the wheels of the Land Rover. Despite my experienced driving, I suddenly feel alone and scared. I try moving some of the stones together to make the downward steps less steep. Time's getting on; it'll be dark in two hours. How far is it still to Barsaloi? I'm so nervous I can't remember anything. I engage the four-wheel drive and know that I mustn't brake or change gear: just let the vehicle climb onward even though it's a steep downhill slope. The car manages the first hurdles even though the steering wheel is almost ripped out of my hand. The car scrapes and bumps, so long in the wheelbase that the rear end is often still on one rock when the front has already bumped down over another. Then halfway down the worst happens. The engine splutters briefly and dies. I'm halfway down a hill of stones, and the engine has croaked. How the hell am I going to bring it back to life? I hit the clutch briefly, and it shunts a couple of feet forward. But I stop immediately; it'll never work like that. I get out and see that one of the rear wheels is up in the air. I drag a big rock behind the other one, but I'm getting hysterical.

Then, climbing back into the car, I spot two warriors on a nearby outcrop watching me with interest. It obviously doesn't occur to them to help me, but even so I feel a bit better not being so completely alone. I try again to start the engine. It clunks into life but then falters again. I try and try again. I want out of here. The pair over on the rocky outcrop just sit there. But how could they help anyhow? They don't know anything about engines.

When I've just about given up hope, suddenly it comes back to life as if nothing had ever happened. Gently, ever so gently, I ease off the clutch and hope that the vehicle can get itself over the remaining stones. After twenty yards or so I'm over the biggest rocks, and I can loosen my iron grip. Then I break into tears with the realization of the danger I was in.

From here on, the track is fairly flat. I catch sight of a few *manyattas* here and there and children who wave excitedly. I slow down for fear of running over one of the large number of goats. About half an hour later I reach the big Barsaloi River, which is not without its dangers in crossing because, although it is dry, there is quicksand. I engage the four-wheel drive again and drive at top speed across the hundred or so yards of its width. The car manages the last upward stretch to Barsaloi, and I drive proudly into the village. People come out from all over to watch, even the Somalis from their shops, and all around me I hear, *"Mzungu! Mzungu!"*

Then all of a sudden Lketinga and two other warriors are standing in the street in front of me. Before I can even stop he's jumped into the car beaming at me radiantly. "Corinne, you come back and with this car!" He stares at me in disbelief, as happy as a child. I just want to embrace him. The two warriors jump in when he invites them, and we drive together to the *manyatta*. Mama runs away in fright, and even Saguna scampers away, but before long the parked vehicle is surrounded by old people and young people alike. Mama doesn't want to leave the car near the tree because someone might deliberately damage it. Lketinga opens the briar fence, and I park the car next to the *manyatta*, which looks even smaller against the big vehicle. The contrast is really quite grotesque.

We unload all the foodstuffs and store them away inside the hut. I'm happy to get some of Mama's chai, and she's delighted by the sugar I've brought. In the meantime the shops have maize meal again but no sugar. Lketinga and the others are admiring the car. Mama talks and talks to me. I don't understand a word, but she seems happy because when I laugh helplessly she joins in.

It's late before we get to bed this evening because I have to tell them everything. When I mention the buffalo everyone looks serious, and Mama keeps muttering, *"Enkai, Enkai,"* which means "God." When the older brother comes back with the goats, he is amazed too. There's a lot of conversation. The car will have to be watched all the time to make sure nobody steals it or damages it. Lketinga volunteers to spend the first night in it. I had somehow imagined our reunion differently, but I say nothing because his eyes are full of pride.

The next day he's already eager to go for a drive, to see his half brother, who keeps cows in Sitedi. I try to tell Lketinga that we can't make any big expeditions because I don't have any reserves of fuel. The indicator is showing half full. That's just enough to get back to Maralal. He only reluctantly understands. I'm sorry too that I can't show off and drive him proudly around the place, but I have to be strict.

Three days later the number two in the local government, known as the assistant chief, is outside our *manyatta*, talking to Lketinga and Mama. I hear the words *"mzungu"* and "car"; they're talking about me. He looks funny in his ill-fitting green uniform. Only the large gun at his side lends him an air of authority. He can't speak English either. Afterward he wants to look at my passport. I show it to him and ask what the problem is. Lketinga translates for me. I have to go to Maralal to register with the government office: Europeans are not allowed to live in *manyattas*.

Back to the Future

The same afternoon Lketinga and I, after discussion with Mama, decide to get married. The little boss man says we'll have to do it in Maralal, at the government office there; the traditional bush wedding won't do. At the end of our discussion the boss man demands to be driven home. As far as Lketinga is concerned, that goes without saying: he is, after all, a "man of respect." It is a status he clearly abuses. But when I start up the Land Rover, I check the fuel indicator and see with horror that the level has dropped, even though the vehicle hasn't been used. I don't understand.

We set off, the boss man in the front passenger seat with Lketinga behind him. I consider it impudence but say nothing, as it clearly doesn't bother Lketinga. When we get to our destination, the boss man says he has to be in Maralal in two days' time and as I have to sort things out with the office there anyhow, I might as well take him with me. In fact, there is only one month left on my visa.

But when we get back to the *manyatta*, I realize that there is not enough fuel left to get to Maralal, quite apart from the fact that I intend to take the longer, less hazardous route. I go up to the Mission, where Father Giuliani opens the door and, slightly more politely this time, says: "Yes?"

I tell him my problem with the fuel. When he asks which route I took, I tell him I took the track through the forest, and for the first time I have the feeling that he treats me with a bit more attention and respect. "That road is very dangerous, don't go there again," he says, and tells me to bring the car around and he'll look at the tank. When I do, he discovers that the tank has dropped two inches on one side and that fuel has been evaporating. Now I also know how I got stuck on the rocks.

Over the next few days the priest fixes the tank, for which I am extremely grateful. He asks me which of the *morans* I'm living with and wishes me *"bon courage"* and strength. He also tells me that getting fuel in Maralal is always hit and miss, and I'd do better to get one or two forty-gallon canisters and keep them in the Mission, as he won't always be able to sell me his fuel. I'm delighted by the offer, especially as he also says I can park the Land Rover up at the Mission. It's not so easy to persuade Lketinga, though, as he doesn't even trust the missionaries.

The next few days pass quietly except that people keep coming by to ask when we're going to Maralal. It seems everybody wants to come. At long last here is a Samburu with a car, so everyone treats it as theirs. I keep having to repeat that on roads like these I'm not prepared to take twenty people.

Eventually we set off, with the little boss man, of course, who thinks he can decide who else may come along. Only men of course, women have to wait behind. When I spot one woman who has a child with tightly shut, septic-looking eyes wrapped up in her kanga, I ask her why she wants to go to Maralal. She answers shyly, looking down at the ground, that she wants to go to the hospital because there's no eye medicine to be had here. I tell her to get in.

When the boss man goes to sit in the front passenger seat, I summon up all my courage and, looking him right in the eye, say, "No, this place is for Lketinga!" He yields, but I know that from now on I'll get no sympathy from him. The journey goes well, everybody talking together and singing. For most of them it's the first time they've ever been in a car.

Three times we cross a river, and I have to engage the four-wheel drive, but the rest of the time I don't need it. Even so, I have to concentrate on the road, which is full of ruts and potholes. It seems to go on forever, and the fuel level drops quickly.

We get to Maralal in the afternoon, the passengers leave, and we head for the filling station right away. I'm deeply disappointed to find out there's still no fuel. Apparently there hasn't been any more fuel in Maralal since I bought the car. The Somali insists it'll arrive today or tomorrow, but I don't believe a word anymore. Lketinga and I find our boardinghouse and spend the night there.

In the meantime, however, it has rained in Maralal, and everything is green, almost as if we were in another country. But the nights are also colder, and for the first time I find out what pests mosquitoes can be. Even during dinner, which we take in our cold little room so that nobody will see us eating together, the mosquitoes attack me incessantly. Before long my ankles and hands have swollen up. For every mosquito I kill, more come in under the roof. Funnily, they seem to prefer white meat because my Masai gets barely half as many bites. In bed they buzz around my head continuously. Lketinga just pulls the sheet right over his head and notices nothing.

After a while I can't take it anymore and turn on the light in annoyance, waking him: "I can't sleep with these mosquitoes," I tell him despairingly. He gets up, goes out, and ten minutes later comes back and puts a green snail-like thing on the floor, a mosquito repellent that he lights at one end. And indeed before long, although it stinks appallingly, the pests have gone, and eventually I fall asleep. I wake at five, however, because the mosquitoes are tormenting me again. The coil has burned out; apparently they last just six hours.

After four days, however, there's still no fuel. Out of boredom, Lketinga starts chewing *miraa* again and secretly knocks back a couple of beers. I don't like it, but what can I say? The waiting is getting on my nerves too. In the meantime we have been to the office to notify them of our intention to get married. We get shunted from pillar to post until they find someone who knows about civil weddings. It's not something that happens often here because most Samburus can have more than one wife when they get married the traditional way. This is to cause quite a bit of a fuss for both Lketinga and me, although for quite different reasons, as I'm soon to find out.

For the moment, however, we don't think much about it. When the official asks for my passport and Lketinga's identity card to note down our details, it turns out that Lketinga no longer has one. It was stolen in Mombasa. The official makes a face and tells us he'll have to order a new one from Nairobi and that is likely to take at least two months. Only when he's got all the details can he register us and then it takes six weeks before the marriage can take place, providing no one raises an objection. But I have to leave Kenya in three weeks at the latest, when my extended visa expires.

With Lketinga still chewing his weed, I decide to discuss the issue of multiple wives with him. He tells me that it would be a problem for him if our marriage would make that impossible. This comes as a bit of a blow to me, but I try to stay calm because, after all, for him it is not something wicked or wrong but perfectly normal, even if from my European point of view it is unthinkable. I try to imagine how he could live with me and one or two other wives. Just the thought makes my blood boil with jealousy.

As I'm thinking all this, he announces that he can't marry me in this office if later on I won't let him marry another Samburu woman in a traditional ceremony. This is too much for me, and I can't hold the tears back any longer. He stares at me in astonishment and asks: "Corinne, what's the problem?" I try to tell him that we white people don't do things that way and I can't imagine living together like that. He laughs, puts his arms around me, and gives me a quick kiss on the mouth: "No problem, Corinne. Now you will get my first wife, *pole, pole.*"

He wants lots of children—eight at least. I have to smile and tell him I don't want more than two. Well, there you are, says my warrior, all the better if there's another wife to have children. In any case, he doesn't even know if I can give him children, and a man without children is worthless. I see his point because, after all, I don't know if I can have children either; until I came to Kenya it never mattered. We talk things through until at last I come to the following proposal: If after two years I still have not had a child, then he can marry again, otherwise he has to wait five years at least. He agrees and I tell myself to calm down: five years is a long time.

We leave the bedroom and wander around Maralal in the hope that the fuel tanker might have arrived, but as usual it hasn't. However, we do run into my eternal savior Tom and his young wife. She's practically a child still and looks at her feet shyly. Not a happy girl. We mention that we've been waiting four days for fuel, and our friend says why don't we drive down to Lake Baringo? It's just two hours away, and there's always fuel there.

I'm delighted by the suggestion, fed up with hanging around, and I suggest he and his wife should come along, as I owe him a trip. He discusses it with me, but says the girl is afraid of the car. Lketinga, however, laughs and manages to persuade her. We agree to set off the next day.

First we go to the local garage, run by a Somali, to buy two empty canisters that will fit into the back of the Land Rover. When we have fastened them down with ropes, I feel well equipped for future journeys and we're happy to be on the road again. The girl, however, seems even smaller and quieter and holds on to the canisters in fear.

For ages we trundle along the dusty, bumpy road without seeing any other traffic. From time to time we spot herds of zebra or giraffes, but there is no sign of any human life or road signs. Suddenly the Land Rover tips forward, and the steering goes—we've got a flat! In ten years of driving this is the first time it's ever happened to me. "No problem," says Tom. We get out the spare tire, the wheel brace, and an ancient jack. Tom crawls under the Land Rover to get the jack into position. He tries to use the brace to loosen the wheel nuts, but the tool is worn and can't get any purchase on the nuts. We try to wedge them in with sand, bits of cloth and wood, and eventually get three of the nuts off but the others won't budge. Tom's wife starts crying and runs off.

Tom tells us not to worry, she'll be back, but Lketinga goes to fetch her because he says we're in another tribal district now: the "Baringos." We're thirsty, dirty, and sweating. We have enough fuel but nothing to drink, because we'd anticipated only a short journey. So we sit down in the shade and hope another vehicle will come along; at least the road looks better used than the one to Barsaloi.

But when nothing arrives after several hours, and even Lketinga on a reconnaissance tour has failed to spot either Lake Baringo or any huts, we decide to spend the night in the Land Rover. A night that seems to last forever. We're so cold, hungry, and thirsty we hardly sleep. In the morning the men have another go at the car, but to no avail. We decide to wait until midday. My throat is dry and my lips cracked. The girl is crying again, and Tom has completely lost patience with her.

Suddenly Lketinga hushes us; he thinks he can hear a car. Minutes pass before I can hear the engine sounds too. To our enormous relief we see a safari bus. The African driver stops and lowers his window. The Italian tourists stare at us in curiosity. Tom tells him the problem, but the driver says he's sorry, he's not allowed to pick anyone up. He hands us his wheel brace, but it doesn't fit. I try to soften him up by even offering him money, but he rolls up his window and drives off. The whole time the Italians said nothing, looking at me somewhat distantly. Clearly I'm too dirty, and the others are too exotic. Furious, I shout the worst swearwords I can think of after the departing bus. I'm ashamed of the white people, because not one of them tried to persuade the driver to help.

Tom is convinced that at least we're on the right road and is about to set off on foot when we hear more engine sounds. This time I'm absolutely determined not to let any vehicle leave without taking at least one of us. It's another safari bus, also filled with Italians.

When Tom and Lketinga talk to the bus driver, and again he only shakes his head, I pull open the rear door and shout in despair, "Do you speak English?"

"No, solo italiano," comes the response. But then one young man says, "Yes, just a little bit, what's your problem?" I explain that we have been stuck here since yesterday morning with no food or water and urgently need help. The driver says, "It's not allowed," and tries to shut the door. But, thank God, the young Italian intervenes and says that they've paid for the bus and therefore can decide whether or not anyone can come with them. Tom gets in alongside the driver, whether he likes it or not, and I thank the tourists in relief.

We have to stick it out for nearly three hours by the roadside until we see a cloud of dust in the distance and Tom comes back in a Land Rover with its owner. To our delight, he's also brought cola and bread. I want to guzzle the drink, but he warns me just to take little sips or I'll be ill. Like someone brought back from the dead, I swear never again to set out on a journey without drinking water.

Tom has to use a hammer and chisel to loosen the last nut, but then we change the wheel rapidly and, with one nut less on our wheel, set off again. It takes just one and a half hours to reach Lake Baringo finally. The filling station is right next to a grandiose garden restaurant for tourists. After the nightmare we've been through, I invite everyone into the restaurant. The girl is astounded to discover this new world but feels uncomfortable. We sit down at a nice table with a view over the lake and thousands of pink flamingos. Looking into the wondering faces of my guests, I'm thrilled to have been able to offer them something more than just trouble.

Two waiters come to the table, but not to take our order. They tell us that we won't be served because the restaurant's only for tourists. I tell them I am a tourist and I want to treat my friends. The black waiter tries to calm me down, saying I can stay but the Masai must leave the premises. We get up and go. I sense almost physically how demoralized these otherwise proud people feel.

At least we get the fuel. When the owner sees that I want to fill up the two canisters as well, he demands to see my money first. Lketinga inserts the nozzle into the canister, and I retire some distance to smoke a cigarette to calm me down. All of a sudden he shouts out, and I see the gas erupting like a fountain. I rush to the car and pull the trigger back on the pump; the cut-off trigger had gotten jammed and the fuel kept flowing even when the canister was full. Several quarts have spilled on the ground and inside the vehicle, but when I see how bad Lketinga feels, I try to calm myself down. Tom and his wife are standing off to one side, wishing the earth would swallow them. We're told to pay and go, without being allowed to fill the other canister. I wish we were back at home in the *manyatta*, even without the car. Up until now it's brought only trouble.

We drink tea in the village and set off again. The whole car stinks of gas, and it's not long before the girl's sick. Then she refuses to get back into the car and wants to walk home. Tom gets furious and threatens to send her back to her parents in Maralal and take another wife instead. That would obviously be a great disgrace because she gets back in. Lketinga has said nothing. I feel sorry for him and try to console him. By the time we get back to Maralal it's dark.

The other pair say good-bye quickly, and we retire to our boardinghouse. Even though it's quite cold, I take a quick, inadequate shower to get rid of some of the dust and dirt. Lketinga washes up too. Then we wolf down a huge portion of meat in our room. This time even I enjoy the meat, and we both wash it down with beer. Afterward I feel really good, and we make love; and for the first time with him, I reach a climax. Not completely silently, which scares Lketinga, who holds me and says: "Corinne, what's the problem?" When I can breathe normally again, I try to explain my orgasm to him, but he doesn't understand and laughs disbelievingly. It has to be something that happens only to white people, he believes. Tired and happy, I fall gently asleep.

Early the next morning we do some serious shopping: rice, potatoes, vegetables, fruit, even pineapples. We also manage to fill the second canister, for ironically the gas has finally arrived in Maralal. Loaded up, we set off for home. With another couple of Samburu men on board.

Lketinga wants to take the shorter road through the bush. I have my doubts, but with him there they soon disappear. The journey is easy until we get to the steep bit. Because the full canister makes the vehicle less stable and I'm afraid it could tip over, I ask our two passengers to put themselves and all our shopping on the uphill side. Nobody says a word as I tackle the two-hundred-yard stretch. But we manage it, and the conversation in the vehicle resumes. When we get to the scree, everybody else gets out, and Lketinga directs me well over the rocks. With that successfully behind us as well, I feel both relieved and proud, and we roll into Barsaloi without further ado.

The Daily Grind

The next few days are pure pleasure. We have enough to eat and more than enough gasoline. Every day we use the car to either visit relatives or fetch wood. Occasionally we drive down to the river for our washing ritual and bring back water canisters for half of Barsaloi, sometimes as many as twenty. However, all these little expeditions soon begin to eat into the fuel supply, and I begin to raise objections, which every time ends up in a long debate.

This morning one of the *morans* tells us one of his cows has given birth. This is something we have to see, so we drive to Sitedi. This is not officially a road, so I have to be careful not to drive over thornbushes. We drop in on his half brother in the corral where the cows are kept at night, which means plowing our way through endless cow pies swarming with flies. Lketinga's half brother shows us the newborn calf. The mother cow is kept in the corral on the first day after the birth. Lketinga beams while I battle the flies. My plastic sandals are sinking into the cow dung. Now I see the difference between our corral, which doesn't have cows, and this one, and I know which I prefer.

We're invited to chai, and Lketinga leads me into the hut belonging to his half brother and his young wife, who has a two-week-old baby. She seems pleased to see us, and the conversation is lively, although I don't understand a word. The swarms of flies are driving me mad. I keep one hand continuously over my cup to make sure I don't swallow any. The baby is naked, lying in his mother's kanga, and when I point out that nobody has noticed the infant is doing its business in it, the wife laughs and takes the child out, cleaning his backside by spitting on it and rubbing the mess off. She shakes the kanga and her skirt and rubs sand into both to dry them. I feel sick at the idea that this happens several times a day with the same lack of hygiene. I mention it to Lketinga, but he says it's normal. In any case the flies deal with what's left.

I decide it's time to go home, but Lketinga says that won't do: "Tonight we're sleeping here." He wants to stay with the cow, and his half brother wants to slaughter a goat for us because his wife could do with the meat after giving birth herself. The thought of spending the night here almost sends me into a panic. On the one hand, I don't want to offend their hospitality; on the other, I really feel uncomfortable.

Most of the time Lketinga is with the other warriors looking at the cows, and I'm left sitting in the dark hut with three women to whom I can't say a word. They talk among themselves, quite obviously about me, or giggle. One of them touches the white skin of my arm; another puts her hand in my hair. The long fair hair disconcerts them; they all have shaved skulls, although they're wearing pearl headbands and long earrings.

The wife has quieted her baby down and hands it over to me. I take it in my arms but can't feel quite comfortable because I keep expecting the same thing to happen as before. I know that they don't have diapers here, but I still can't quite get used to it. After looking at the baby for a while I'm relieved to hand it back.

Lketinga sticks his head into the hut, and I ask him where he's been all this time. Laughing, he tells me that he's been drinking milk with the other warriors. After that they're going to kill the goat and bring some good bits back for us. He's going off to eat in the bush again. I want to go too, but this time it's not okay: the settlement is enormous, and there are too many women and warriors. So we have to wait for some two hours before our share of the meat is brought back.

In the meantime it has grown dark. The wife cooks the meat for us: three women and four children to share half a goat. Lketinga and his half brother have eaten the other half. When I've had my fill, I crawl out of the hut and stroll over to my Masai and the other warriors who're hanging around among the cows. I ask Lketinga when he's coming to bed. He laughs: "Oh, no, Corinne, here I cannot sleep in this house together with ladies. I sleep here with friends and the cows." There's nothing for me to do but to crawl back in with these strange women. It's my first night out here without Lketinga, and I miss his warmth. Inside the hut there are three little newborn goats tethered by my head, and they bleat all night. I don't sleep a wink.

Early next morning it's much busier than back in Barsaloi. Here they don't just have the goats to milk but the cows as well. There's an impatient mooing and bleating everywhere. The milking is done by women or girls. After our chai we finally set off. I'm almost on a high thinking of our clean *manyatta* with lots to eat and the river. Our Land Rover is full of women who want to sell their milk in Barsaloi and are happy that for once they don't have to walk all the way. It's not long before Lketinga says he wants to have a go at steering. I do everything I can to dissuade him, but there's not a lot I can say because obviously the women are all teasing him. He keeps grabbing the steering wheel until eventually I get angry and stop. He climbs proudly into the driver's seat, and all the women clap. I'm miserable and try at the very least to explain to him about accelerating and braking, but he dismisses me with "I know, I know," and starts up, beaming with happiness. I'm able to share his happiness for just a few seconds because within a couple of hundred yards I'm shouting, "Slowly, slowly!" But Lketinga accelerates instead of braking and is heading straight for a tree. He seems to get it all the wrong way around. I shout out, "Slowly, more to the left!" Just before we hit the tree I grab the steering wheel in panic, but one wing crashes into it, and the motor conks out.

I've had enough now. I climb out, inspect the damage, and kick the damn car. The women are all shrieking, not because of the damage to the car, but because I'm shouting at a man. Lketinga stands next to me, totally dejected. He hadn't meant it. Distraught, he grabs his spears and sets off to go home on foot. He'll never get into the car again. When I look at him, so miserable when a few minutes earlier he'd been so happy, I feel sorry for him. I reverse the Land Rover and, seeing as everything still works, persuade Lketinga to get back in. The rest of the journey passes in silence, and I can already imagine my disgrace in Maralal the next time the *mzungu* turns up with a dent in her car.

In Barsaloi Mama is waiting for us happily, and even Saguna greets me enthusiastically. Lketinga goes and lies down in the hut. He's not feeling well and is worried about the police because he shouldn't have been driving. He's in such a bad state that I fear he could go mad again and calm him down by promising to say nothing to anybody. We'll say it happened to me and get it repaired in Maralal.

I want to go down to the river to wash. Lketinga won't come with me; he won't leave the hut. So I go on my own, even though Mama grumbles, afraid to let me go down to the river without a chaperone. She hasn't been there herself for years. Nonetheless, I head off, taking the water canister with me. I wash where we usually do, but I don't feel quite so comfortable on my own and don't dare take all my clothes off. I waste no time, but when I get back and crawl into the hut, he asks me what took me so long at the river and who I ran into. I answer in surprise that I don't really know anybody, and in any case I was as quick as I could be. He says nothing.

I discuss my journey home with him and Mama, for my visa runs out soon and I have to leave Kenya within two weeks. Neither is very happy. Lketinga asks worriedly what will happen if I don't come back, seeing as we've already told the government office about our marriage plans. "I come back, no problem!" I tell him. But because I don't have a valid ticket and no flight reservation I plan to set off in a week's time. The days themselves fly by. With the exception of our daily washing ritual we spend the time at home discussing our future.

On the day before my departure, as we're loafing around in the hut, a lot of women start screaming outside. "What's that?" I ask in astonishment. Lketinga listens carefully to the noise outside, and a dark shadow falls across his face. "What's the problem?" I ask again, and feel that there's something wrong. Suddenly Mama appears in the hut, all hot and bothered. She exchanges a couple of sentences with Lketinga, giving him angry looks. He goes out, and I hear a loud argument. I want to go out too, but Mama holds me back, shaking her head. My heart is pounding as I lie there. It has to be something dreadful. Eventually Lketinga comes back and sits down beside me, extremely worked up. The noise outside has abated, and I want to know what's going on. After a long silence I'm told that the mother of his old steady girlfriend is standing outside the hut with two friends.

I feel sick with worry. This is the first I've heard of a girlfriend. In two days I'll be leaving. I want to know for sure what's going on, right now: "Lketinga, you have a girlfriend; maybe you must marry this girl?" Lketinga gives a tortuous laugh and says: "Yes, many years I have a little girlfriend, but I cannot marry this girl!" I don't understand. "Why?" Now I'm told that virtually every warrior has a girlfriend to whom he gives pearls, and over the years he's obliged to give her lots of jewelry so that she looks as pretty as possible when she gets married. But a warrior is never supposed to marry this girlfriend. They can make love as often as they want up to the day before her marriage, but then she is sold by her parents to someone else. It's only on her wedding day that the girl learns who is to be her husband.

Shocked by what I've just learned, I say that must be awful. "Why?" says Lketinga. "This is normal for everybody." He tells me the girl ripped off all her jewelry when she heard I was living with him before she was married. That's what was awful for her. I'm slowly starting to get jealous, and I ask him when he last saw her and where she lives. Far away, toward Baragoi, he says, and swears he hasn't seen her since I arrived. I think things over and suggest that while I'm away he go to see her to clear things up. If necessary, he should buy jewelry for her, but when I get back the business has to be over. He doesn't answer, and so on the day I'm due to leave, I still don't know what he's going to do. But I trust in our love.

I say farewell to Mama and Saguna, who've both clearly become very fond of me. "*Hakuna matata,* no problem." I laugh with them, and then we drive to Maralal in our Land Rover, as I intend to get it fixed in the garage while I'm away. Lketinga will go back home on foot. In the bush we come across a small group of buffalo, but as soon as they hear the engine they flee. Even so, Lketinga immediately grabs for his spear and grunts at them. I look at him, laughing, and he settles down again.

We park directly in the garage so that as few people as possible see the dented wing. The Somali manager comes out and looks at the damage. He reckons it'll cost six hundred Swiss francs to fix. I'm horrified: that's a quarter of what it cost to buy. I do some serious haggling and in the end the price comes down to three hundred and fifty francs, which is still far too much. We spend the night in our usual boardinghouse but don't sleep much, partly because of my impending departure and partly because of the mosquitoes. Saying good-bye is hard, and I leave Lketinga looking lost behind the bus. I cover my face, so as not to arrive in Nairobi covered in dust.

A Stranger in My Own Country

In the Igbol backpackers' hotel I find a room and have a really good meal. I check through all the airlines until at last I find a flight with Alitalia. For the first time in months I call home. My mother is very excited when I tell her I'm coming home for a short while. The two days in Nairobi before I fly out are an absolute curse. I wander through the streets to kill time, giving change to the cripples and beggars who stand on every corner. In the evenings back at the Igbol I chat with lifelong backpackers and avoid the Indians and Africans offering to be my boyfriend.

At long last I'm in the taxi to the airport, but when the plane takes off I can't properly look forward to "going home" because I know Lketinga and the rest of the family are worrying about whether I'll come back.

After the initial joyful reunion with my mother, I can't quite feel at home in Meiringen, the little town in the Alps near Bern where she and her husband live. Everything follows a European timetable again. In the shops I almost feel sick at the sight of the excess of food, and even things out of the fridge no longer agree with me. I keep getting stomach cramps.

I get a certificate from the local council to confirm my single status so that at least my paperwork will be in order. As a special wedding present my mother buys "my warrior" a magnificent cowbell. I buy a few smaller bells too for my goats. For Mama and Saguna I sit down and sew two new skirts and buy wonderful woolen blankets for Lketinga and me: a bright red one for him and a striped one to cover us both.

Packing again is no easy job. Right at the bottom of my bag goes the long white wedding dress that I was given as a present from a supplier when I closed down the shop. I promised him that when I got married I would wear it, so it has to go in, including the headdress and veil. On top of the wedding dress go pudding bowls, sauces, and soups. Then come the presents. The spaces get filled with medicines, Band-Aids, bandages, antiseptic ointment, and vitamin tablets. The blankets go over everything. Both bags are absolutely stuffed.

The departure day comes closer. My whole family has recorded wedding greetings for Lketinga, so a small radio-cassette player has to be squeezed into the luggage too. I turn up at Zurich's Kloten airport with seventy pounds of luggage. I'm delighted to be going home. Yes, when I listen to my inner self, I have no doubts where my real home now is. Of course, leaving my mother again is hard, but my heart already belongs to Africa. I have no idea when I'll be back.

African Homeland

In Nairobi I take a taxi to the Igbol. The driver notices the Masai jewelry on my arms and asks me if I know the Masai well. "Yes, I go to marry a Samburu man," I reply. The driver shakes his head and says he cannot imagine why a white woman of all people should want to marry a man from what he calls "a primitive race." I leave off the conversation and am glad to get to the Igbol. But I'm not so lucky—all the rooms are taken, and I have to find somewhere else that's cheap and cheerful.

There is a place two streets away, but dragging my luggage even that short distance is an enormous effort, and then I have to hump it up three floors to my room. It's nowhere near as congenial as the Igbol, and I'm the only white. The bed sags, and there are two used condoms underneath it. At least the sheets are clean. I hurry back around to the Igbol because I want to telephone the Mission in Maralal. They can then tell the Mission in Barsaloi in their regular morning radio call that I'll be back in Maralal in two days, and that way Lketinga will know I've arrived. This idea occurred to me on the plane, and I want to try it out, even though I don't know the missionaries in Maralal. Even after our conversation, I'm not sure if it'll work. My English has improved, but there are a few misunderstandings during the conversation, and I'm not sure the good missionary got my drift.

That night I don't sleep well. This is obviously an hourly rental hotel for the locals because from the rooms on either side there's continual squeaking, moaning or laughing, and doors banging. But in the end it's just one night.

There are no problems on the bus journey to Nyahururu. I look out of the window and soak in the scenery. I'm getting ever nearer to home.

In Nyahururu it's cold and raining. I have to spend another night there before I can catch the dilapidated bus to Maralal the next morning. The departure is delayed an hour and a half so that the luggage on top of the bus can be covered with plastic sheeting. My big black bag is up there too. I keep the smaller one with me.

Soon the tarmac road gives way to the dirt track, and the red dust has turned to red mud. The bus goes more slowly than before to avoid falling into the huge potholes, which are now full of water. It weaves its way slowly, sometimes swerving diagonally across the road before getting back on track. It's going to take twice as long as normal. The track is getting worse all the time, and every now and then the bus gets stuck in the mud and people get out to push it free. In places the surface of the road is twelve inches below the level of the mud, and there is nothing to be seen through the splattered windows.

About halfway there the bus sways and the rear end swerves, leaving it diagonal with the rear wheels stuck in a ditch. It's completely immobile with the rear wheels spinning. All the men get out, and initially the bus lurches a couple of yards to one side before getting stuck again. Now everybody has to get out. The instant I leave the bus I'm over my ankles in mud. We find a piece of higher ground and watch the futile attempts to free it. I join in pulling branches from the bushes and sticking them under the wheels, but none of it helps: the bus is still stuck. A handful of people pack their few belongings together and set off on foot. I ask the driver what happens next. He shrugs his shoulders and says we'll have to wait until tomorrow. Once again I find myself close to despair in the middle of nowhere with no food or drink—just custard powder, which isn't much use. It quickly gets cold, and I'm freezing in my wet clothes. I go back to my seat; at least I've got a warm blanket. Lketinga will be waiting in vain in Maralal, if he did somehow get my message.

One by one people begin to get out food. Everyone who has anything offers to share. I'm offered bread and fruit, which I accept with embarrassment because I have nothing to offer in return even though I have more luggage than anyone else. Everybody tries to make themselves as comfortable as possible to get to sleep. The few empty seats are given to women with children. During the night a Land Rover passes but doesn't stop.

About four in the morning it's so cold that the driver runs the engine for nearly an hour to warm us up. The time drags but eventually the sky glows red, and the sun hesitantly shows itself. It's just after six. The first few leave the bus to do what they have to behind the bushes. I climb out and stretch my stiff limbs. It's still as muddy as yesterday. We'll have to wait until the sun warms up properly before trying again to get the bus out of the ditch. From ten o'clock until midday we push and shove, but we can't move it more than a hundred feet. The idea of another night out here is horrific.

Suddenly I see a white Land Rover plowing its way through the mire, partly off road. In despair I run up and stop it. There's an elderly English couple inside, and I explain my situation and plead with them to take me with them. The wife agrees straightaway, and delightedly I rush back to the bus and get my stuff down. In the Land Rover I tell my story to the lady, who's horrified and gives me a sandwich, which I wolf down.

We've barely gone half a mile when we meet a gray Land Rover coming the other way. The road is narrow, and we have to be careful that neither skids into the other. We're going slowly, but the other one is getting closer fast when suddenly I think I've seen a mirage. "Stop, please, stop your car," I shout, "this is my boyfriend!" At the wheel of the other car, driving along this nightmare road, is Lketinga.

I wave like mad out of the window to get him to see me, but Lketinga is totally concentrating on the road. I don't know which is the greater: my huge joy to see him and pride in his achievement, or my terror as to how he might bring the car to a standstill. Then he spots me and laughs at us proudly through the windshield. The car comes to a stop twenty yards farther on. I charge out and run to him. It's a magnificent reunion. I can hardly hold back my tears of joy. He has two companions but happily hands over the keys: he'd much rather I drive back. We fetch my luggage and load up. I thank the English couple, and the gentleman says that having seen what a good-looking man I have he now understands why I am here.

On the way back Lketinga tells me that he was waiting for the bus. Father Giuliani had passed on the message, and he had immediately set off on foot to Maralal. It was nearly ten P.M. when he heard that the bus had become stranded and there was a white woman on board. When the bus didn't arrive in the morning, he went to the garage, picked up our repaired car, and had set off, just like that, to save his woman. I can hardly imagine how he managed. The track was fairly straight but seriously muddy. He had gone the whole way in second gear and every now and then had to restart the stalled engine, but all in all "*hakuna matata,* no problem."

We get to Maralal and go to the boardinghouse. All three sit on the bed with me facing them. Lketinga obviously wants to know what I've brought back, and the two warriors look eager too. I open my bags and first of all get out the blankets. Lketinga beams at the sight of the soft, bright red blanket—I'd got that one spot on. The striped one he wants to give to his friend, but I protest. I want that for myself in the *manyatta*; the Kenyan ones itch. I have sewn three new kangas, and I don't mind if he wants to give those away to his friends who're staring so much. The radio-cassette player with the recordings of my family knocks Lketinga flat because he recognizes the voices of Eric and Jelly. He is immeasurably happy, and so am I because I've never seen such genuine pleasure and amazement from everyday European things. My darling rummages around in the luggage to see what else there might be and is delighted when he comes across the cowbell that my mother sent as a wedding present. Now the other pair liven up too, and each one in turn rings the bell, which to me sounds louder and better here. The other pair would like one too, but I have only the one, so in the end I give them two of the little goat bells, which please them too. When I tell my darling that that's everything, he continues to search and is amazed to find the pudding bowl and medicines.

At long last we try to catch up with each other's news. All's well at home because the rain has come at last, but there are lots of mosquitoes. Saguna, Mama's little girl, is sick and has stopped eating while I've been gone. I'm so pleased to be going home tomorrow.

First of all we all go for something to eat, tough old meat again of course, plus flat bread and a type of leaf spinach, and before long there are bones all over the floor. The world is a completely different place than it was three days ago, and already I feel content again. It's late before the other pair leave, and at last we're alone together in the room. The continuous rain has meant it's cold in Maralal now, and showering outside is out of the question. Lketinga fetches me a big basin full of hot water so that at least I can wash in our room. I'm happy to be so close to my darling again. I can hardly sleep, however, because the bed is so narrow and sags so much that it will take me a while to get used to it.

The next morning we go to the government office to see if there has been any progress with Lketinga's identity card. Unfortunately there hasn't been any. Because we can't produce his ID number, everything is held up, the official says. This is depressing news because on entry I got only a two-month visa, and getting married in such a short space of time is going to be a problem.

We decide to go home for now. Because of the rains we can't use the jungle track and have to take the long way. This has big rocks and branches everywhere, and large ruts run across the road. Even so we do well enough. The scrubland is blooming, and there's even grass growing in some places. It's incredible how fast that can happen here. Here and there zebras graze peacefully or whole families of ostriches run from the noise of our engine. We have to ford a small river and then a larger one, both with flowing water, but thanks to the four-wheel drive we get through and without getting stuck in quicksand.

We're still an hour or more from Barsaloi when I hear a soft hissing and shortly afterward the car tilts over. I take a look: a flat! First of all we have to unload everything to get at the spare, then I crawl under the filthy vehicle to get the jack into place. Lketinga helps and after half an hour we manage to get going again and eventually get back to the *manyattas*.

Mama is standing laughing in front of the hut, and Saguna throws herself into my arms, a fabulous reunion; Mama even kisses me on the cheek. We drag everything into the *manyatta*, almost filling it. Mama makes chai, and I give her and Saguna the skirts I made. Everyone is happy. Lketinga plays the cassette, and that sets everyone off talking. But when I give Saguna the brown doll that my mother bought for me, everyone's jaw drops, and Saguna runs screaming out of the hut. I have no idea what's happened, but even Mama has recoiled from the doll. Lketinga asks me in all earnestness if it really is a dead baby. After my initial astonishment I burst out laughing and say, "No, this is only plastic." But the doll with its hair—and above all its eyelids that open and close—disconcerts them for some time. Other children come to stare at it, and it's only when another girl goes to lift the doll that Saguna pushes in and grabs it for herself. From then on nobody else is allowed to touch the doll, not even Mama. From now on Saguna will only sleep with her "Baby."

At sunset the mosquitoes descend on us. Everything is so damp, they seem perfectly at home, and even though there's a fire burning in the hut, they swarm around our heads. I'm forever waving my hand in front of my face. How can I sleep in this? They're even attacking my feet through my socks. My joy at being home is distinctly diminished. I sleep in my clothes and pull my new blanket over me, but unlike the others I can't cover my head. I'm almost hysterical by the time I get to sleep, just before dawn. In the morning I'm so bitten that I can hardly open my eyes. I don't want to catch malaria, so I'm going to have to buy a mosquito net, even though that could be dangerous with the open fire.

Up at the Mission I ask the Father if there's any chance he could repair my tire. He says he has no time but gives me a spare and advises me to travel with two, because it's not unknown to get two punctures at once. I take the opportunity to ask him what he does about the mosquitoes. He has fewer problems in his well-built house and makes do with a spray. He says the best thing would be to build a house: it wouldn't cost much and the local government man could allocate us a piece of land that we'd then have to register in Maralal.

I can't get the idea out of my head: it would be tremendous to have a properly built hut. Taken with the idea, I go back to the *manyatta* and tell Lketinga, but he's not so sure. He doesn't know if he'd feel at home in a house. We can think about it. Even so I want to go to Maralal, because I'm not spending another night without a mosquito net.

Within a short time there's a crowd around the Land Rover again: everybody wants to go to Maralal. A few of them I know by sight, but others are complete strangers. Lketinga decides who can come. Once again it takes nearly five hours until, late in the afternoon, we reach our destination, although without punctures. First of all we have the tire repaired, which turns out to be a lengthy business. While it's being done I take a closer look at the other tires and notice that hardly any of them have any tread left. I ask at the garage about new tires and am horrified by the price. For a set of four new tires they want one thousand Swiss francs. That's the same price as in Switzerland. Here it represents three months' wages, but I'll have to get them if I want to keep from having accidents.

While we're waiting I find a mosquito net in the shops and also buy boxes full of repellent coils. That evening in the boardinghouse bar I get to know the chief government official for the Samburu District. He's an amiable character and speaks good English. He'd already heard of my existence and had planned to drop in on us one of these days. He congratulates my Masai on finding such a brave woman. I tell him about my plans to build a house, our wedding, and the identity card problem.

He promises to do what he can to help but says the house could be a problem, as there's very little wood available.

At least he will look into the identity card problem. The next day he comes with us to the government office. There's a lot of discussion, forms filled out, and various names mentioned. If he knows everything about Lketinga's family, the card can be issued in Maralal within two to three weeks. We fill in the wedding preregistration document at the same time. If no one objects, we can get married in three weeks, but we have to have two literate witnesses. I don't know how to thank the man enough, I'm so happy. There's money to be handed over for this and that, but within a couple of hours everything has been put in motion. We have to drop in again in two weeks and bring all our documents. In good humor, I invite the government man to join us for dinner. He's the first person who's helped us out of the goodness of his heart. Even Lketinga generously pushes some money in his direction.

After the one night in Maralal we set off home again. Just before we leave the town I bump into Jutta. Obviously we have to have chai together and swap news. She wants to come to our wedding. She's currently living with Sophia, another white woman who's recently moved to Maralal with her Rasta boyfriend. She tells me to call in. We whites need to stick together, she says jokingly. Lketinga's in a bad mood; we're laughing a lot, and he doesn't understand anything because we're speaking German. He wants to go home, so we say good-bye. This time I risk the jungle track, but the surface is appalling and when we get to the steep—and now slippery—slope, I scarcely dare to breathe. But this time my prayers are heeded, and we get to Barsaloi without incident.

The next few days pass quietly in measured routine. People have enough milk, and there's corn flour and rice to be had in the run-down shops. Mama is busy with preparations for the big Samburu festival. They will celebrate the end of the warrior stage for my darling's age group; after the festival—in a month's time—the warriors will officially be able to look for wives and marry. One year later, the next generation—today's boys—will be officially elevated to "warriors" in a big festival marked by circumcision.

The coming festival, which happens at a particular place attended by all the mothers with warrior sons, is very important for Lketinga. In two or three weeks Mama and we will leave the *manyatta* and move to the festival site, where the women will build new huts just for the event. The exact date for the commencement of the three-day festival we'll only find out closer to the time because the phase of the moon plays an important part. I think that we should contact the government office about two weeks before because if anything should go wrong, I won't have much time left before my visa runs out.

Lketinga is on the road a lot now because he has to find a black bull of a specific size. That means visiting lots of relations and doing barter deals. Sometimes I go with him, but I sleep at home under my mosquito net, which protects me well. During the day I do the usual chores. Each morning, with or without Lketinga, I go down to the river. Sometimes I take Saguna along, who thinks it's great fun to bathe; it's her first time! While we're there I wash our smoky clothes, which once again hurts my knuckles. Then we drag our water containers back home and go and look for firewood.

More Red Tape

Time passes quickly, and soon we must go to Maralal to get married. Mama is unhappy about Lketinga going away so soon before the ceremony, but we think that a week should really be more than enough. Mama herself leaves the same day, heading off with all the other mothers and some heavily laden donkeys. There's no way she wants to come with us: she's never been in a car and has no intention of trying the experience. So I just pack my things into the car and leave the rest to Mama.

Lketinga brings Jomo along, an older man who speaks some English. I don't particularly like him, and he keeps pestering us to be a witness to the wedding or help in some way. Then they talk about the upcoming festival. Mothers are coming from all over to be there, between forty and fifty *manyattas* will be built, and there'll be lots of dancing. I'm looking forward immensely to this big festival, which I'm allowed to attend. Looking at the moon, our passenger thinks it'll be in two weeks' time.

In Maralal we first of all go to the identity card office, but the official on duty isn't there, and we're told to come back tomorrow morning. Without the card we can't set a date for the wedding. We search Maralal for two potential witnesses, but it's not that easy; the people Lketinga knows either can't write or don't understand English or Swahili. His brother is too young, and some people are in any case afraid to go near the government office because they don't understand what it's all about. Only on the second day do we run into two *morans* who've lived in Mombasa and also have identity cards. They promise to stay in Maralal for a couple of days.

When we turn up in the office that afternoon, Lketinga's identity card really is there; all he has to do is add his fingerprint. Then it's off to the civil registration office. The official there examines my passport and the certificate confirming that I am single. From time to time he uses Swahili to ask Lketinga questions that he obviously doesn't understand. This makes him nervous. I dare to ask when we can get married and give the names of the two witnesses. The official says we'll have to speak directly to the district officer because he's the only man who can carry out the ceremony.

We sit down in the line of people waiting to talk to this important man. It's two hours before we get to see him: an enormous man seated at a stylish, modern table. I put our papers on the table and tell him we want a date for our wedding. He leafs through my passport and asks me why I want to marry a Masai and where we're going to live. I'm so nervous that I find it hard to speak in proper sentences. "Because I love him and we're going to build a house in Barsaloi." His gaze wanders back and forth between Lketinga and me, and eventually he tells us to come back in two days' time at two P.M. with the witnesses. We thank him happily and leave.

All of a sudden everything seems to be happening more normally than I could ever have dreamed. Lketinga buys *miraa* and settles down with a beer in the boardinghouse. I advise him against it, but he thinks he needs it. At about nine o'clock there's a knock on the door, and our companion is standing there, chewing *miraa* also. We talk over everything again, but the longer the evening goes on, the more restless Lketinga gets. He's not sure if this is the right thing to do. He doesn't know anybody who's got married in a registry office. This time I'm glad that Jomo can explain it all to him. Lketinga just nods. Here's hoping he sticks it out for the next two days. Visits to government offices don't agree with him.

The next day I go looking for Jutta and Sophia. Sophia lives in grand style in a two-story house with electric lighting, running water, and even a fridge. They're both delighted about the wedding and promise to turn up at the registry office the next day at two. Sophia lends me a pretty hairclip and a smart blouse. We buy two nice new kangas for Lketinga. Everything is ready.

On the morning of our wedding, however, I start getting nervous. By midday our witnesses still haven't turned up and don't even know that their presence is needed in two hours' time. We have to find two others. There's always Jomo, and under the circumstances I don't mind as long as we can find a second. In despair I ask the boardinghouse landlady, who's delighted to agree. At two o'clock we're standing in front of the office. Sophia and Jutta are there, with cameras even. We sit on the bench and wait with everyone else. The mood is somewhat tense, and Jutta keeps teasing me. Truth to tell, I had imagined the minutes leading up to my wedding as somewhat jollier.

After half an hour we still haven't been called. People go in and out, and one of them in particular strikes me because I notice he has been in three times. Time's getting on, and Lketinga's getting worried. He's afraid there'll be something wrong with his papers and he'll be put in jail. I try my best to reassure him, but because of the *miraa* he hasn't slept. "*Hakuna matata,* we're in Africa, *pole, pole,*" says Jutta, as the door suddenly opens, and Lketinga and I are called in. The witnesses have to wait outside. Now even I'm getting butterflies.

The district officer is once again behind his great baronial desk, and sitting at the long table in front of him are two other men, one of them the one I had noticed going in and out. They introduce themselves as plainclothes police and demand to see my passport and Lketinga's identity card.

My heart is beating like thunder. What is going on? They inundate me with questions, and I'm terrified that I'm not understanding their bureaucratic English properly. How long have I been living in the Samburu District? How did I get to know Lketinga? And when? What are we doing for a living? What is my profession? How do we communicate? And so on, and so on. Endless questions.

Lketinga keeps asking what we're talking about, but I can't explain that to him here: not in the way we're used to communicating. At the question of whether or not I've been married before, I finally erupt. Angrily I tell them that my birth certificate and my passport both show the same name and that I even have a certificate from the local authority in Switzerland written in English. One of them says this cannot be accepted unless it is confirmed by the embassy in Nairobi. "But there's my passport!" I insist furiously. But it doesn't do any good. The officer says that might be a forgery too. Now I'm beyond myself with anger. The district officer asks Lketinga if he already has a Samburu wife, and he answers truthfully, "No." But the officer wants to know how he can prove it. Everybody in Barsaloi knows it, he says; "But we're in Maralal," comes the answer. In which language do we think we can get married, then? I suggest in English with translation into Masai. The officer gives a snide laugh and says he doesn't have the time for special cases like that and in any case he doesn't speak Masai. We should come back when we can both speak the same language, either English or Swahili, when I've had my papers stamped in Nairobi and Lketinga can bring a paper signed by the local chief to say he is unmarried.

I flip my lid completely at this pantomime and scream at the officer, why didn't he tell us all this in the first place? Spiffily he declares that here he can decide when he tells people anything, and if I don't like it he can have me thrown out of the country tomorrow. That does it! "Come, darling," I say. "We go. They don't want give the marriage." Furious and in tears, I storm out of the office with Lketinga behind me. Outside Jutta and Sophia are clicking with their cameras: they think it's all over!

In the meantime a crowd of about twenty people has gathered. I wish the earth would swallow me. "What's wrong, Corinne? Lketinga, what's the problem?" "I don't know," he says in confusion. I storm over to the Land Rover and race at full speed to the boardinghouse. I want to be alone. I throw myself onto the bed and burst into sobs that shake my whole body. "These goddamn pigs!"

Sometime later Lketinga is sitting next to me, trying to calm me down. I know he can't cope with tears, but I can't help myself. Jutta pops her head in and brings me a local brandy. Reluctantly I force it down, and gradually the crying fit subsides. I feel exhausted and insensible. At some stage Jutta leaves. Lketinga drinks beer and chews his *miraa*.

Later still, there's a knock at the door. I'm lying in bed staring at the ceiling. Lketinga opens the door, and the two plainclothes policemen come in. They apologize politely and offer their assistance. When I ignore them, one, a Samburu, talks to Lketinga. When eventually I realize that all these bastards want is a load of money to let us get married, I lose my temper again and shout at them to get out of the room: I will marry this man in Nairobi or wherever I have to and without any of their grubby help. They leave the room in embarrassment.

Tomorrow we'll go to Nairobi to get my form stamped and have my visa extended just in case. Now that I have my wedding application forms, that ought not to be a problem. Then we'll have another three months in which to get the relevant paper from the local chief. It would be absurd

that we can't do it without bribery! Just as I'm getting ready to go to
sleep, the unlovable Jomo sticks his head in. Lketinga tells him our plan,
and he says he should come with us because, he assures us, he knows
Nairobi like the back of his hand. Because the road via Nyahururu is still
in a bad state, we decide to go via Wamba and Isiolo and take the public
buses from there. But because of the upcoming festival we've only four or
five days.

It's a new route for me, but everything goes according to plan. It takes
us five hours to get to Isiolo. I ask my way to the local mission in the hope
of being allowed to park the car there, which I am. If the car were just left
on the street, it wouldn't be there long.

As it's another three to four hours to Nairobi we decide to spend the
night here and set off first thing in the morning in order to get to the
office in the afternoon. But now Jomo tells me he has no money left,
leaving me no option but to pay for his room, food, and drink. I do it with
ill grace because I still don't like him. In our room I fall into bed and am
asleep before nightfall. The other two are drinking beer and nattering. I
wake up with a thirst, and we have breakfast before boarding the bus for
Nairobi. It takes an hour until it fills up, and we finally set off, arriving in
Nairobi just before noon.

First of all we track down the Swiss embassy to get them to certify my
certificate from the local council, but they say they don't do that sort of
thing. In any case, although I was born in Switzerland and have always
considered the country home, because my father was German I have a
German passport. Therefore, they say, I need to go to the German embassy.

I have my doubts that the Germans will deal with a Swiss document,
but they insist that's my only option. The German embassy is in a different
part of town, and we drag ourselves across bustling sticky Nairobi. The
German embassy is busy, and we have to line up. When I finally get to the
front, the official on duty shakes his head and tries to send me to the Swiss
embassy. When I tell him exasperatedly that we've just come from there,
he lifts the telephone and calls them. Shaking his head, he comes back and
says he can't see the point in any of it, but it will satisfy them in Maralal
if there are as many stamps and signatures as possible on the piece of
paper. I thank him and leave.

Lketinga wants to know why nobody likes my papers. I can't answer
him, and he looks at me doubtfully. Now we head off to another part of

town where the Nyayo Building is located to renew my visa, which runs out in ten days. My legs are like lead, but I am determined to get the visa in the one and a half hours we have left. In the Nyayo Building there are more forms to fill out. Now I'm actually grateful for our companion because my head's spinning and I understand only every other question. Everyone stares at Lketinga, so he has pulled his kanga down over his head. We wait until I am called. Time is ticking on, and we've already been sitting for more than an hour in this stifling hall. I can barely stand the stink of sweat from the crowds. The office will be closing in fifteen minutes, and coming back tomorrow means starting all over again.

At long last my passport is held up. "Miss Hofmann!" a stern woman's voice calls out. I push my way to the counter. The woman looks at me and asks me if I want to marry an African. "Yes," I answer abruptly. "Where is your husband?" I point toward Lketinga. The woman asks with amusement if I really want to marry a Masai. "Yes," I say. "Why not?" She disappears and comes back with two colleagues who also take a look at me and then at Lketinga, and all three of them laugh. I stand there proudly and refuse to let their attitude annoy me. Eventually the rubber stamp comes down on a page of my passport, and I have my visa. I say thank you and leave the building.

Malaria

The air outside is clammy and the exhaust fumes worse than I've ever noticed before. It's four P.M., but all my paperwork is correct. I want to celebrate, but I'm too tired. We have to get back to the part of town where we can find somewhere to stay, but we've barely gone a few hundred yards when I feel faint and my legs threaten to fold beneath me. "Darling, help me," I call. "Corinne, what's the problem?" asks Lketinga. My head is spinning, I have to sit down, but there isn't a restaurant nearby. I lean against a shop front and feel suddenly ill and incredibly thirsty. Lketinga gets cross because people are stopping to stare. He wants me to move, but I can't, not without help. They half carry me to the boardinghouse.

All of a sudden I get agoraphobia. The people coming toward me are blurred, and everything stinks. On every corner somebody is cooking fish, corncobs, or meat. I feel sick. If I don't get out of the street immediately, I'm going to throw up. There's a beer bar close by, and we go in, but I want to lie down. At first they say it's impossible, but when Jomo tells them I can't move any farther, they take me to a room upstairs.

It's a typical rent-by-the-hour hotel. The Kikuyu music is almost as loud in the room as it is downstairs in the bar. I collapse on the bed and suddenly feel dreadful. I make clear I'm about to be sick, and Lketinga lifts me and drags me to the toilet. But I don't make it. We're still in the corridor when the first geyser erupts out of my mouth, and when we reach the toilet it keeps coming until there's nothing left to bring up but yellow bile. I stagger back to the bedroom on wobbly legs, embarrassed by my awfulness. I lie down on the bed feeling as if I'm dying of thirst. Lketinga fetches me a Schweppes tonic water, and I finish off the bottle in one gulp, then another and another. All of a sudden I'm freezing. It's as if I'm sitting in a fridge, and it gets worse and worse; my teeth are chattering so hard my jaw hurts, but I can't stop. "Lketinga," I say, "I feel so cold, please give me blankets." Lketinga gives me the blanket, but it doesn't do any good. Jomo goes back to the boardinghouse and fetches two more blankets. But even draped in the blankets I pull my stiff, shivering body up from the bed and demand tea, steaming hot tea. It seems like hours before it arrives, and then I'm shivering so badly I can hardly drink it. After just two or three sips my stomach starts churning again, but I have no strength to get out of the bed. Lketinga fetches me one of the basins from the shower rooms, and I throw up what little I've drunk.

Lketinga doesn't know what to do. He keeps asking me what's wrong, but I haven't a clue either. I'm scared. The shivering stops and I collapse like jelly on the pillows. My whole body aches, and I'm as exhausted as if I've been running for my life for hours on end. Then I start getting hot, and within minutes, my whole body's dripping with sweat. My hair's sticking to my head, and I feel as if I'm burning up. Now all I want is cold cola, and once again I knock back the whole bottle. Then I need the toilet. Lketinga takes me and immediately diarrhea seizes me. Even though Lketinga doesn't know what to do, I'm glad he's there. Back in bed I try to sleep. I can't speak and doze on and off with the voices of the two men in my ears, even though the noise from the bar downstairs is much louder.

Then a new attack hits me. A chill runs through me, and within seconds I'm shivering again. I clutch the bed in panic and beg, "Darling, help me!" Lketinga leans over me, covering me with his chest, but I keep shivering. Jomo, standing there, reckons I've got malaria and need to go to the hospital. The word echoes in my head: malaria, malaria, malaria! In the space of a second I stop shivering and start sweating from every pore. The sheets are soaking. I'm thirsty, thirsty. I need something to drink. The boardinghouse landlady sticks her head in, and when she sees me I hear the words, "*Mzungu*, malaria, hospital!" But I shake my head. I don't want to go into a hospital here in Nairobi. I've heard such terrible stories, and then there's Lketinga. He's lost on his own in Nairobi.

The landlady disappears and comes back with antimalaria powder, which she mixes with water. I drink it and fall asleep. When I wake again, it's dark, and my head's buzzing. I call for Lketinga, but nobody's there. A

few minutes later—or it might have been hours—Lketinga comes back
into the room. He'd been downstairs in the bar. I smell the beer fumes,
and once again my stomach turns. It's one shivering fit after another the
whole night long.

When I wake in the morning I hear the two of them talking about
the festival back home. Jomo comes over to the bed and asks me how I
feel. Bad, I tell him. Can we go back today? he asks. Not me. I'm going
to the toilet. My legs are shaking, and I can hardly stand. I ought to eat, I
tell myself.

Lketinga goes downstairs and comes back with a plate of lumps of
meat. When I smell the food, however, my stomach, which has started to
ache, goes into cramps. I throw up again almost immediately, but all that
comes up is some yellow liquid, and the vomiting sets off the diarrhea
again. I'm as sick as a dog and feel as if I'm on my last legs.

On the evening of the second day I start falling asleep whenever the
sweating starts and lose all sense of time. The endless noise is driving me
so mad that I start crying and covering my ears. It's all too much for Jomo,
who announces he's off to see some relatives but will be back in three
hours' time. Lketinga gives him some of our cash, which I resent, but I
don't really care because it's rapidly becoming clear that if I don't do
something I'll never get out of Nairobi alive, and maybe not even out of
this awful room.

Lketinga goes off to get some vitamins and the local malaria medicine.
I force the tablets down, and every time I throw up force myself to take
another one. It's midnight by now, and Jomo still isn't back. We worry
about him because this part of Nairobi isn't safe. Lketinga hardly sleeps for
taking care of me.

The medicine has done something to reduce my attacks, but I'm so
weak I can barely raise an arm. Lketinga is in despair. He wants to find Jomo
as quickly as possible, but it's madness in this city that he doesn't know. I
plead with him to stay with me or I'll be all alone. We have to get out of
Nairobi as soon as possible. I'm swallowing vitamin tablets like candy, and
gradually my head's clearing. If I don't want to die here, I've got to summon
the last reserves of my strength. I send my darling off to get fruit and bread
for me, anything that doesn't smell like cooked food, and force it down bit
by bit. My cracked lips burn like mad when they touch the fruit, but I need
strength to get out of here. Jomo has left us in the lurch.

The fear that Lketinga could completely lose it gives me strength. I try to wash in order to feel better. My darling carries me to the shower, and with a lot of effort I manage to clean myself. Then I insist on changing the three-day-old bed linen. While they're changing it all I try to take a few paces. Out on the street I feel faint again, but I want to do it. We go about fifty yards, but to me it seems like five miles. I have to go back; the stink on the street is torturing my stomach. Even so I'm proud at what I've managed and promise Lketinga that tomorrow we'll leave Nairobi. But when I'm lying back in bed, I wish I were at home with my mother in Switzerland.

The next day we take a taxi to the bus station. Lketinga is worried that we're leaving Jomo behind, but after waiting two days we have every right to leave, not least because Lketinga's festival is getting closer.

The journey to Isiolo takes forever. Lketinga has to support me to stop my falling out of my seat when we turn corners. When we get there, Lketinga suggests we spend the night, but I want to get home. At least as far as Maralal, where I might see Jutta or Sophia. I drag myself to the Mission and crawl into the car while Lketinga says good-bye to the missionaries for us. He wants to drive, but I can't let him; this is a small town with traffic police everywhere.

I set off but can hardly manage to press the clutch down. The first few miles are metaled road, but after that it's a dirt track. We stop en route and pick up three Samburus who want to get to Wamba. I concentrate on driving and shut out everything else. I can see the potholes from miles away. I'm paying no attention to what's going on in the car until someone lights a cigarette and I ask him to put it out or I'll throw up. I can feel my stomach rebelling. But to stop now and start vomiting would rob me of what strength I have. The sweat is pouring off me, and I have to keep wiping my forehead with the back of my hand to stop it from getting into my eyes; I just look straight ahead and dare not lift my eyes from the road for a second.

It starts to get dark, and lights are coming on; we've got to Maralal. I can hardly believe it—I'd been driving with no sense of time. I park straightaway in front of our boardinghouse, turn off the motor, and turn to Lketinga. Then I notice how light my body feels, and suddenly everything goes dark.

In the Hospital

I open my eyes and think I'm awakening from a nightmare. But a glance around me shows that the crying and moaning are real. I'm in the hospital, in a huge room with beds packed together. On my left is an old, emaciated Samburu woman, and on my right is a pink child's cot with a railing. Something inside it keeps hitting the woodwork and crying out. Everywhere I look there's nothing but misery. What am I doing in the hospital? I don't know how I got here. Where is Lketinga? I start to panic. How long have I been here? Outside the sun is shining. My bed is made of iron with a thin mattress and a dirty gray sheet.

Two young doctors in white coats pass by. "Hello!" I wave to them, but my voice isn't loud enough to compete with the groaning, and I can't sit up. My head is too heavy. Tears gather in my eyes. What's going on? Where's Lketinga?

The Samburu woman says something to me, but I don't understand, and then at last I see Lketinga coming toward me. The sight of him calms me down and almost makes me happy. "Hello, Corinne, how you feel now?" I try to smile, and say, "Not bad." He tells me that as soon as we arrived I fell unconscious. Our landlady called the ambulance immediately, and I've been here since yesterday evening. He was by my side all night, but I didn't come to. I can hardly believe that I didn't know what was going on. The doctor had given me a sedative.

After a while the two medics come over to the bed. I have acute malaria, but there's not much they can do because they don't have the drugs. All they can do is give me pills. I should eat and sleep as much as possible, but just the word "eat" makes me feel ill, and I can hardly imagine sleeping amid all this crying and groaning. Lketinga sits on the edge of the bed and looks at me helplessly.

Suddenly I detect the strong smell of cabbage, and my stomach turns over. I need a container of some sort. In despair I grab the water jug and throw up into it. Lketinga holds the jug and supports me; I could hardly manage on my own. Immediately a dark nurse appears, grabs the jug, and replaces it with a bucket. "Why you make this? This is for drinking water," she snaps at me. I feel miserable. The smell is coming from the food cart. There are tin bowls on it filled with a mound of rice and cabbage; one is delivered to each bed.

Totally exhausted from the effort of vomiting, I lie on the bed and hold my arm in front of my nose. There's no way I can eat. It's an hour since I swallowed the first tablets, and my whole body is starting to itch. I start scratching like mad all over. Lketinga notices spots and pimples on my face. I lift up my skirt, and we find my legs are also covered with little lumps. He calls the doctor. It seems I have an allergic reaction to the medicine, but there's nothing else he can give me because everything else has been used and they've been waiting for days for supplies from Nairobi.

In the evening Lketinga leaves: he wants to get something to eat and see if he can find someone from home to tell him when the big festival is due. I'm dead tired and just want to sleep. My whole body is bathed in sweat, and the thermometer says I have a temperature of 105.8. After drinking so much water I need the toilet, but how am I to get there? The toilet cubicles are some ninety feet from the ward entrance. How can I get that far? I slowly lower my feet to the floor and step into my plastic sandals. Then, holding on to the bed frame, I stand up, but my legs are trembling and I can hardly stand. I pull myself together. The last thing I want to do is collapse. Feeling my way from bed to bed, I get as far as the door. But the ninety feet seems an impossible distance, and I end up crawling the last few with nothing to hold on to for support. I grind my teeth together and with the last of my strength reach the toilet. But there's nowhere to sit down: I have to squat. Holding on to the stone walls, I do the best I can.

Just how bad this malaria is dawns on me as I realize that, despite never having been really sick in my life, I am incredibly weak. There's a heavily pregnant Masai woman outside the door, but when she notices that I can't let go of it without falling backward, she helps me silently back to the ward entrance. I'm so thankful that I cry tears of gratitude. With enormous effort I drag myself back into bed and sob. The sister comes to ask if I'm in pain, but I shake my head and feel even more miserable. At some stage I fall asleep.

I wake up in the middle of the night. The child in the cot is screaming appallingly and banging its head against the railing. Nobody comes, and it's driving me mad. I've been here for four days now and am feeling really sorry for myself. Lketinga comes often, but he doesn't look well either; he wants to go home but not without me because he's afraid I'll die. The nurses curse me because every time I eat something I throw up. My stomach aches terribly. One time Lketinga brings me a whole leg of kid, already roasted, and pleads with me to eat it and it'll make me better. But I can't, and he leaves disappointed.

On the fifth day Jutta comes. She'd heard there is a white woman in the hospital. She's horrified when she sees me. She says I have to get out of here straightaway and get into the missionary hospital in Wamba. But I don't understand why I should move to another hospital; they're all the same. And in any case I wouldn't survive a four-and-a-half-hour trip in a car. "If you could see yourself, you'd understand that you have to get out of here. Five days and they haven't given you anything? You're worth less than a goat out there. Maybe they don't want to help you," she says. "Jutta," I say, "please take me to the boardinghouse. I don't want to die here, and on these roads I wouldn't make it to Wamba. I can't even sit up!" Jutta talks to the doctors. They don't want to let me leave and only prepare my discharge papers when I sign a form absolving them of all responsibility.

In the meantime Jutta fetches Lketinga to help bring me to the boardinghouse. They take me between them, and we make it slowly into the village. Everywhere people stand and stare at us. I'm ashamed to have to be dragged so helplessly through the village.

But I want to fight and survive. So I ask the pair of them to take me to the Somali restaurant, where I'll try to eat a piece of liver. The restaurant is at least two hundred yards away, and my legs are folding under me. I keep telling myself: "Corinne, you can do it! You have to get there!" Exhausted but proud, I sit down at the table. The Somali is horrified too when he sees me. We order the liver. My stomach rebels as soon as I see the plate, and I summon up all my strength and slowly begin eating. By the end of two hours I've nearly cleaned my plate and convince myself I feel fantastic. The three of us go to the boardinghouse, where Jutta leaves us. She'll drop by again tomorrow or the day after. I spend the rest of the afternoon sitting in front of the boardinghouse in the sun. It's wonderful to feel the warmth.

That evening I lie in bed, slowly eating a carrot and proud of my achievements. My stomach has calmed down, and I can keep it all down. "Corinne, onward and upward," I think to myself as I fall asleep.

Early the next morning Lketinga finds out that his ceremony has already begun. He's very worked up and wants to go home immediately, or rather to the site of the ceremony. But there's no way I can go that far, and if he goes on foot it'll take him more than a day.

He's worried about his mama, who'll be waiting there in despair, not knowing what's going on. I promise him we'll go tomorrow, my darling. That way I have a whole day to build up at least enough strength to hold on to the steering wheel. When we get out of Maralal, Lketinga can drive, but it's too dangerous here with the police.

We go back to the Somali's, and I order the same thing. Today I managed to get halfway there without assistance and find eating easier. I'm slowly beginning to feel life returning to my body. My stomach is flat, no longer concave. In the boardinghouse I take a look at myself in the mirror for the first time: my face has changed enormously. My eyes seem enormous, and my cheekbones protrude. Before we set off Lketinga buys a few pounds of chewing tobacco and sugar, and I get some fruit and rice. The first few miles exhaust me because I have to keep changing from first to second gear and need strength to work the clutch. Lketinga, sitting next to me, helps by using his arm to reinforce mine. Once again I'm driving as if in a dream, but after several hours we reach the ceremony site.

Rites of Passage

Even totally exhausted, I'm overwhelmed by the site of the encampment. The women have built an entire village out of nothing: more than fifty *manyattas*. There's life everywhere, smoke spiraling up from every hut. Lketinga goes to find Mama's *manyatta* while I wait by the Land Rover. My legs are trembling, and my skinny arms ache. Before long a crowd of women, children, and old people have gathered around me staring. I wish Lketinga would come back soon, and then here he comes with Mama. She frowns when he points to me and says, "Corinne, *jambo . . . wewe* malaria?" I nod and suppress my welling tears.

We unload everything and leave the vehicle locked outside the encampment. We have to go past about fifteen *manyattas* before we reach Mama's. The whole path is covered in cow pies. Everyone of course has brought all their animals with them, although at the moment they're all out grazing and will come home only in the evening. We drink chai, and Mama has an animated conversation with Lketinga. I find out later that we've already missed two of the three days of the festival. My darling is disappointed and upset. I feel sorry. There will have to be a council of the elders in which the most important will decide if he is allowed to take part and what will happen next. Mama, who also belongs to this council, scuttles around trying to find the most important men.

The festivities begin only when it gets dark and the animals are back. Sitting in front of the *manyatta*, I watch all the comings and goings. Lketinga gets filled in by two other warriors who give him jewelry and decorate him artistically. There's a huge feeling of anticipation in the encampment. I feel left out and forgotten. Nobody has spoken a word to me in hours. Soon the

goats and cows will be home, and then it will be night. Mama comes back
and talks over the situation with Lketinga. She seems a bit drunk. All the
elders are drinking vast quantities of home-brewed beer.

I want to find out what's going to happen. Lketinga tells me that he
has to slaughter a big ox or five goats for the elders, and then they'll allow
him to take part in the ceremony. They will give their blessing in front of
Mama's *manyatta* this evening, and then he'll be allowed to join the
warriors' dance. In that way everyone will know officially that this gross
lateness, which would normally mean exclusion, has been forgiven. I'm
relieved. But the problem is that right now he doesn't have five goats. He
has two at most, and one of them is pregnant and can't be killed. I suggest
he buys some from his relatives and bring out a big bundle of notes. He's
not sure because today every goat will cost double, but Mama has a
serious talk with him, and when the first bell rings to say the animals are
coming back he takes the money and goes out.

Bit by bit our *manyatta* fills up with other women. Mama is cooking
ugali, a sort of maize porridge, and everybody's talking. The hut is barely
illuminated by the fire. Every now and then one of the women tries to
talk to me. A younger woman with a little child sits down next to me and
first admires my arms, which are covered with Masai jewelry, and then
plucks up the courage to run her fingers through my straight hair. Then
there's laughter again, and she points at her bald head, decorated with only
a band of pearls. I shake my head; I can't imagine myself bald.

Outside it's already pitch black when I become aware of a grunting
sound, the typical sound of the men when they are excited, either by
danger or sex. Immediately it falls quiet in the hut. My warrior sticks his
head in the hut, but at the sight of so many women he disappears again.
I hear voices rising steadily, and then suddenly there's a shout, then a
group of people start up a sort of humming or cooing. I creep out
curiously and am amazed to see how many warriors and young girls have
assembled in front of our hut for the dance. The warriors are exquisitely
painted and wear red loincloths. Their chests are bare and crisscrossed with
pearl chains. The red war paint stretches from their throat to a point in the
middle of their chest. There are at least three dozen warriors moving to
the same rhythm. The girls, some of them very young, from nine up to
about fifteen years old, are dancing in a row, facing the men, moving their
heads in time to the same rhythm. The tempo increases but only very

slowly, and it's an hour before the first warriors start to jump into the air in the typical Masai leap.

My warrior looks wonderful. He leaps high, floating ever higher like a feather, his long hair flowing behind with every leap. The naked bodies glisten with sweat. It's hard to see everything clearly in the starry night, but it's all too easy to feel the eroticism built up in these hours of dancing. The faces are serious, the eyes staring straight ahead. From time to time a wild scream erupts, or some leader starts to sing and everyone joins in. It is magnificent, and for hours on end I forget my sickness and exhaustion.

The girls choose one warrior after another bobbing up and down in front of them with their rows of necklaces and naked breasts. Looking at them depresses me as I realize that, at twenty-seven, I'm relatively old here, and maybe later on Lketinga will take one of these young girls as his second wife. Plagued by jealousy, I feel out of place and excluded.

The whole group merges into a sort of conga with Lketinga at the head of the column. He looks wild, unapproachable. Gradually the dance comes to an end. The girls, giggling slightly, draw aside. The elders sit on the ground in a circle wrapped in their woolen blankets. The *morans* form themselves into a circle too. Now it is time for the elders to give their blessing. One of them utters a sentence, and all the others repeat *"Enkai"*: the Masai word for God. This goes on for half an hour, and then the whole festival is over for today. Lketinga comes over to me and says I ought to go and sleep now, with Mama. He and the other warriors are going out into the bush to slaughter a goat. None of them will sleep, they will talk about old times and things to come. I understand perfectly and wish him a wonderful night.

In the *manyatta* I make myself as comfortable as I can among the others. I lie awake for ages; there are voices to be heard coming from all over, and in the distance an occasional goat bleats or a lion roars. I pray that I will be fully well again soon.

The next morning, at six o'clock, the day begins in earnest. So many animals in one place create a tremendous noise. Mama goes out to milk our goats and cows. We make chai. I sit wrapped in my blanket because it's cool, waiting impatiently for Lketinga. I've needed to go to the toilet for ages, but with so many people around I don't dare leave the encampment. They'd all be watching me, especially the children, who follow me everywhere when I go out without Lketinga.

At last he arrives and sticks his head into the hut beaming from ear to ear: "Hello, Corinne, how are you?" Then he unfolds his kanga and reaches out to give me a roasted leg of lamb wrapped in leaves. "Corinne, now you eat slowly. After malaria this is very good." It is nice that he thought of me, because it's not normal here for a warrior to bring his wife already cooked meat. When he sees me holding the leg weakly, he sits beside me and cuts bite-sized pieces off with his big bush knife. I have absolutely no desire for meat, but there isn't anything else, and I have to eat if I'm to regain my strength. I force myself to eat a couple of pieces, and Lketinga is happy. I ask him where we can wash, and he laughs and says it's a long way to the river and you can't get there by car. The women fetch just enough water to make chai, nothing else; we'll have to wait a couple of days before we can wash. I find the thought unappealing. At least there are no mosquitoes but more than enough flies. When I clean my teeth outside the *manyatta*, people gather to watch in curiosity, and when I spit out the froth they all get very excited. It's my turn to laugh.

Today an ox is to be slaughtered in the middle of the square. It's quite a spectacle. Six men try to wrestle the ox onto the ground from the side. It's not easy as the terrified animal thrusts around with its horns. Only after several attempts do two warriors manage to grab the horns and turn its head to one side, and the beast slowly sinks to the ground. Immediately its legs are tied, and three people set about slaughtering it while the others hold its legs. It's appalling, but for the Masai it's the only way they know to kill an animal. When the animal stops moving, its artery is cut, and all the men standing around try to drink the blood. It must be a great delicacy because there's a lot of pushing and jostling. Then the butchery begins. Old men, women, and children are already lining up for their share. The best bits go to the old men, and only then do the women and children get theirs. Four hours later there's nothing left but a pool of blood and the splayed-out hide. The women have withdrawn into their huts and are cooking. The old men are sitting in the shade under the trees, drinking beer and waiting for their cooked meat to arrive.

Late in the afternoon I hear the sound of an engine, and shortly afterward Father Giuliani turns up on his motorbike. I greet him warmly. He's heard that I'm here and have malaria and wanted to see if I was okay. He has brought home-baked bread and bananas. I'm overjoyed and feel as if it's Christmas. I tell him the whole story from our wedding plans to the malaria. He advises me strongly to go to Wamba or back to Switzerland until I've fully recovered. He gives me such a penetrating look that I realize I'm not over the hill yet, not by a long way. Then he gets back on his motorbike and roars off.

I think of home, my mother, a warm bath. Yes, right now that would be wonderful, even though it's not all that long since I was back in Switzerland. Even so it seems like forever. But one look at my darling, and I forget even the thought of Switzerland. He asks how I am, and I tell him about the priest's visit. I learned from him that today the schoolchildren come home from Maralal. Father Roberto is bringing some of them in his car. When Mama hears, she immediately hopes that James is among them. I'm pleased too at the thought of being able to speak English for a couple of weeks.

Slowly I manage to eat a few pieces of meat after brushing off a swarm of flies. The drinking water looks more like cocoa, but unless I want to go thirsty I've no choice but to drink it. I'm not given any milk because Mama reckons that with malaria it could be dangerous and cause a relapse.

The first schoolboys arrive, including James and two friends. They're all dressed the same in short gray trousers, a light blue shirt, and a dark blue pullover. He greets me cheerfully and his mother respectfully. As we sit drinking chai together I notice how much his generation is different from that of Lketinga and his age group. They don't look right in these *manyattas*. James looks at me and says he heard in Maralal that I had malaria. He says he's amazed that a white person can live in Mama's *manyatta*. Even as a Samburu he finds it difficult when he comes home for the holidays: everything is so cramped and dirty.

The children's arrival makes a change, and the day flies by. Soon the goats and cows are back home. In the evening there's a big dance in which even the old women will take part, dancing just with themselves. Even the schoolboys dance, outside the encampment, some of them still in uniform. It looks funny. Late in the evening the kings of the festival, the warriors, assemble again. James stands next to them and records their song with our radio-cassette player. I wouldn't have thought of it. After two hours the cassette is full.

The warriors' dance gets wilder and wilder. One of the *morans* suddenly gets a sort of fit. He shakes as if in ecstasy until he falls to the ground thrashing around noisily. Two of the warriors break loose from the dance and forcibly hold him to the ground. I ask James worriedly what's going on. He says this warrior has probably drunk too much blood and gone into a sort of trance and imagines he's fighting a lion. It's not too drastic, and eventually he'll snap out of it and become normal again. The man is squirming and screaming on the ground, his eyes staring at the heavens and foam coming from his mouth. It looks awful, and I just hope nothing like that happens to Lketinga. Apart from the two holding him down, nobody else pays any heed. The festival goes on as before, and I watch Lketinga and notice again how elegantly he leaps into the air. I soak in the spectacle because today is the official end of the festival.

Mama sits in the *manyatta*, half drunk. The boys play back the cassette, and everybody gets very excited. The warriors gather around the machine, which James has placed on the ground. Lketinga is the first to understand, and his whole face lights up when he recognizes one or another of the *morans* singing or shouting. Some of the others stare at the machine with wide eyes, and a few dare to touch it. Lketinga lifts it proudly onto his shoulders, and some of the *morans* start to dance again.

It's slowly getting cold, and I go back into the *manyatta*. James will sleep with a friend, and my darling will go off with the others into the bush. Once again I hear noises everywhere. The entrance to the hut isn't closed, and from time to time I see feet passing by. I'll be glad to be back in Barsaloi. My clothes are dirty and smoky, and my body could do with feeling water, not to mention my hair.

The boys are in the hut the next morning before Lketinga. Mama's making chai when Lketinga sticks his head in. At the sight of the boys he says something crossly. Mama repeats it, and the boys disappear without their chai. In their place Lketinga and another *moran* come in and sit down. "What's the problem, darling?" I ask, somewhat shocked. After a lengthy pause he tells me that this is a warrior's hut and uncircumcised boys shouldn't be in it. James has to eat and drink in another hut where the Mama has a son his own age and not a warrior. Mama keeps an embarrassed silence. I'm disappointed to lose the English conversation and sympathize with the banished boys. But I have to accept these rules.

I ask how much longer we're staying here. Two or three days, comes the reply, and then each family goes back to where they were living. I'm horrified at having to stick it out here for so long with no water to wash with and all the cow pies and flies. The thought of Switzerland comes creeping back, and once again I feel weak. I don't dare venture any farther than a couple of yards into the bush to answer the call of nature. I would prefer to live a more normal life again with my boyfriend.

That afternoon Father Giuliani looks in and brings me some bananas and a letter from my mother. The letter cheers me up, even though my mother is very worried because she hasn't heard from me for so long. The priest and I exchange a few words, and then he's off again. I take the opportunity to write a letter back, mentioning my illness only briefly and playing it down so as not to worry my mother. Nonetheless I hint that I might be back in Switzerland soon. I intend to post the letter when we get back to the Mission. My mother will have to wait three weeks to receive it.

Eventually we depart. We pack up quickly, piling as much as possible into the Land Rover with the rest loaded onto two donkeys. Naturally we get to Barsaloi long before Mama, and so I drive directly to the river. Because Lketinga won't leave the car unattended, we drive along the dried-up riverbed until we get to an isolated spot. I get out of my smoky clothing, and we wash each other thoroughly. The soap suds run black off my body, and there's a layer of soot on my skin. Lketinga washes my hair several times.

I haven't seen myself naked for some time, and I notice how skinny my legs are. After washing I feel as if I've been reborn. I wrap myself in a kanga and begin washing the clothes. It's as hard work as ever getting the dirt out with cold water, but with enough Omo it eventually works. Lketinga helps me and shows how much he loves me by helping wash my skirts, T-shirts, and even underwear. No other man would wash the clothes of a woman.

I really enjoy this togetherness. We hang our wet clothing over bushes or on the hot rocks and sit down in the sunshine, me in the kanga, Lketinga completely naked. He gets his little mirror out and starts painting his clean face artistically with orange-colored ochre and a little stick. His long elegant fingers do this so exactly that it's a joy to watch. He looks fantastic. He turns to me and laughs: "Why you look always to me, Corinne?" "Beautiful, it's very nice," I reply. But Lketinga shakes his head and says you shouldn't say such things, it's bad luck.

Our clothes dry quickly, and we pack everything up and set off. We stop in the village and go to the teahouse, where there's not only chai but also *mandazi,* little sweet spiced pastries. The building is a mishmash between a big *manyatta* and a wooden shed. There are two fires on the ground with chai boiling on each. Along the walls planks serve as benches for three old men and two *morans*. "Hey, *Supa Moran*," they greet us. "*Supa*," Lketinga replies. We order chai, and the two *morans* look at me as Lketinga takes up the conversation with the same habitual phrases that by now I understand. People start by asking a stranger the name of their tribe, where they live, how their family and animals are, where they've just come from, and where they're going. Then they talk about recent events. That's how the work of the newspaper or telephone gets done out in the bush. When we're walking somewhere, we have this conversation with everyone we meet. These two *morans* also want to know who the *mzungu* is. Then the conversation is over and we leave the teahouse.

Mama is back by now and busy cleaning and renovating our old *manyatta*. The roof has to be repaired with cardboard or sisal matting; there's no cow dung to be had for the moment. Lketinga and James go off into the bush to chop down some more thornbushes to repair and raise our fencing. Some of the people who stayed in Barsaloi were followed home a few days ago by two lions that ripped apart their goats. They came in the night and leaped over the thornbush fencing, seized the goats, and disappeared into the night. Because there were no warriors, there was no one to pursue them. So all the fences have been built higher. Everyone is talking about the event and saying we have to watch out because they'll be back. Our corral would be more difficult because we have the Land Rover parked in front of the hut, taking up half the space.

In the evening our animals come back. We can hear them from miles off, thanks to their Swiss cowbells. Lketinga and I go to meet them. It's a pretty sight watching the animals driven back home: the goats in front, the cows behind.

Our evening meal consists of *ugali*, which Lketinga will eat only late at night when everyone is asleep. At last we can make love, even though it has to be quietly because Mama and Saguna are sleeping just five feet away. Even so it's good to feel his silky skin and touch again. After this lovemaking, Lketinga whispers: "Now you get a baby!" I have to laugh because he sounds so convinced. At the same time I suddenly realize I haven't had a period for ages. But I put it down to my poor health rather than a pregnancy, though the thought of a baby sends me to sleep happy.

In the night I feel a stomach cramp and suddenly realize that the diarrhea is starting again. I panic and gently nudge Lketinga, but he's sound asleep. Oh my God, I'll never find the gate in the fence! And then there might be lions around! I crawl silently out of the *manyatta* and look around to see if there is anyone about. Then I squat behind the Land Rover and let go. It seems endless, and I'm ashamed because I know it's a serious misdemeanor to answer a call of nature like this inside the corral. On no account can I use paper, so I clean myself with my underwear and hide it in the undercarriage of the Land Rover. I cover up the mess I've made with sand and hope that in the morning there'll be no evidence of this nightmare. Worried, I crawl back into the *manyatta*, but nobody wakes. Lketinga just grunts.

As long as it doesn't happen again. I last until the morning and then have to rush off into the bush. The diarrhea keeps coming, and my legs start shaking again. Back inside the corral I glance around the Land Rover and am relieved to see that there is no sign of my accident in the night. A stray dog has probably dealt with the rest. I tell Lketinga that I still have problems and go to the Mission to ask for some medicine. But despite the charcoal pills, the diarrhea lasts all day. Mama brings me home-brewed beer and tells me to drink a pint or so of it. It looks disgusting and tastes that way too, but after a couple of cups the alcohol has its effect, and I doze on and off all day.

At some stage the boys come by. Lketinga is in the village, and I can enjoy an unhindered conversation. We talk about God, the world, Switzerland, my family, and the wedding, which I hope will take place soon. James is amazed at me and is proud that his brother, whom he sees as difficult, is going to get a good wife, and a white one at that. They tell me lots about the strict school and how life can be completely different when you have the chance to go to school. There are lots of things at home they don't understand anymore. They give me examples, and we all laugh.

During the conversation James asks me why I don't do business with my car. I could fetch maize or bags of sugar for the Somalis, transport people, etc. I'm not keen on the idea because of the state of the roads but mention that after the wedding I'd like to do something to bring in money. I'd most like to open a shop to sell all sorts of food. The boys are fascinated by the idea of a shop. James promises that when he's finished school in a year's time, he'll help. The idea is attractive, but a year is a long time.

Lketinga comes back, and shortly afterward the boys bid a respectful farewell. He wants to know what we talked about. I tell him of my vague idea of opening a shop. To my surprise, he's enthusiastic too. It would be the only Masai shop for miles, and the Somalis would have no customers anymore because everyone would use the shop of a fellow tribesman. Then he looks at me and says this would cost a lot of money and do I have that much? I reassure him that there is still some in Switzerland. We'll have to think it all through.

"Pole, Pole"

For some time now I've been dealing with injured people. Since I used some antiseptic ointment to cure a festering sore on the leg of a neighbor's child, mothers have been bringing children to me with sometimes horrifying abscesses. I clean them, put ointment on them, and bandage them up as best I can. But so many keep coming that I've run out of ointment and can't help them anymore. I send them to the hospital or the Mission, but the women go away silently and don't take my advice.

In two days' time the children return to school. I'm sorry to see them go because they've been good company. In the meantime we've worked on the shop idea, and one day I make up my mind to go back to Switzerland for a bit, to gain some energy and put on a few pounds. The opportunity of a lift to Maralal with either Father Roberto or Giuliani is tempting. I can leave our Land Rover here and won't have the problem of driving myself in my weakened condition. Shortly beforehand I tell Lketinga. He is very annoyed by my intention to leave him in two days' time. I promise him I'll think about the shop and bring more money back. He can find out how we should build it and where. Even as we discuss it the idea of running a shop together reinforces itself in my mind. All I need is time to prepare everything and build up my strength.

Naturally Lketinga is worried once again that I'm going to leave him, but this time the boys are on my side and can translate for him, word for word, my promise that I'll be back in good health in three or four weeks' time. I'll tell him the exact day as soon as I've got my ticket. I'm going to set off for Nairobi in the hope of getting a flight to Switzerland as soon as possible. With a heavy heart he gives his agreement. I leave him some money, about three hundred Swiss francs.

With as little baggage as possible I wait outside the Mission with several schoolchildren. Just when we'll be off nobody knows, but anyone who isn't there will have to go on foot. Mama and my darling have come too, and while Mama gives her final instructions to James, I console Lketinga. He says a month without me is a long, long time. Then Father Giuliani comes. I get to sit next to him while the boys squeeze into the back. Lketinga waves and shouts after me: "Take care of our baby!" I have to smile at how convinced he is that I'm pregnant.

Father Giuliani speeds along, and I have to hold on tight. We don't talk much, except when I tell him that I'll be back in a month, and he says I'll need at least three months to recover. But for me that is out of the question.

There's chaos in Maralal. The little town is filled with departing schoolchildren, being sent all over Kenya so that the different tribes are thrown together. James is lucky and can stay in Maralal. One boy from our village has to go to Nakuru, so he and I can share part of the journey. But first of all we have to get a bus ticket, and that seems impossible for the next two days. All the seats are full. A few folk from far away have even driven into Maralal with open-backed pickups to make money offering overpriced rides, but even these are booked up. Maybe tomorrow morning at five, somebody offers. We make the reservation but don't hand over any money.

The boy stands there helplessly because he doesn't know where he can spend the night, as he has no money. He is very shy and helpful. He keeps carrying my bag, and I suggest we go into my usual boardinghouse to get something to drink and ask about rooms. The landlady greets me cheerily, but when I ask if she has any rooms, she shakes her head sorrowfully. But she says that because I'm a regular customer she can make one free by the evening. We drink chai and trawl round the other boardinghouses. I'm prepared to pay the relatively tiny sum for the boy. But they are all full. Meanwhile it's grown dark and colder. I wonder whether I should offer to let the boy sleep in the second bed in my room. I wouldn't find it a problem, but I don't know what other people might think. I ask him what he's thinking of doing. He tells me he'll have to look for some *manyattas* outside Maralal and if he finds a mama with a son his age, she'll be obliged to take him in.

That seems to me to be leaving too much to chance, especially as we have to leave at five. On the spur of the moment I offer him the second bed, against the opposite wall. His first reaction is to give me an embarrassed look and say thanks but no. He says that he couldn't possibly sleep in the same room as a warrior's bride: it would cause problems. I laugh, not taking it too seriously, and tell him he should just keep quiet about it. I go into the boardinghouse first, giving the watchman a few shillings and asking him to waken me at four-thirty the next morning. The boy turns up half an hour later. I'm already in bed, fully clothed, even though it's only eight o'clock. There's nothing going on after dark except in a few bars, which I avoid.

The naked lightbulb shows the whole horrid little room for what it is. The blue paint is peeling from the walls, and everywhere there are brown patches with thin trickle lines beneath them: disgusting remnants of spat-out tobacco. Back home in the *manyatta* Mama and all our visitors used to do the same thing until I complained about it. Since then Mama spits under one of the flints. I find the boardinghouse room particularly nauseating. The boy lies down on the bed with his clothes on and immediately turns to face the wall. We turn off the light and don't speak.

There's a thunderous knocking at the door. I start in shock from a deep sleep and ask what's happening. But before anyone can answer, the boy says it's nearly five A.M. We have to go! If the pickup is full, it'll simply leave. We grab our stuff together and run to the rendezvous spot. There are little groups of schoolchildren everywhere. Some are getting into a vehicle; the rest waiting in the cold and dark. I'm absolutely freezing. The dew at this hour of the morning makes Maralal cold and damp. We can't even drink chai because none of the boardinghouses have opened up.

At six A.M. the overcrowded regular bus trundles by blaring its horn. Our driver hasn't even turned up yet. He seems to be in no hurry, as we're captive passengers. It's getting light, and we're still waiting, and I'm getting angry. I want out of here, to get to Nairobi today. The boy despairingly asks around for a lift, but the few cars are crammed full, and our only possibility is a truck laden with cabbages. I jump at the chance, as it's the only one we've got. But after the first few yards I'm already wondering if I made the right choice. It's absolute torture sitting on the things because they're hard and keep moving. I can only hang on by grabbing the side rail, and that keeps hitting me in the ribs. Every pothole throws us into the air and then we fall back down onto the hard cabbages. There's no way to talk, it's much too noisy and too dangerous—the bumps are so hard you could easily bite through your lip. But somehow or other I survive the four and a half hours to Nyahururu.

Completely wrecked, I climb out of the truck to say good-bye to my young traveling companion. I want to go into a restaurant to find a toilet. When I pull down my jeans I see big violet bruises on my thighs. My God, before I get to Switzerland the whole of my skinny legs will have turned blue. It's going to be a shock for my mother because, since my last visit just two months ago, I've changed enormously physically. She still doesn't know that I'm coming home, still unmarried and in a bad state.

In the restaurant I order cola and a proper meal. There's chicken, and I wolf down a whole half bird with some floury chips. It's too early to think of spending the night here, so I drag my bag to the bus station, which is still busy. I'm in luck: a bus for Nairobi is about to go. The road is tarmac, which is a blessing, and I fall asleep in my seat. When I next look out of the window, we're only an hour from my destination. If I'm lucky, we'll reach the metropolis before dark. The Igbol isn't exactly in the safest part of town, and it's already turning to dusk as we drive through the suburbs.

People start piling out with their possessions while I'm still sitting with my face against the window trying to get used to the sea of lights. I still don't recognize anything. There are just five people left on the bus, and I'm wondering if I shouldn't just get out because I don't want to go all the way to the bus station, which is too dangerous for me at this time of day. The driver keeps looking back at me in his mirror wondering why the *mzungu* doesn't get out. Eventually he asks me where I want to get to. "To Igbol Hotel." He shrugs his shoulders. Then I remember the name of a huge cinema very close to the Igbol. "Mister, you know Odeon Cinema?" I ask hopefully. "Odeon Cinema? This place is no good for *mzungu* lady," he lectures me. "It's no problem for me. I only go into the Igbol Hotel. There are some more white people," I reply. He changes lanes a couple of times, takes a left, a right, then stops right in front of the hotel. Thankful for his help, I tip him a few shillings. In my exhaustion I'm pleased for every few feet I don't have to walk.

It's mad busy in the Igbol. All the tables are laid, and there are backpacks everywhere. The man at reception, who's got to know me by now, greets me with "*Jambo,* Masai lady!" He still has one bed free in a three-bed room.

In the room I find two English girls studying a guidebook. I go straight out again to have a shower, taking my passport and money purse with me. I strip off and am horrified to see the state my body is in. My legs, lower back, and underarms are covered in bruises. But the shower makes me feel human again. Then I find a table in the restaurant to get something to eat at last and watch the tourists, but the more I look at the Europeans, in particular the men, the more I long for my handsome warrior. It's not long before I retire to bed to rest my weary bones.

After breakfast I make my way to the Swissair office, but to my disappointment they don't have a free seat for five days. That's too long. With Kenya Airways the wait would be even longer. Five days in Nairobi, that would depress me deeply. So I try around the other airlines until I find an Alitalia flight in two days' time, although it involves a four-hour stopover in Rome. I check the price and book it. Then I go to the nearby Kenya Commercial Bank to draw out money.

There's a line at the bank. Two policemen armed with machine pistols are guarding the door. I join the line and within half an hour reach the counter. I have written a check for the sum, but it's going to be a huge bundle of cash to carry through the streets to the Alitalia office. The man at the counter turns the check over and asks me whereabouts Maralal is. Then he goes off and comes back to ask me if I'm sure I want to withdraw so much cash. "Yes," I answer with annoyance. I'm worried myself about it. After I've filled out various forms I'm handed heaps of banknotes, which I immediately conceal in my backpack. Luckily there's next to nobody about. The bank clerk asks me what I want to do with so much money and whether I need a boyfriend. I say thanks but no thanks and leave.

I reach the Alitalia office without incident. Once again I have to fill out forms, and my passport is checked. One of the staff asks why I don't have a return ticket to Switzerland. I explain to her that I live in Kenya and am just going back to Switzerland for two and a half months' holiday. The woman says politely that surely I am a tourist, however, because it doesn't say anywhere on my passport that I live in Kenya. All these questions confuse me. I simply want a ticket and to pay for it in cash. But it turns out that's the problem. I have a form that says I've withdrawn the money from a Kenyan bank. As a tourist, I'm not allowed to have a bank account and must be able to prove that the money has

Lketinga

Lketinga in traditional headdress
with hair freshly dyed red

Fetching water down by the river

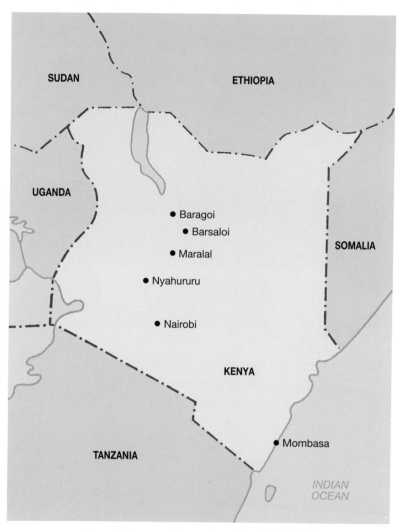

Map of Kenya with major places identified

Our first home, where I lived with Lketinga and
his mother for over a year

In front of our new manyatta

My "White Samburu-Wedding"

Our daughter Napirai with her proud parents

With the family animals

Slaughtering a cow out in the bush; Lketinga's sister
in the center of the picture

Mama Masulani (Lketinga's mother) with Saguna
and three more of her grandchildren

been brought in from Switzerland; otherwise, she'd have to assume that it's illegal earnings. Tourists are not allowed to work in Kenya. I'm speechless. My mother did the transfers, and the paperwork is all in Barsaloi. I'm standing in front of this woman with a heap of money, and she won't take it. The African woman at the counter tells me that, regrettably, unless I can prove where the money came from, they can't issue the ticket. I burst into tears of fury and say I'm not leaving the office with all this money because it would be suicide.

The African woman stares at me in shock and drops her arrogance at the sight of my tears. "Wait a moment," she says kindly, and disappears. A few minutes later a second lady appears, tells me the same thing, and assures me she's just doing her duty. I ask her to call the bank in Maralal, where the manager knows me well. The two of them talk it over. Then they simply make a photocopy of my exchange slip and my passport and ten minutes later I leave the office with my ticket. Now I have to find an international telephone to tell my mother to expect a surprise visit.

On the flight my feelings keep swinging between happy anticipation of the comforts of civilization and homesickness for my African family. At Zurich airport my mother can hardly conceal her horror at my appearance, but I'm grateful that she doesn't mention it. I'm not hungry because I've eaten on the plane, but I'd love to drink some good Swiss coffee before we drive back to the mountains. Over the next few days I'm spoiled by my mother's cooking and gradually become a bit more presentable. We talk a lot about my future, and I tell her about my plans for a shop. She understands that I need a job and an income.

On the tenth day I have an appointment with a gynecologist for an examination. Unfortunately the results are negative: I'm not pregnant. I'm far too anemic and undernourished for that. Afterward I realize how disappointed Lketinga will be, but I console myself with the thought that we've got plenty of time to have children. Every day I walk through the green landscape, thinking of Africa. After two weeks I'm already planning my departure and book my flight for ten days' time. Once again I buy lots of medicines, various herbs, and packets of pasta. I send a telegram to Lketinga via the Mission to tell him I'm on my way back.

The next nine days pass without event. The only big thing is my brother Eric's wedding to Jelly, but for me the whole event is like something experienced in a trance, and I find the luxury and the lavish meal unappealing. Everybody wants to know what life is like in Kenya, and each and every one of them tries to bring me to my senses. But for me common sense is in Kenya, where my great love and a life with meaning are. It's time for me to get out of here.

Farewell and Welcome

I arrive at the airport heavily laden. Leaving my mother is particularly hard for me this time because I don't know when I'll be back. On June 1, 1988, I land back in Nairobi and take a taxi to the Igbol Hotel.

Two days later I arrive back in Maralal, drag my luggage to the boardinghouse, and think about how I'm going to get back to Barsaloi. Each day I trawl through the village, looking for a car. I think of calling on Sophia but discover that she's on vacation in Italy. On the third day I hear that in the afternoon a truck with maize meal and sugar is leaving for the Mission in Barsaloi. I wait all morning next to the wholesaler where the bags are to be loaded. And indeed the truck turns up around noon. I do a deal with the driver and settle a price to sit up front, and that afternoon we finally leave. Our route is via Baragoi, so it will take six hours and it will be late before we get to Barsaloi. There are at least fifteen people on board the truck: good money for the driver.

The journey takes forever. This is the first time I've done it on a truck. We cross the first river in pitch darkness, only the beam of the headlights feeling our way across the broad emptiness. By ten P.M. we're there and stop in front of the Mission compound, where lots of people are waiting for the "lori." They've spotted the lights in the distance, and all Barsaloi is excited. Many people plan on earning money offloading the sacks.

Tired but happy, I climb down. I'm home, even if the *manyattas* are a few hundred yards away. A few people say a friendly hello. Father Giuliani turns up with a flashlight to give instructions, says hello briefly, and then vanishes again. I'm standing helplessly with my heavy bags, unable to drag them in the dark as far as Mama's *manyatta*. Two boys, who obviously don't go to school because they're wearing traditional garb, offer to help me, but halfway there someone comes toward us with a flashlight. It's my darling. "Hello!" He beams. I throw my arms around him with joy and press a kiss on his lips. The emotion takes away my breath and silently we make our way to the *manyatta*.

Mama too is delighted to see me. Immediately she lights the fire to make the obligatory chai. I hand out my presents. Later Lketinga taps lovingly on my stomach and asks, "How is our baby?" I feel uncomfortable as I tell him that unfortunately there is no baby. He frowns: "Why? I know you have baby before!" As calmly as possible I try to explain to him that it was only because of the malaria that I missed my period. Lketinga is very disappointed, but nonetheless that night we make wonderful love.

The next few weeks are very happy; life takes its usual course until at last we set off again for Maralal to see about the wedding. Lketinga's brother comes with us, and this time we're in luck. When we have our appointment and hand over my forms with their stamps, as well as the paper from the chief that Lketinga has managed to get in the meantime, there seem to be no more problems.

Registry Office and Honeymoon

On July 26, 1988, we get married. There are two new witnesses: Lketinga's older brother and some other person I don't know. The ceremony is conducted by a nice official: first in English, then in Swahili. Everything goes without a hitch, except that at the decisive moment my darling fails to say his "Yes" until I kick his leg. Then the wedding certificate is signed. Lketinga takes my passport and says I need a Kenyan one, as my name is now Leparmorijo. The officer tells us that this has to be done in Nairobi because Lketinga will have to apply for my permanent residency. Now I'm confused again. I thought we'd done everything and the battle with red tape was over. But no, the wedding notwithstanding, I'm still a tourist until I have a right of abode stamp in my passport. My joy fades, and Lketinga doesn't understand it all either. In the boardinghouse we decide to go to Nairobi.

The next day we set out for Nairobi along with both of our witnesses. Lketinga's brother has never been on such a long journey before. We take our Land Rover as far as Nyahururu and then catch the bus to Nairobi. The brother just gapes at everything. For me it's entertaining to be with someone who, at the age of forty, is seeing a city for the first time. He is speechless and even more helpless than Lketinga. He can't even cross a road without our help. If I didn't take his hand, he would almost certainly stay rooted to the same spot until nightfall because he's afraid of all the traffic. He looks at the big blocks of apartments and doesn't understand how the people can live on top of one another.

Eventually we get to the Nyayo Building. I stand in the line to fill out more forms. When I finally finish, the woman at the counter tells us to check back in three weeks or so. I protest and try to explain to her that we've come a long way and there's no way we are leaving without a valid stamp in my passport. I almost beg her, but she says everything has to take its course and she'll try to get it done in a week or so. When I realize that that's her last word on the subject, I say thank you and go.

Outside we debate what to do. There are four of us, and we have to wait a week. Hanging around in Nairobi with my three men is inconceivable. Instead I suggest we go to Mombasa so Lketinga's brother can see the sea. Lketinga agrees because he'll feel safe in their company, and so we set out on the eight-hour journey—which will have to make do as a honeymoon.

The first thing we do in Mombasa is go to see Priscilla. She's delighted about our marriage and thinks everything will be fine now. Lketinga's brother is eager to see the sea, but when he's confronted with the vast expanse of water he has to hold on to us. He won't go closer than thirty feet from the sea, and after ten minutes he's so afraid that we have to leave the beach. I show him a tourist hotel too, but he doesn't believe what he sees. On one occasion he asks a man if we're really still in Kenya. It's a remarkable feeling to be able to show the world to someone who can still be amazed. Later we go for a meal and drinks, and for the first time he tastes beer, which has a bad effect on him. We find ourselves a shabby little boardinghouse in Ukunda.

These days in Mombasa cost a fortune. The men drink beer, and I have to just sit there because I don't want to go to the beach on my own. Gradually it starts to grate on me to be paying the bar tab for three people, and so we have our first few quarrels. Lketinga, who is now officially my husband, doesn't understand and says it's my fault we have to wait such a long time before going back to Nairobi. He doesn't understand in any case why I need a stamp. He's married me, hasn't he? That should be enough to make me a Leparmorijo and a Kenyan. The others agree, and I'm left sitting there wondering how to explain bureaucracy to them.

After four days we set off sullenly. With a lot of effort I drag Lketinga one more time—the last, he says—to this office in Nairobi. I keep hoping that the stamp will be there. Once again I explain our situation and ask for someone to check if it's been done yet. Once again I'm told to wait. The other three look at one another and me nervously. Everyone else stares at us in curiosity: a white woman with three Masai is not something you see every day in a government office.

At long last my husband and I are called out and told to follow a woman. When we stop at a lift I already guess what's going to happen if Lketinga has to get in. The elevator doors open, and a horde of people pile out. Lketinga looks at the empty cabin with horror and says: "Corinne, what's that?" I try to explain to him that this box will take us up to the twelfth floor. The woman is already waiting impatiently inside. But Lketinga doesn't want to get in. He's scared of going up so high. "Darling, please, this is no problem; if we are in the twelfth floor you go around like now," I say, begging him to get in before the woman gets fed up, and in the end, with bulging eyes, he does it.

We're taken into an office where a stern African lady is waiting for us. She asks me if I am really married to this Samburu. She wants to know from Lketinga if he is really able to provide food and shelter for me. He turns to me and asks, "Corinne, please, which house I must have?" My God, I think to myself, just say "yes." The woman looks back and forth between us. My nerves are so stretched that I'm sweating from every pore. She stares straight at me and asks, "You want to have children?" I answer promptly: "Oh, yes, two." There's a silence. Then eventually she goes over to her desk and picks out one of a multitude of rubber stamps. I hand over two hundred shillings and get my passport back, stamped. I could weep with joy. At last, at last, it's done! I can stay in my beloved Kenya. All we have to do now is get out of here, back to Barsaloi, back home!

A Hut of Our Own!

Mama is delighted that everything has gone well. Now it's time to plan the traditional Samburu wedding. Apart from anything else we have to build our own *manyatta* because after the wedding we wouldn't be allowed to live in her house. Now that I'm free from red tape I stop thinking about having a proper house and ask Lketinga to find the best women to build us a nice, big *manyatta*. I can fetch branches with the Land Rover, but I don't know how to build a hut. We can pay them with a goat. Quickly four women, including his sister, volunteer to build our *manyatta*. It's to be twice the size of Mama's and taller, so that I can almost stand up inside.

The women spend ten days on it, and I can hardly wait to move in. The hut will be approximately sixteen feet by eleven. First they mark the outline with thick posts around which willow branches are woven. The interior will be divided into three areas: the fireplace right in front of the entrance with a support to hang pots and cups. Then five feet in there'll be a woven partition wall. Half of the space behind that is for my darling and me, with a cowhide on the ground and then a straw mat and on top of that my striped Swiss woolen blanket. We'll hang the mosquito net over our sleeping area. Opposite will be a second sleeping area intended for two or three visitors, and right at the back, where their heads would be, a rack for me to hang my clothes.

The bare bones of our super hut go up fast. The only thing missing now is the plasterwork—cow dung, which still has to be delivered. There are no cows in Barsaloi, so we drive over to Lketinga's half brother in Sitedi and load up the Land Rover with cow pies. We have to make three trips before we have enough.

Two-thirds of the hut is plastered inside with the dung, which soon dries in the heat. One-third and the roof are plastered on the outside so that the smoke can seep out through the porous roof. It's riveting watching the construction work. The women smear the dung on just using their hands and laugh at my turned-up nose. When it's finished, we have to wait a week before moving in so that the dung can harden and lose its smell.

Wedding, Samburu-Style

We're into our last few days in Mama's hut. All the talk now is of our forthcoming Samburu wedding. Every day old men or women arrive to discuss possible dates with Mama. Our calendar doesn't depend on dates or days; everything depends on the moon. I would like to get married at Christmas, but the Samburu don't know anything about that and in any case they wouldn't know what the moon might be like then. But we've planned roughly around that date. As there's never been a wedding between a black and a white here before, nobody knows how many people will turn up. The news will be passed from village to village, and only on the wedding day itself will we see who pays us the honor. The more people, particularly old people, who turn up, the more respect we'll get.

One evening the game warden comes by, a strapping lad but calm and immediately likable. Unfortunately he speaks only a little English but has a long chat with Lketinga. Eventually I get curious and ask what they're talking about. My husband tells me that the warden wants to rent out his newly built shop, which is only used as a store for Father Giuliani's maize. Excitedly I ask how much it would cost. He suggests that we go and take a look at it tomorrow and discuss terms afterward. I spend a sleepless night, since Lketinga and I already have plans.

After our morning wash down by the river, we stroll through the village to the shop. My husband talks to everyone we meet, mostly about the wedding. Even the Somalis come out of their shops and ask when it's going to be. But the elders still haven't given us anything definite. For now I just want to see the shop and drag Lketinga off.

The game warden is already waiting for us in this opened-up empty building. I'm speechless. It's a building with walls near the Mission, which I always assumed belonged to Father Giuliani. It's huge with a gate that opens to the front; left and right are windows, and in the middle there's what could be a shop counter and proper wooden shelving. Behind another door there's a similarly large room that could be used as a store or even a living space. I can imagine with a bit of effort turning this into the smartest shop in Barsaloi and for miles around. But I have to play down my enthusiasm so as to not to drive the rent through the roof. We agree on the equivalent of fifty Swiss francs, as long as Lketinga gets the license to run a shop. My experiences with the bureaucracy make me reticent about putting money up front.

The game warden agrees, and we go back to Mama. Lketinga tells her everything, and they end up arguing. Later he tells me with a laugh: "Mama's afraid that there'll be problems with the Somalis because people won't go to their shops anymore. The Somalis are dangerous, and they could cause us trouble. She wants to get the wedding over with first."

Then Mama takes a long, hard look at me and says I ought to cover up my upper body a bit better so that not everybody sees I have a baby in my belly. When Lketinga tries to explain to me, I'm speechless. Me? Pregnant? But then I think about it and realize that my period is nearly three weeks late, and I hadn't noticed. But pregnant? No, I'd have noticed.

Why does Mama think that? I ask Lketinga. She comes over to me and traces with her finger the lines of the arteries running down to my breasts. Even so I can't believe it and don't know if it will fit in with our shop plans. Apart from that, of course, I want to have babies with my husband, a daughter in particular. Mama is convinced she's right and warns Lketinga he should leave me alone now. Surprised, I ask, "Why?" With great difficulty he manages to tell me that if a pregnant woman has sex with a man the children will have blocked-up noses. Although he apparently means it seriously, I have to laugh. Until I'm certain myself, I don't want to live without sex.

Two days later when we're on our way back from the river, there's a group of people sitting gossiping under Mama's tree. We're in Mama's hut, but in three days ours will be ready, and that means I will have to light the fire myself and be responsible for fetching firewood. I can fetch water from the river with the Land Rover, unless I can persuade anyone else to do it for some small change. I find it hard to make do with just one gallon, though, and want to have a four-gallon canister in the house.

Mama comes into the *manyatta* and says something to Lketinga. He seems worked up by it, and I ask him, "What's the problem?" "Corinne, we have to make the ceremony in five days because the moon is good." Just five days until the wedding? We'll have to set off straightaway to Maralal to get rice, tobacco, sweets, drinks, and other stuff.

Lketinga is upset because now he can't get his hair braided properly. This takes several days from morning to night. Even Mama is in a tizzy because she has to brew vast quantities of maize beer, and that takes nearly a week. She doesn't want to let us leave, but there isn't any sugar or rice in the village: just maize meal. I give her some money so she can get started on the brewing. Lketinga and I set off.

In Maralal we buy eleven pounds of chewing tobacco, which is an absolute must for the older people; two hundred pounds of sugar, the tea would be unimaginable without it; and thirty-two pints of sterilized Long-life milk because, although it's normal, I have no idea how many women might bring milk with them. I don't want to take any risks. It has to be a good party, even if not many people turn up. We still need rice, but there isn't any right now. I pluck up the courage to ask at the Maralal Mission, and luckily the missionary sells us his last forty-pound sack. Finally we have to go to the school to tell James. The headmaster tells us the school holidays start on December 15, and since we're getting married on December 17, it won't be a problem. I'm pleased he'll be there. Last of all I decide to buy an old gas container, which we can clean out and use for water. By the time we've bought sweets for the children it's already five P.M.

Even so, we decide to drive back straightaway and manage to get through the dangerous jungle stretch before dark. Mama is relieved to see us back. The neighbors come around immediately to beg for some sugar, but this time Lketinga is firm. He even sleeps in the car to make sure nothing disappears.

The next day he takes off to buy a few goats, which we'll slaughter. I don't want to kill ours because I've gotten to know them all. We need an ox too. Down at the river I try to get the smell out of the old gas container, but it's not so easy. I spend the whole morning rolling the barrel filled with Omo and sand up and down until it's relatively clean. Three children use tin cans to help me fill the barrel with water. Mama's out in the bush all day brewing beer, because it's not allowed in the village.

In the evening I go to the Mission, tell them about the wedding, and ask to borrow a couple of church benches and some crockery. Father Giuliani is not surprised; he's already heard the news from one of his employees and reassures me that I can come and collect the things I want on the day of the wedding. I remind him that, a while earlier when they let me store my gas canisters up at the Mission, I also left my wedding dress and ask him for permission to get changed there. He is surprised that I'm planning to get married in white here, but he agrees.

Only two days to go, and Lketinga still isn't back from his "goat safari." I'm gradually getting nervous because there's nobody here I can talk to properly and everyone's rushing around busily. In the evening at least the schoolchildren arrive, which is good news. James is really excited about the wedding, and I have him explain the Samburu ceremony to me.

Normally, he tells me, the ceremony starts early in the morning: with a clitorectomy for the bride. I feel as if I've been shot down from the sky. "Why?" I ask. Because without such she's not a proper woman and won't have healthy babies, the otherwise so well educated James answers me in complete earnestness. Before I can recover, Lketinga appears in the hut. He beams his smile at me, and I'm glad to see him. He's brought four fat goats, which wasn't an easy task because they kept trying to escape back to their herds.

After the usual chai, the boys leave us and I can ask Lketinga what all this about "female circumcision" is and tell him in no uncertain terms that I will go along with everything but not that! Under no circumstances. He looks at me calmly. "Why not, Corinne? All ladies here make this." At that I go as stony as a statue and tell him that if that's the case I would rather not get married. But he takes me in his arms and calms me down: "No problem, my wife. I have told to everybody, white people have this"—and he points between my legs—"cut, when they are babies." I look at him doubtfully, but when he taps my tummy lovingly and asks, "How is my baby?" I throw my arms around him in relief. Later I find out that he's even told his mother this fairy tale, and I think all the more of him for saving me from this rite.

One day before our wedding, guests arrive from far away and settle down in various *manyattas* all around. My darling fetches the ox from his half brother, which takes the whole day. I drive into the bush with the boys to chop enough firewood. We have to do a lot of driving before we can fill the car with wood, but the boys work hard. In the evening we drive down to the river and fill up the big barrel and every canister we can find. On the way home I ask James to pop into the teahouse to order *mandazi,* the little spiced pastries, for tomorrow. While I'm waiting in the car, the owner, a likable young Somali, comes out and gives me his congratulations.

The night before our wedding is our last in Mama's *manyatta*. Ours is already finished, but I prefer to move in on the day of my wedding because with Lketinga out and about a lot I didn't want to sleep alone in our new home.

We wake early. I'm very nervous. I go down to the river to wash myself and my hair. Lketinga drives the boys up to the Mission to pick up the benches and crockery. When I get back everything's already bustling. The benches have been put out under the shadiest tree. Lketinga's older brother is making tea in a huge pot. Now it's Lketinga's turn to go down to the river to get ready. We agree to meet in one hour up at the Mission. In the Mission building I put on my wedding dress and all the accessories. The dress is tight and only just fits, so that for a moment I wonder if I really am pregnant. It's a bit stretched across the stomach and breasts. When I'm all done up, I find Father Giuliani standing dumbstruck in the doorway. For the first time in ages I actually get a compliment. He laughs and says this long ankle-length dress is not exactly right for the *manyattas* and certainly not for the thornbushes. Then my darling is there too, painted magnificently, ready to collect me. He asks me with minor irritation why I want to wear a dress like that. Slightly embarrassed, I laugh back: "To look pretty." Thank God I'm wearing white plastic sandals rather than European shoes with high heels. Giuliani accepts our invitation to join us.

When I get out of the car both children and grown-ups are amazed. None of them have ever seen a dress like this. I feel a bit unsure of myself, not knowing what to do next. People are cooking everywhere. The goats are taken out and slaughtered. It's just past ten A.M., and already there are more than fifty people. The old men are sitting on the benches drinking tea while the women sit a bit apart under another tree. The children jump up and down around me. I hand out chewing gum, and the old men stand around James, who's handing out tobacco. There are people pouring past in every direction, the women giving their calabashes of milk to Mama, others tying goats up to the trees. Rice and meat are being boiled up in a big cauldron over an enormous fire. The water is disappearing fast as vast quantities of chai are brewed. By midday the first meal is ready, and I begin to hand it out. Father Giuliani has arrived and is filming everything.

Gradually I start to lose track of events. In the meantime some two hundred and fifty people have turned up, not counting the children. I keep hearing that this is the biggest ceremony there's ever been in Barsaloi, which makes me very proud, particularly on behalf of my darling, who took the risk of marrying a white woman, despite the fact that far from everyone was in favor. James comes to tell us the rice is all gone and lots of women and children haven't had any yet. I tell Giuliani about this "disaster," and he immediately drives off and comes back with a forty-pound sack as a wedding present. While the warriors, set apart from everyone else, start dancing, there's more cooking going on for the others. Lketinga spends most of the time with his warriors, who won't get to eat anything until tonight. As time goes by I start to feel somewhat neglected. It's my wedding after all, but there are none of my relatives here, and my husband spends more time with his warrior mates than with me.

The guests start dancing, each group on its own: the women beneath their tree, the boys separately, and the warriors off in the distance. A few women from the Turkana tribe do a dance for me. I'm supposed to dance along with the women, but after the first few dances Mama takes me to one side and says I shouldn't jump up and down too much on account of the baby. Meanwhile, a little bit away from the festivities the ox is being slaughtered and hacked into pieces. I'm relieved to see that we'll have enough to eat and drink for everyone.

Before dusk people hand over their presents or make promises to us. Everyone who wants to give us a present, whether to my husband or me, stands up and announces it. They have to announce which of us the gift is for because it is the Samburu custom for men and women to own their possessions—in other words, their animals—separately. I'm overwhelmed by how much people give me: fourteen goats, two sheep, one chicken, a cockerel, two young calves, and a little camel, all for me alone. My husband gets about the same. Not everyone has brought their presents with them, so Lketinga will have to go and collect them later.

The party comes to an end, and for the first time I retire to my own *manyatta*. Mama has fixed everything nicely for me, and at last I can unpeel my tight dress. I sit down in front of the fire, waiting for my husband, who's still out in the bush. It is a beautiful night, and I am alone in my own *manyatta*, beginning life as a proper housewife.

The Shop

A week after the wedding we go to Maralal to find out about getting a shopkeeper's license for Lketinga. This time a friendly official says things ought to go quickly. We fill out all the forms and are told to look in again in three days' time. As we'll urgently need weighing scales for the shop, we head off to Nyahururu. I also want to buy wire netting so that we can display our wares on the shelves better because I want to offer our customers potatoes, carrots, cabbage, oranges, bananas, and other things.

But we can't find any scales in Nyahururu. It turns out they're very expensive and only to be had in Nairobi. Lketinga is not very happy, but we definitely need scales, so we catch the bus to our despised Nairobi. There are scales everywhere there but at widely differing prices. In the end we buy the cheapest on offer—three hundred and fifty Swiss francs for a heavy set of scales with all the weights—and head back to Maralal. Once there we start going around to all the wholesalers and markets to find out the best available prices for what we want. My husband finds everything too dear, but I suppose that with a bit of sharp haggling we can get the same prices as the Somalis. The biggest wholesaler offers to organize a truck to deliver our goods to Barsaloi.

Hoping for the best, we go into the office on the third day only to find the official says there's just one little problem: we have to get a certificate from the veterinary surgeon in Barsaloi that the shop is clean, and also before he can give us a license we have to have a portrait of the president, which has to hang in every shop. Lketinga wants to curse the man, but I restrain him. In any case I want to go back home to settle the rental agreement for the shop and arrange things so that we can stock up properly. We also need to find a shop assistant because my command of the language is too poor, and my husband can't add.

That evening we go to visit Sophia and her boyfriend. She has just come back from Italy, and we have lots of news to exchange. In passing she lets me know that she is three months pregnant. I'm really pleased to hear it because I've come to believe that I'm in the same situation myself. I'm just not one hundred percent certain like she is. Sophia has regular morning sickness, which I don't. She's astonished to hear about my business plans. But I have to earn money because the car is a huge drain on my cash reserves.

We do the rental deal in Barsaloi and are now happy shop owners. I spend days cleaning the dusty shelving and nail the wire netting to it. I'm throwing out the old planks in the back room when I hear a hissing and see a green snake's head disappear behind the remaining bits of wood. I run out in panic shouting: "Snake, snake!" A few men take a look, but when they see what I'm talking about, nobody dares go into the room anymore.

It's not long before half a dozen people have gathered, but no one knows what to do until a big Turkana man with a long stick comes along. He goes in and carefully starts poking around in the woodpile. He knocks one piece of wood after another out of the way until eventually a snake about a yard long shows itself. The Turkana attacks like a madman in an attempt to kill it, but the snake eludes his blows and slithers out of the door toward us. Like greased lightning a Samburu boy stabs the creature with his spear; and it's only then, when I realize how dangerous the situation was, that my knees start to shake.

My husband comes back about an hour later, having been to see the vet, who gave him the certificate on the condition that within a month we install an earth closet toilet outside the shop. Another thing! A few people, mostly Turkanas, volunteer to dig the nine-foot-deep hole and build the rest, but, including their materials, the bill comes to six hundred Swiss francs. There's no end to the expenditures, and I hope I start to see some income soon.

I tell Fathers Giuliani and Roberto about my plans to open a shop. They're delighted because for half the year there's not even maize to be had. I don't mention my pregnancy, not even in a letter home to

Switzerland. Although I'm very happy, I know how easy it is to become sick here, and I don't want to upset anybody.

At long last the great day is here, and we set off intending to come back with a truckload of goods. We've found a pleasant shop assistant, Anna, the wife of the village policeman. She's sturdy and has already worked in Maralal and with a bit of effort can even manage some English.

In Maralal we go to the Commercial Bank to find out if the money I'd asked for from Switzerland has arrived yet. We're in luck, and I withdraw the equivalent of nearly five thousand francs to buy our supplies. Lketinga has never seen so much money in his life. We ask the Somali wholesaler when a truck will be available to come out to Barsaloi. He says because the riverbeds are all dry at the moment the journey is no problem for the heavy trucks and there'll be one available in two days.

We stock up. The truck costs three hundred francs, so we have to make the most of its ten-ton fully laden capacity. I order eighty two-hundred-pound sacks of maize meal, fifteen two-hundred-pound sacks of sugar: an absolute fortune for here. When I go to pay the bill, Lketinga takes back the bundle of notes and says I'm giving the Somalis too much. He wants to be in charge of everything. I'm on the verge of getting annoyed with him for running down everybody else when he can't even count. He stacks the money up in piles, and nobody else understands what he's playing at. In my best angelic tones I persuade my husband to give me the money back, and in front of him I count out the money again. When there's three thousand shillings left over he says angrily, "See, it's far too much!" I calm him down, explaining that this is the rent for the truck. He looks crossly at the three Somalis, but in the end the goods are paid for and put aside for us until the truck gets here. I drive around the village, buying two hundred pounds of rice here, two hundred pounds of potatoes there, and cabbage and onions somewhere else.

By the end of the afternoon our truck is finally loaded. It'll be close to eleven before we reach Barsaloi. I put the breakable items—such as bottles of Fanta, cola, and mineral water—into the Land Rover along with the tomatoes, bananas, bread, Omo, margarine, tea, and a few other bits and pieces. The car is jam-packed. I plan to take the jungle route rather than the main road so that I can get back to Barsaloi in two hours. Lketinga is going with the truck driver because he believes with some justification that otherwise things might disappear en route.

The game warden and two women come with me. The car is so loaded up I soon have to switch to four-wheel drive to manage the uphill stretch leading to the forest. It takes time to get used to driving with so much on board, nearly 1,540 pounds in all. Every now and then we lurch into puddles of water, which in the thick forest never quite dry out.

The meadow where I came across the buffalo is empty. I struggle in Swahili to talk to my front-seat passenger about our business plans. Just before the oblique "drop of death" there's a sharp S-bend, and when I turn into the narrow bit suddenly there's a huge gray wall in front of us. I brake like mad but the weight gives the vehicle so much momentum that it rolls on steadily—toward a great bull elephant. "Stop, stop the car!" screams the game warden. I try everything, including the hand brake, but that no longer works very well. Eventually we come to a halt just ten feet away from the animal's enormous backside. The elephant slowly tries to turn around on the narrow path. Quickly I put the Land Rover in reverse. In the back the women are screaming; they want to get out. By now the elephant has turned around and is staring at us with its big button eyes. He swings his trunk high in the air and trumpets, the powerful tusks making him even more threatening. Our car slides slowly backward, we're now twenty feet away, but the game warden believes we'll only be out of danger when he can no longer see us: in other words, once we get around the bend. Because the car is packed full and doesn't have a rearview mirror, I can't see behind us and the game warden has to give me directions. I only hope I'm interpreting them correctly.

At last we're far enough back that, although we can still hear the elephant, we can no longer see him, and only now do I realize my knees are knocking. I daren't think what would have happened if we'd crashed into the monster or if the engine had conked out when I tried to back up.

The game warden can still smell the elephant. Ironically this is the one day he doesn't have his gun with him. We're about ninety yards away now, but we still can hear him bending back trees. When it goes silent, we wait, and then the game warden creeps forward to the bend in the road. He comes back to tell us that the elephant is defending his turf and quietly grazing along the path, having knocked over small trees on either side.

Gradually it grows dark, and horseflies start sticking to us and biting. Nobody but the game warden dares to get out. After an hour the big bull elephant is still blocking the path. I'm getting annoyed because we still have a long way to go, and I'm going to have to negotiate the scree slope heavily laden in the dark. Since nothing has happened to change things, the warden picks up some big stones and creeps along to the bend where he starts throwing them into the thick forest, causing thumps and rustling. It works: before long the elephant has left the path.

When we reach Barsaloi I drive directly to the shop and unload in the light of the headlamps. Thank God a few people help me out. Then I go to our *manyatta*. A while later the boy from next door comes and tells me there are two lights in the distance. Lketinga's big brother is on the lookout as well. Now everyone is excited: Our truck is coming. A Samburu truck!

I go into the shop with the brother to wait there. The vet turns up too and brings an oil lamp from his log cabin. We set it on the counter, and immediately the place feels homely. I wonder where to put everything and what to display. More and more people stroll by, waiting for the truck.

At last it rolls up with a threatening roar. It's an overwhelming sensation for me, and I'm supremely happy that from now on Barsaloi will have a shop that will always have food. Nobody need go hungry anymore because there'll always be enough to buy. Lketinga climbs out of the truck proudly and says hello to a few people, including the game warden. He listens to his story with horror but then comes up to me laughing and says: "Hello, wife, really you have seen an elephant?" "Yes, sure!" He puts his hand on his head and says: "Crazy, this is very dangerous, really, Corinne, very dangerous!" "Yes, I know, but now we are okay," I reply, looking for someone to help with the unloading.

We do a deal with three men who sometimes also work for the Somalis. First of all, the rice and potatoes have to be stored away, and the back room, which is to be our storeroom, is filled with the sacks of maize and sugar. Everything else is piled up in the shop.

Everyone works hard, and in half an hour the truck is empty and disappears into the night back toward Maralal. We're standing in total chaos surrounded by Omo and tea chests. The first customers arrive, wanting to buy sugar. But I refuse to start selling; it's too late and we have to sort everything out first. We lock up the shop and go off to our *manyatta*.

The next morning as usual we're sitting in the sun with the animals when a few women come up to the *manyatta*. Lketinga asks what they want: they want to know when the shop will be opening. Lketinga wants to open up immediately, but I tell him to explain that nothing will be sold before noon, because we have to unpack everything first and Anna isn't here yet.

Anna has a good eye for arranging things on the shelves, and after a couple of hours the shop looks perfect. There are already some fifty men and women waiting outside for us to open. The wire netting works well. Below the counter I've laid out potatoes, cabbage, carrots, onions, oranges, and mangos. Two hands of bananas are hanging from the ceiling on a rope. On the shelves behind are different-size packets of Omo, tins of Kimbo brand fat, powdered tea, toilet paper, which is later to sell remarkably well, various soaps, all sorts of sweets, and matches. Next to the scales we place a sack each of sugar, maize meal, and rice. We clean the floor once again and open the doors.

For an instant the sunlight blinds us, and then the women pour in, a multicolored wave of people washing toward me. The shop is full to bursting. Everyone extends their kangas or homemade cloth bags. Anna begins to dole out maize meal, while I also serve meal or sugar. Most people just throw money down on the counter and ask for various things, which means we have to do some speedy sums.

In barely an hour the first big sack of meal has been sold and half the sugar. I'm glad that I wrote prices on everything first. Even so, everything is all over the place. The box that we're using as a till is overflowing by evening, and we've sold nearly 1,350 pounds of maize meal, 450 pounds of sugar, and all sorts of other things. As it starts to get dark we try to close, but one child or another turns up looking for sugar for supper. Eventually we close at seven. I can barely stand up or move my arms anymore. Anna goes home equally tired and exhausted.

On the one hand, it's been a huge success; on the other, the rush has got me thinking, Is it going to be like this tomorrow from morning to night? I have to go down to the river to wash, but when will I find the time?

By eight the next morning we're back at the shop where Anna's already waiting. Business is slow to start with, but from nine o'clock until noon the shop is packed full. The boxes of mineral water, Coke, Fanta, and Sprite are soon emptied. People here have had to do without for so long.

A lot of the warriors or boys just hang around for hours, either in the shop or just outside, chatting. The women and girls sit against the walls in the shade. Even the wives of the vet, the doctor, and the bush teacher come to buy pounds of potatoes and fruit. Everyone is delighted to have such a great shop. Of course I can see that it lacks a few things.

Lketinga is with us most of the time and talks to people or sells simple things like soap or Omo. He helps as well as he can. For the first time in ages Mama comes into the village to see our shop.

On the second day I've already learned all my numbers in the Maa language. I've put up a board where we can quickly check the price of different amounts of maize or sugar, which makes adding up easier. Today too we work right through and crawl off home, tired and weary. Once again of course we haven't managed a hot meal. My back is aching from bending over all day. Today alone we weighed out and sold the contents of eight sacks of maize and nearly 675 pounds of sugar.

Mama cooks up some maize meal with a bit of meat for me, and Lketinga and I discuss the situation: It can't go on like this. Anna and I need time off to eat and wash. We decide that tomorrow we'll close the shop from noon until two P.M. Anna is also pleased by this new rule, and we fetch nine gallons of water so I can at least wash in the back room.

Gradually our stocks of fruit and vegetables disappear. Even the expensive rice is soon gone. I brought only seven pounds back home for us. Giuliani and Roberto look in for the first time today and say they are amazed, which cheers me up. I ask them if I can lodge the money I've made with them because I can't think of anywhere to keep such a large sum. Giuliani agrees, and so every evening I drop by the Mission and leave an envelope full of money.

The new opening times puzzle people because most of them don't have watches. Either we have to almost throw them out by force, or there are so many we just work through anyway. By the end of nine days, the shop is almost empty. We've got five sacks of maize left, but there's been no sugar for the past two days. So we have to go back to Maralal. With any luck we'll return with another truckload in three days' time. Anna stays on her own in the shop; with no sugar there are far fewer customers.

In Maralal, however, there's a shortage of sugar too. Supplies have not arrived; there are no one-hundred-kilogram (220-pound) sacks to be bought, and it's not worth going back to Barsaloi without sugar.

Eventually, after three days, the sugar arrives, but the sacks are rationed and instead of twenty we get just eight. On the fifth day we can set out with a truck again.

During my few days in Maralal I've stocked up on a few other things—the much-prized kangas, chewing tobacco for the older folk, and even twenty pairs of car tire–soled sandals in every size. Unfortunately the money we've made doesn't cover all the new stuff, and I have to draw money from the bank. I decide to put up the price per pound of maize and sugar, even though it's set by the state. But with the high cost of transport it's not possible to charge the same prices as in Maralal. We also have to fill up the forty-gallon gas tank.

This time Lketinga won't let me go in the Land Rover alone because he's afraid I'll run into elephants or buffalo again. But who's to go with the truck? Lketinga chooses an acquaintance he thinks he can trust. We set off around noon and get to Barsaloi without incident. It's really strange: when my husband is with me there are never any problems.

It's deadly quiet back at the shop. A bored Anna comes to meet us. In the past five days she's sold the rest of the maize meal. Only occasionally does someone drop by to buy powdered tea or Omo. The till is half full of money, but I can hardly check it. I trust Anna.

We go back to our *manyatta* to find two warriors sleeping in it. I'm not exactly delighted to find my *manyatta* occupied, but I know that the rules of hospitality demand it. All men of the same age as Lketinga have the right to rest or spend the night in our hut. I even have to offer them chai. While I'm lighting the fire, the three men chat among themselves. Lketinga translates for me that a warrior in Sitedi has had his thigh cut open by a buffalo and he has to go immediately with the Land Rover to take him to a doctor. I have to stay behind because the truck should arrive in the next two hours. Reluctantly I hand over the car keys to my husband. It's the same road on which a year ago he crashed!

I go down to Anna, and we sort out the shop, getting everything ready for unloading the new supplies. As it gets dark we light the two new oil lamps. I've also bought a little charcoal grill so that from time to time I can cook or make tea in the back room.

At last the truck arrives, and soon there's a crowd around the shop again. Unloading doesn't take long, and this time I count the sacks to make sure they're all there, but it turns out my mistrust is misplaced. It's chaos when everything's unloaded: cardboard boxes everywhere that have to be cleared away.

All of a sudden my husband's in the shop. I want to know if everything's all right. "No problem, Corinne, but this man has a big problem," he replies. He's taken the wounded man to the bush doctor, who's cleaned the eight-inch wound and stitched it up without anesthetic. But now he's in our *manyatta* because he has to go for a checkup every day.

Lketinga bought *miraa* by the pound in Maralal and is selling it at good prices. Everybody from the town comes in for the plant, and even two Somalis come in for the first time. They're after the *miraa* too. My husband gives them a dirty look and asks them dismissively what they want. His attitude annoys me because they're friendly enough and we've done their business enough damage. They get their *miraa* and go. By nine P.M. the shop is ready for us to resume business as usual the next day.

When I crawl into my hut, there's a stocky warrior with a heavily bandaged leg lying there, groaning softly. I ask him how he is. Okay, he says. But that means nothing here. No Samburu would ever say anything else even if he were about to breathe his last. He's sweating heavily, and there's a smell of sweat mixed with iodine. When Lketinga comes in a little later, he's got two bunches of *miraa* with him. He says something to the injured man but gets only a halting response. It looks as though the man's running a fever. After a bit of argument I'm allowed to take his temperature. The thermometer shows 104.9 degrees F. I give the warrior some medicine to bring his fever down. That night I don't sleep well. My husband spends the whole night chewing *miraa* while the wounded warrior groans and sometimes calls out.

The next morning I leave Lketinga with his companion and go to the shop. Business is hectic—news that more meal and sugar have arrived has spread like wildfire. Today Anna doesn't look well. She keeps sitting down and has to run out a couple of times to be sick. I ask her worriedly what's wrong. But she says it's fine, maybe just a touch of malaria. I send her home, and her husband, the one who accompanied our truck, offers to work in her place. I'm glad for his help because he works really hard. After a couple of hours, my back is aching terribly again but whether it's on account of the pregnancy or just bending over all the time I don't know. I suppose I must be at about three months, but apart from a small bump there's not much to see. In the meantime my husband has started to doubt that I'm pregnant and thinks I might just have a stomach ulcer.

Eventually Lketinga turns up in the shop. Right away he starts at the sight of the man behind the counter and asks him what he's doing there. I keep serving. The man tells him about Anna's illness and says she's had to go home. We work on while my husband sits there still chewing his *miraa*, which starts to get me annoyed. I send him to the vet to find out if a goat's been slaughtered today because I'd like to make a good meal with meat and potatoes. I want to close at midday so that I can wash and cook in the back room. But Lketinga and our new helper want to work through. So I use my charcoal burner to cook up a tasty stew and enjoy a nice meal on my own. I keep half for Lketinga, but I can work better on a full stomach.

We set off for home after seven P.M. The injured man is hobbling around our hut; he seems a bit better. But what a mess! There are chewed *miraa* stems and lumps of chewing gum everywhere; the cooking pot is next to the fire with maize stuck inside it; and there are bits of food all around with ants climbing all over them. There's also a foul smell in the hut. I take a sharp intake of breath: here I am just back from work and now I have to clean the hut, not to mention the pot to make chai, which I have to scrape clean with my fingernails.

When I complain to my husband, he doesn't understand. On his *miraa* high, he thinks I'm getting at him and don't want to help his friend, who barely escaped with his life. All I'm asking for is a bit of tidiness. My husband and the warrior leave the hut grumpily and say they're going off to Mama. I hear them talking loudly and feel lonely and excluded. To keep my composure I get out my radio-cassette player and put some German music on. After a while Lketinga sticks his head in and looks at me mistrustfully. "Corinne, what's the problem? Why you hear this music? What's the meaning?" Oh, God, how am I to tell him that I feel misunderstood and taken advantage of and am just looking for a bit of comfort? He wouldn't understand.

I take his hand and ask him to sit beside me. We listen to the music together, staring into the fire, and slowly I feel an erotic charge building between us and relish it. Lketinga looks fantastic in the firelight. I put my hand on his dark naked thigh and feel his excitement too. He turns and looks at me wildly, and suddenly we're in each other's arms, kissing, and for the first time I get the feeling that he likes it. Although I keep trying, Lketinga has up until now never really enjoyed it, and my attempts usually are given up pretty quickly. But now he's kissing me more and more passionately. Eventually we make love, magnificently. When his passion subsides, he strokes my stomach tenderly and asks: "Corinne, you are sure, you have now a baby?" I laugh happily: "Yes." "Corinne, if you have a baby, why you want love? Now it's okay. I have given you a baby, now I wait for it." This is a fairly sobering line of reasoning, but I don't take it too seriously. We fall asleep contentedly.

The next day is Sunday. Our shop is closed, and we decide to hear Father Giuliani say mass. The little church is packed, almost exclusively with women and children, just a few men—the vet with his family, the doctor, and the bush teacher, sitting on one side. Giuliani reads the mass in Swahili, and the teacher translates into Samburu. In between, the women and children sing and drum their fingers. By and large everything is very jolly. Lketinga is the only warrior, and this visit to the church is his first and last.

We spend the afternoon together down by the river. I wash clothes, and he cleans the car. Eventually we have time for our ritual of washing each other, just like before, and I think back nostalgically. Of course, I like the shop, and we have more variety in our meals, but we don't have as much time for ourselves. Everything is much more hectic. Even so, after each Sunday I'm pleased about the shop; I've made friends with some of the townswomen and a few of their husbands who speak English. Gradually I'm getting to know who belongs to whom.

I've also really taken a shine to Anna. Her husband is on vacation and has been helping out in the shop for a few days. I don't mind, but Lketinga does, and every time Anna's husband has a soft drink he asks me if Anna is paying for it.

It's time to sort out some more sugar. For a couple of days now the sacks have been empty, and as a result we've had fewer customers. Also the school holidays are about to start, so I can go to Maralal, get sugar, and bring James home. Lketinga will stay in the shop and help Anna since we've still got twenty sacks of maize meal left to sell to get enough money to pay for the use of the truck.

I take our trusty helper with me. He's a good worker and can stow the heavy sacks in the Land Rover for me. As ever, another twenty people want to come with us. Because there's always an argument I decide to ask for some money to help meet the cost of the gas. That way only the ones who really need to come will want to. When I tell them, the crowd quickly disappears except for five people who are ready to pay my price. The Land Rover can cope with that. We set off early because I want to get back the same evening. The game warden is one of the group, but he has to pay too.

In Maralal everyone gets out, and I drive down to the school. The headmaster tells me the boys don't get out until four. I agree with him to take three or four boys back to Barsaloi. Meanwhile my helper and I get hold of three sacks of sugar and some fruit and vegetables. I can't take any more. That leaves a couple of hours to kill, so I go to see Sophia.

Sophia is delighted to see me. Unlike me, she's put on several pounds, and she looks well. She makes some spaghetti for me: a real treat after so long without any pasta. No wonder she's putting on weight so quickly! Her Rasta friend drops by with a couple of friends and takes off again. Sophia grumbles that since she became pregnant she hardly ever sees him. He has no intention of working and just spends her money on beer and his friends. Despite all the comforts she has, I don't envy her. Sophia's case makes me appreciate how much Lketinga does.

I say good-bye, promising to drop by every time I'm in Maralal. I pick up my helper and the game warden at our agreed rendezvous and drive down to the school, where three boys are waiting for us. James is pleased to be collected, and we set off immediately because we want to be home before dark.

Jungle Tracks

The car snakes its way up the dusty red track, and just before the S-bend the game warden and I break into laughter thinking of our experience with the elephant. The boys in the back are chatting and laughing too. Just before we get to the steep descent I brake, ready to engage the four-wheel drive, and brake again, but nothing happens as the car rolls ever forward toward the deadly drop. I scream out in horror, "No brakes!" and at the same time I see there's no way of turning right because, masked by the trees, the steep ravine has already begun. Without a second thought I throw the steering wheel to the left—the game warden's already struggling to open the door.

As if by a miracle the car bangs over the edge of the wall of rock, falling away evermore sharply. Where I've gone over, the drop is barely a foot, but if we'd gone just a bit farther, there would have been no choice but to plunge down the slope headfirst. I pray that the car will get stuck in the undergrowth here where there's a platform of fifty feet or so, after which it falls away steeply into the jungle.

The boys are on an adrenaline rush, and the game warden has gone gray. At last the car stops, barely a yard from the end of the plateau. I'm shaking so much all over that I can't get out.

The boys climb out through the windows since we don't dare move forward and the rear doors are locked. With weak knees I manage to get out too and go to inspect the damage, and at that very moment the car starts to slowly roll forward. With presence of mind I grab the nearest large stone and shove it in front of a wheel. The boys have discovered that the brake cable has been ripped out. Shocked and stunned, we stand next to the vehicle, less than three yards from a fatal plunge.

The game warden says there's no way we can stay out here in the bush, even though he's got his gun this time. Apart from anything else, it'll be bloody cold when it gets dark. There's also no way we can drive on to Barsaloi with no brakes. The only option is to go back to Maralal, which I can manage without brakes, in four-wheel drive all the way if need be. First of all we have to turn the long vehicle around on this narrow plateau. We get some big rocks, and I start the engine carefully. I can't go more than a couple of feet forward, so the boys have to use the stones to stop each wheel. Then we do the same thing in reverse, where I can see next to nothing. The sweat is running down my face, and I pray to God for help. After this experience, when we could all have died, I'm quite certain of His existence. It takes more than an hour to complete the second miracle, but at last the car faces the other way.

It's already dark in the jungle by the time we can set off, in four-wheel drive and first gear all the way. When we start downhill, the car is going far too fast and the engine screams horribly, but I don't dare change gear. At critical moments I automatically step on the nonfunctioning brakes. At the end of an hour with great relief we arrive back in Maralal. Here there are people ambling across the road in the blithe assumption that the few cars will brake for them. I can only sound my horn, and people leap aside with a curse. As we approach the garage I turn off the ignition and let us roll up to it. The Somali boss is about to close, but I explain my problem and tell him the car is full of goods that I can't leave out on the street. He opens up his iron door, and a few men push the car in.

We go off for chai, still in shock, to discuss what to do. First we have to find somewhere to stay. The game warden can sort himself out, but I obviously offer to pay for my helper and the boys. We take two rooms, the lads saying they can easily share one bed. I want to be on my own. After we eat I retire, miserable for my husband, who won't know what's happening and will be worried about us.

Early the next morning I head to the garage, where the workers are already repairing our vehicle. Even the Somali boss is puzzled as to how it could have happened. By eleven we're ready to leave, but this time I don't dare take the jungle route. I have a deep terror of it now and in any case I'm four months pregnant. We take the detour via Baragoi, which takes nearly four and a half hours; I think all the time about how worried my husband must be.

We get on well, though. Despite the strewn rubble, this road is a lot less demanding. We're at least halfway there when, just as we're crossing a dried-up riverbed, a hissing noise I had already noticed suddenly becomes louder. Of all the bad luck, now we've got a flat! Everyone gets out, and the boys dig the spare out from under the sacks of sugar. My helper puts the jack in position, and within half an hour it's all done. For once I had nothing to do and could sit in the warm sun. We set off again and get to Barsaloi during the afternoon.

We park next to the shop, and I'm just about to get out when my husband comes up with a nasty frown on his face and stands in front of the car door shaking his head: "Corinne, what is wrong with you? Why you come late?" I explain, but he turns away without listening and demands to know who I spent the night with in Maralal. That gets me mad: we've barely escaped with our lives and my husband thinks I've been unfaithful. I had never imagined he might react like that.

The boys come to my aid, describing the journey. He crawls under the car and examines the cable. When he discovers the traces of brake oil, he declares himself satisfied. But I'm deeply disappointed in him and decide to stomp off to my hut. They can sort themselves out. At least James is there. I say a brief hello to Mama and Saguna and then hide myself away, exhausted and disillusioned.

By evening I'm freezing, but I don't worry about it and make chai. Lketinga comes in and has a cup. We don't talk much, and late in the evening he sets off to visit a distant encampment to collect the rest of our wedding-present goats. He'll be back in two days. He wraps his red blanket around his shoulders, grabs his two spears, and, saying little, leaves the *manyatta*. I hear him exchange a few brief words with Mama, and then all is silence save for the cries of a baby in a neighboring hut.

My own condition is getting worse, however. During the night I panic: Is this another malaria attack? I get out my Fansidar antimalaria pills and read the instructions carefully. Three pills to be taken on suspicion of an attack, but in case of pregnancy consult a doctor. Oh, God, the last thing I want is to lose my baby, which is something that up to the sixth month malaria can easily cause. I decide to take the three tablets and put wood on the fire to warm up.

The next morning I waken only when I hear voices outside. I crawl out of the hut into blinding sunlight. It's nearly eight-thirty. Mama's sitting outside her hut and laughs at me. "*Supa* Corinne," comes the call. "*Supa* Mama," I reply, and head off into the bush to deal with my morning needs.

I feel weak and worn out. When I get back to the *manyatta* there are already four women there asking about the shop. "Corinne, *tuka!*" I hear Mama call. She wants me to open the shop. "*Ndjo, ja*—later!" I reply. Understandably they all want the sugar we brought back yesterday, and half an hour later I drag myself to the shop.

There are already twenty people waiting, but Anna isn't there. I open up and immediately the bedlam breaks loose. Everybody wants to be first. I serve them mechanically. Where's Anna? My helper hasn't turned up either, and there's no sign of the boys. While I'm serving I suddenly have an urgent need for the toilet. I grab the toilet paper and rush for the earth toilet. I've already got diarrhea. I'm completely worked up now. The shop is full of people. The till is just a box, open to anybody who goes behind the counter. With no strength I still force myself to go back to the nattering women, but again and again the diarrhea forces me back to the toilet.

Anna has left me in the lurch; she hasn't turned up. So far there hasn't been a single familiar face to whom I could even half explain the situation in English and ask for help. After lunch I can't stand on my feet any longer.

At last the teacher's wife turns up, and I send her to Mama to see if the boys are at home. Luckily James turns up with the boy who'd spent the night in the boardinghouse with me. They're both prepared to run the shop so I can go home. Mama looks at me in surprise and asks what's wrong. What am I to tell her? I shrug my shoulders and say, "Maybe malaria." She looks at me in shock and grabs her stomach. I take her meaning but am worried enough myself and don't know what to do. She comes into my *manyatta* and makes black tea for me, because milk would be dangerous. While she's waiting for the water to boil she talks quietly to Enkai. Mama is praying for me in her own way. I'm really fond of her sitting there with her long breasts and dirty skirt. At a time like this I'm pleased my husband has such a loving, caring mother and don't want to let her down.

When our goats come home, the older brother looks in on me and tries to start a conversation in Swahili. But I'm too tired and keep falling asleep. In the middle of the night I wake up bathed in sweat, hearing footsteps and the spears being thrust into the ground outside our hut. My heart is pounding madly when I hear the familiar grunting noise and shortly afterward a shape appears in the hut. "Darling?" I ask hopefully in the darkness. "Yes, Corinne, no problem," replies the familiar voice of my husband. I explain what's wrong with me, and he's very worried. As I haven't had the shivering fit yet, I still hope that taking the Fansidar right away may have done the trick.

The next few days I stay home, and Lketinga and the boys run the shop. Gradually I get on my feet again; after three days even the diarrhea has stopped. After a week of lying around I've had enough, and that afternoon I go back to work. But the shop is in a state: there's been next to no cleaning done, everything is covered with maize meal dust, and the shelves are almost empty. The four sugar sacks have long since been emptied, and there are barely one and a half sacks of meal left. That means another trip to Maralal. We plan to make it next week, because the boys' short holidays will be over then and I can take a few of them with me.

The shop is quiet. As soon as the basic foodstuffs are sold the customers from far away stop coming. I go to see Anna. When I get to her house, I find her lying in bed. When I ask what's wrong, she initially won't say anything, but eventually I get out of her that she's pregnant too. She's only in her third month but a while ago had some bleeding and that's why she stayed away from work. We agree that she'll come back when the boys have gone.

The start of school is getting closer, and it's time for us to go. This time we'll leave the shop shut. Three days later we send a whole truckload back to Barsaloi with our helper on board. Lketinga and I take the jungle road, and luckily nothing goes wrong. Just before dark we're standing waiting for the truck, but instead two warriors arrive to tell us it's got stuck in the last riverbed. We drive the short distance in our car to see what can be done. The truck has got one left wheel stuck in the sand just before it could reach the riverbank, and spinning the wheel has only caused it to sink deeper.

There are already a few people at the scene, and some stones and branches have already been pushed under the wheel. But the truck's heavy load keeps tipping it farther over, and the driver says there's nothing for it but to unload here. I'm not very happy about this idea and go to ask Father Giuliani what he thinks. He's not particularly delighted to see me because he's already heard what's happened, but nonetheless he gets into his car and comes with me.

He uses a towrope, but our two four-wheel-drive vehicles together fail to pull the truck out. So the one hundred sacks, each weighing 224 pounds, have to be transferred to our vehicles. We can take eight at a time. Father Giuliani makes five trips before he's had enough and goes back to the Mission. I do another seven before we've got everything to the shop. It's night now, and I'm exhausted. The shop is an unimaginable mess, but we close up and leave sorting it out to the next morning.

Frequently people offer to sells us goatskins or cowhides, but up until now I've always declined, and the women get upset and leave the shop, cursing, to sell their fleeces to the Somalis. Recently, however, the Somalis have been buying only from those who get their maize or sugar from them. This gives us something else to think about, and so I decide that I'll buy skins too and store them in the back of the shop.

Barely two days pass before the sly little local boss man turns up and asks for our license to trade in animal skins. Of course we don't have one because we didn't know it was necessary. Then he announces he could close the shop because it's forbidden to store skins in the same building as foodstuffs. There has to be a distance of at least one hundred and fifty feet between them. I throw back that the Somalis up until now have kept their fleeces in the same room, but the boss man says this isn't so, and now I know who's put him on to us. As I've accumulated some eighty skins in the meantime, with the intention of selling them next time we're in Maralal, I need to win time to find a lockable storage place. I offer the boss man a couple of fizzy drinks and ask him to give me until tomorrow.

After a long discussion with my husband we agree that by tomorrow we'll have the hides out of the shop. But where? Hides like these are effectively cash. I go up to the Mission for advice. Only Father Roberto is there, and he says he has no room and we'll have to wait for Giuliani. That evening he comes by on his motorbike and delights me by offering us his old water-pumping shed, where he keeps old machinery. There's not much room, but it's better than nothing because we can fit the lot in. Once again I realize how much I owe to Father Giuliani.

Business in the shop is going well, and Anna is better and now turns up on time. Then one ordinary afternoon there's complete pandemonium. The boy from next door rushes into the shop and starts talking excitedly to Lketinga. "Darling, what happened?" I ask. He tells me that two goats from our herd have gone missing and he'll have to set out right away to find them before it gets dark and the wild animals take them. He's just about to set off armed with his two long spears when the bush teacher's servant girl turns up with a pale face and says something to him. I gather that it's to do with our car and Maralal. Worried, I ask Anna, "What's the problem?" and she replies hesitantly that the teacher's wife is expecting a baby and urgently needs to be taken to the hospital, but there's no one at the Mission to help.

A Matter of Life and Death

Darling, we have to go with her to Maralal," I urge my husband, but he says that's not his business, he has to go after his goats. I simply don't understand him and ask angrily if the life of a human being isn't more important than that of an animal. He doesn't see what I'm talking about; it's not his wife, and if he doesn't find his goats within two hours at most they'll have been eaten. With that, he leaves the shop. I'm left speechless and can hardly believe that my good-natured husband can be so heartless.

Anna says I should go to see the woman and then decide what to do. Her wooden cabin is just two minutes from the shop. I nearly have a heart attack when I enter the house: there are blood-soaked cloths everywhere; the young woman is lying bent double on the bare floorboards groaning loudly. I speak to her because I know from the shop that she speaks English. Haltingly she manages to tell me that the bleeding began two days ago but that she couldn't go to the doctor because her husband is very jealous and opposed an examination. Now that he's away she wants to go.

She looks at me for the first time, and I see blind fear in her eyes. "Please, Corinne, help me. I am dying!" She lifts her skirt, and I see a small blue arm hanging from her vagina. I summon all my strength and promise to fetch the Land Rover immediately from home. I charge out of the house and tell Anna in the shop that I'm off to Maralal straightaway and that if my husband isn't back by seven o'clock she's to close the shop.

I race back to the *manyatta*, barely noticing the thornbushes tearing my legs. Tears of grief and anger at my husband are rolling down my face. If only we can get to Maralal in time! Mama's at home and doesn't understand why I grab all our woolen blankets and even the cowhide out of the *manyatta* and lay them out in the back of the Land Rover. I've no time to tell her the story. Every minute counts. I'm hardly thinking clearly as I roar off in the Land Rover. One glance at the Mission tells me there's nobody there; both cars are gone. I stop outside the wooden house, and the girl and I help the woman into the car.

It's difficult because she can't stand up. We lay her out on the two blankets, which at least shield her from the cold metal but will be no protection against hard jolts. The girl gets in too, and we set off. At the "doctor's hut" I stop to see if the local doctor will come with us, but he isn't there either. Where is everybody when you need them? Instead of him there's a stranger there who comes from Maralal and wants a lift. He's not a Samburu.

It's a life-and-death mission, but I can't go too quickly or the woman in the back would be tossed from side to side. Every bump causes her to cry out. The girl talks to her gently, holding her head on her lap. I'm dripping with sweat and have to keep wiping tears out of my eyes. This teacher has almost killed his wife through his jealousy! The man who translates the mass every Sunday in church, who can read and write. I could hardly believe it if I hadn't seen the reaction of my own husband. The life of a woman obviously matters less to him than that of a goat. If it had been a warrior in distress, like the one we had in our hut a month ago, Lketinga would no doubt have reacted differently. But this was only a woman, and not even his. What would happen if I developed complications?

All of this is flying through my head as we make our slow progress in the car. The woman keeps drifting in and out of consciousness, and her groaning has ceased. We're at the rocks now, and I feel sick at the thought of the car bouncing to and fro. There's no point in driving slowly here. I tell the servant girl to hold on to the woman as tightly as she can. The man sitting next to me hasn't said a word. In four-wheel drive the car climbs up over the rocks. The woman is screaming horribly. When we get to the top she quiets down for a bit, and I drive through the jungle as quickly as possible. Just before the "death slope" I have to engage the four-wheel drive again, and the car crawls up the hill. Halfway up, the engine starts to splutter. I immediately glance at the gas gauge but am reassured. It settles down and then splutters again but makes its way to the top, then conks out, right beside the plateau where I was previously stuck.

In despair I try to fire the engine up again, but there's nothing doing.

Now the man next to me comes to life, and we get out to inspect the engine. I take out all the spark plugs, and they're okay. The battery is topped up. What is the problem with this damn machine? I tug all the cables, look underneath, but I can't see what's wrong. I try and try again to spark the ignition, but it's no good. Nothing's working, not even the dashboard light.

By now it's dark, and the giant horseflies are eating us alive. I'm starting to get really afraid. The woman in the back is groaning; the blankets are covered in blood. I tell the stranger that we're as good as lost here because next to nobody uses this road. The only chance is for him to get to Maralal and get help. On foot, I expect he can do it in an hour and a half, but he refuses to go on his own without a weapon. I lose my temper completely and swear at him angrily. Doesn't he understand that it's dangerous anyway and the longer he waits here the darker and colder it'll get? Our only chance is if he gets going. Eventually he sets off.

The soonest help can get to us is in two hours. I open the rear doors and try to talk to the woman, but she's lost consciousness briefly. It's getting cold, and I pull my jacket on. Then she wakes up and asks for some water. She's very thirsty; her lips are all cracked. My God! In my mad haste I've made another colossal mistake; I've forgotten to bring drinking water. I search the whole car and can find only an empty Coke bottle but set off to find her some water. Everything is so green here there must be water somewhere. After a hundred yards I hear splashing, but I can't see anything through the thicket. Carefully, step by step, I venture into the jungle. In two yards the ground suddenly falls away, and down below is a little stream, but I can't get to it because I'd never be able to get back up the rocky wall. I run back to the car and fetch the rope from the gas containers. The woman is screaming like mad with pain. I cut one end of the rope and tie the bottle to it to lower it to the stream. It fills up, but incredibly slowly. As I hold it to the woman's mouth I notice that she's glowing with heat and at the same time so cold that her teeth are chattering. She empties the whole bottle, and I go back to fetch more.

Back at the car I hear a scream the likes of which I've never heard before. The girl is holding the woman tight and sobbing. She's so young, maybe just thirteen or fourteen years old. I look into the woman's face and see the fear of death. "I'm dying, I'm dying, Enkai!" she stammers. "Please, Corinne, help me!" she begs. What am I to do? I've never been present at a birth. I've never even been pregnant before. "Please, take out this child, please, Corinne!" I lift her skirt and see the same picture again, except that the violet blue arm is now hanging out as far as the shoulder.

This baby is dead, I'm thinking. It's sideways and can't be born without a cesarean. Sobbing, I tell her that I can't help but with luck help will be here in half an hour. I take my jacket off and lay it over her shivering form. My God, why do you leave us so alone? What have I done that this car should once again let us down today of all days? I don't understand the world anymore, and at the same time I can no longer stand her piercing screams and run despairingly, unthinkingly, into the dark jungle, only to turn around almost immediately and head back to the car.

Terrified she is dying, the woman demands my knife. Feverishly I try to decide what to do and make up my mind not to give it to her. Then suddenly she rises up from the blankets and gets into a squat. The girl and I stare in horror at this woman battling for her life, as she sticks both hands into her vagina and pulls at the arm until eventually a blue-violet underdeveloped baby is lying on the woolen blanket. Immediately she falls back in exhaustion and lies there stock-still.

I come to first and wrap up the bloody, dead, seven-month fetus in a kanga, then I give the woman some more water. Her whole body is shaking, but even so she exudes complete calm. I try to clean her hands and talk to her reassuringly. At the same time I strain my ears toward the bush, where after a while I can hear the distant sound of an engine.

Shortly thereafter I make out headlights coming through the jungle, and relief overcomes me like a stone falling from my heart. I wave my flashlight in the air so that they can see us. It's a Land Rover ambulance from the hospital. Three men get out, and I tell them what's happened. They put the woman on a stretcher and load her into their vehicle and take the bundle containing the baby too. The girl goes with them also. The driver takes a look at my car, turns the key, and knows immediately what's wrong. He shows me a cable hanging down behind the steering wheel. The ignition cable has come out. In a minute he's fixed it, and the car starts up.

While the others go on to Maralal, I turn around and head home. I reach our *manyatta* totally exhausted and shaken. My husband wants to know why I'm so late back. I try to explain to him but see that he doesn't believe me. I despair at his reaction and fail to understand why he has so little trust in me. It's not my fault at the end of the day that the car keeps breaking down when he's not there. I lie down to go to sleep and refuse any further discussion.

The next day I go to work with no enthusiasm. I've barely opened when the teacher comes by and thanks me effusively for my help but doesn't once ask how his wife is. What a hypocrite!

A bit later Father Giuliani comes in and has me tell him everything. He regrets what we had to go through and generously pays me for the journey, although that's not what I care about. He's heard over the radio link, however, that the woman is as well as can be expected in the situation.

The stress in the shop is taking more out of me than I know. Ever since this event I've been sleeping badly and having horrible dreams about my own pregnancy. The third morning afterward I'm so wrecked that I send Lketinga to the shop on his own. He can work with Anna, and I'll sit at home with Mama under the big tree. That afternoon the doctor comes by and tells me the teacher's wife is over the worst but will have to spend a couple more weeks in Maralal.

We talk about what happened, and he tries to ease my conscience by telling me it happened only because she didn't want to have the baby. She brought the car to a standstill using her mental powers. When he's leaving he asks me what's wrong. I mention my weak state of health, which I put down to recent events, but he warns me to beware of the chance of malaria. My eyes, he says, have a yellow taint.

Fears for My Child

In the evening we slaughter a sheep. This is the first time I have eaten lamb or mutton out here, and I'm curious. Mama prepares our share. She simply boils a few pieces in water, and we drink the bland fatty broth from cups. Mama believes it's good for when you're pregnant and need strength. But it's obviously not good for me because during the night I get diarrhea. I manage to waken my husband, however, and he helps me to open the gate in the thorn stockade. I barely make it twenty yards farther. Then I drag myself back to the *manyatta* to find Lketinga seriously worried about me and the baby.

It's the same story the next morning, and I throw up afterward. Despite the incredible heat I'm shivering, and now I notice my yellow eyes and send Lketinga to the Mission. I'm afraid for the child because I'm certain this is the beginning of a new malaria bout. Barely ten minutes pass before I hear the Mission car engine, and Father Giuliani comes into the hut. When he sees me he asks what's happened, and I tell him for the first time that I'm five months pregnant. He's surprised because he hadn't noticed. He immediately suggests taking me to the Mission hospital in Wamba because otherwise the child could be premature and I might lose it. I gather a few things together and we set off, leaving Lketinga behind because the shop is open.

Father Giuliani's car is more comfortable than mine. He drives at breakneck speed because he knows the roads so well, but even so I struggle to hold on because I'm using one hand to support my stomach. We don't talk much on the three-hour trip to the hospital. Two white nurses are waiting for us, and they help me to an examination room, where I can lie down on the bed. I'm astounded by the tidiness and cleanliness, but then, lying there on the bed, I'm overcome by a deep sadness. When Giuliani comes to say good-bye, I can't hold back the tears. He's shocked and asks me what the matter is, but I don't even know myself. I'm afraid for my child. And then I've left my husband alone in the shop. He tries to calm me down, promising to check the accounts every day and keep the sisters informed by radio. Overwhelmed by his sympathy, I burst into tears again.

He fetches one of the nurses, who gives me an injection. Then the doctor turns up to examine me. When he hears how many months pregnant I am, he shows concern that I'm far too thin and haven't enough blood. That's why the baby is so small. Then he makes his diagnosis: early stages of malaria.

I ask him worriedly what that might mean for the baby. He dismisses the question and says the first thing is for me to rest, that'll be best for the baby. If I had delayed coming any longer, my body would have initiated a premature birth itself because of my anemia. But he says he's hopeful; at least the baby's still alive. Those words make me so happy that I determine to do everything to get well again as soon as possible. They put me into a four-bed ward in the maternity department.

It's totally unlike Maralal: outside the window are bushes with red flowers. I'm delighted to have been looked at so quickly. The nurse comes and tells me I'll get two injections a day and at the same time a saline drip, which I need urgently to stop my body from losing fluids. That is also the best way to treat the malaria, and I realize how narrowly I escaped with my life in Maralal. The nurses take tender care of me, and on the third day they remove the drip, but I will still need the injections for another two days.

Back in the shop everything's going really well, the nurses tell me. I feel as if I've been reborn and can't wait to get home again to my husband. On the seventh day he turns up with two other warriors. I'm pleased to see him but wonder how he managed to leave the shop. "No problem, Corinne, my brother is there," he answers with a laugh. Then he tells me he's got rid of Anna because she was stealing from us and giving away food. I can't believe it and ask him worriedly who's going to help us in the future. He's put a boy in, and he and his brother are keeping tabs on him, he says. I can hardly refrain from laughing: I don't see how two men who are unable to either count or read can keep tabs on a former schoolboy.

In any case there's not much left in the shop. That's why he's driven here in the Land Rover and now intends to go on to Maralal, where he and the two warriors will organize another truckload. "With what money?" I ask, and he shows me a bag full of bills. He's picked it all up from Father Giuliani. I'm in a panic about what to do. If he and these two warriors go to Maralal, they'll be treated like turkeys turning up before Christmas. All the money is loose in a plastic bag, and he doesn't even know how much there is.

But while I'm thinking what to do, the doctor arrives and the warriors are sent out. The doctor thinks I've escaped the malaria this time, and I ask to be discharged. He promises I can leave tomorrow but warns me not to work too hard. Three weeks before the due date I'm to be back at the hospital. I'm relieved to be discharged and tell Lketinga. He's pleased too and promises to pick me up in the morning. They'll find somewhere to stay in Wamba.

I take the wheel for the trip to Maralal and as always when my husband is with me, the trip is uneventful. We're able to book a truck for the next day. In the boardinghouse I count out the money that Lketinga has brought and to my horror find we're several thousand Kenyan shillings short of being able to pay for the load. I ask Lketinga about it, and he just says he left some behind in the store. So there's nothing for me to do but draw more money out of the bank instead of paying in our profits. But I'm pleased that we'll be able to get back to Barsaloi so quickly; I've been away from home for ten days now.

The truck, with one of the warriors on board, takes the long route, and we set off through the jungle. I'm happy to be with my husband and feel physically well as a result of the regular meals in the hospital.

The Fatal Plunge

On our way we notice that someone else has been this way recently. Lketinga examines the tire tracks and says they belong to strangers. We get down the "death drop" without difficulty, and I try to suppress my memories of the horrible experience of the stillbirth.

As we come round the last bend before the big rocks, I brake sharply. In the middle of the road are two old military Land Rovers with a group of white people running around excitedly between them. There's no way we can get past, so we get out to see what's going on. From what I can make out it's a group of young Italians with one black native.

One of the young men is sitting sobbing in the heat with two young women talking to him, both of them crying too. Lketinga talks to the Kenyan, and I summon up a few Italian phrases from memory.

Despite the 104-degree heat, their story brings me goose bumps. The girlfriend of the man who's crying went into the jungle to answer a call of nature some two hours ago. They had stopped because they thought they had reached the end of the road. The woman had barely gone two yards before she went over the edge of the hidden precipice. They all heard a sudden cry and then an impact, and since then, for all their shouts and efforts to climb down the steep drop, there's been no sign of life.

My blood runs cold because I know there's no chance for her. The man keeps shouting out his girlfriend's name. I go back to my husband in a state of shock. He's upset too and tells me this woman is certainly dead because the cliff wall here drops three hundred feet to an old dried-up, stony riverbed. Nobody has ever climbed down. The Italians seem to have tried, however, because there are several ropes tied end to end. The two girls are hugging the man, who's completely at the end of his tether: red-faced, soaked in sweat, crouching in the searing heat, shaking his head. I go over to them and suggest they move under the trees, but the man opens his mouth wide and screams.

I look back at Lketinga and see he's thinking of something, so I run over and ask him what he has in mind. He says he and his friend could get down there somehow and bring the woman back up. Filled with panic I grab him and cry, "No, darling, that's crazy. Don't go, it is very dangerous." But Lketinga pushes my hand away.

All of a sudden the sobbing man is standing next to me swearing at me for trying to stop someone helping. Furiously I reply that I live here and this is my husband and in three months' time he's going to be a father and I don't intend to bring up my child without a father.

But already Lketinga and the other warrior have begun the dangerous descent some one hundred and fifty feet back up the track. The last thing I see is their completely expressionless faces. Samburus avoid the dead; they don't even speak of them. I sit down in the shade and sob quietly to myself.

After half an hour we've heard nothing, and my anxiety is becoming unbearable. One of the Italians looks down from where the warriors started their descent, then comes back excitedly and says he caught sight of them both on the other side of the ravine, carrying a sort of stretcher.

The reaction is near hysteria, but another twenty minutes pass before the pair of them emerge from the forest completely exhausted. Immediately people rush toward them to take the stretcher made out of Lketinga's kanga and two branches.

From the Masais' faces I can tell that the woman is dead. I glance at the body and am surprised at how young she is and how peacefully she's lying there. If it weren't for the sweet smell that bodies in this heat exude after only three hours, she might merely have been sleeping.

My husband has a brief chat with the group's black tour leader, and then they move their Land Rovers to one side. Lketinga takes the ignition key because he wants to drive, and in my shocked state there's no point in arguing. Promising to inform the Mission, we drive down the scree slope in absolute silence. When we come to the first river, the pair of them get out and wash for nearly an hour. It is a sort of ritual.

At last we drive on, and the men exchange a few words timidly. It's nearly six P.M. when we reach Barsaloi. Outside the shop nearly half of our goods have already been unloaded. Lketinga's brother and the warrior who went with the truck are keeping an eye on the laborers. I open the shop and find myself in a filthy room with maize meal and empty boxes everywhere. While Lketinga cleans up I go to the missionary. He's astounded by the accident even though he had heard something or other over the radio. He jumps into his Land Cruiser and roars off.

I go back home; after such an emotional upheaval I can't take all the fuss in the shop. Mama obviously wants to know why the truck got back before us, but I can give only the barest details. I make chai and lie down. I make up my mind never to use that road again. In my condition it's ever more dangerous. Lketinga comes home around ten P.M. with two warriors, and together they cook up a pot of maize porridge. They talk of nothing but the terrible accident. Eventually I fall asleep.

The next morning our first customers fetch us to open the shop. I go early, as I'm keen to see our new assistant who's replaced Anna. My husband introduces me to the boy. From the very first I take against him, not just because he looks a mess but because he also gives the impression of being lazy. But I force myself not to let his appearance prejudice me because I really ought to be doing less work if I'm not to lose my baby. He works at only half the speed of Anna, and everyone asks where she is.

Now it's time to find out from Lketinga why we didn't have more money in Maralal, because it took only one glance to see that what was left behind did not make up the difference. Proudly he goes and fetches an exercise book and shows me the credit accounts opened for various people. Some of them I know, but I can't even read the names of others and I get cross because when we opened the shop I told him, "No credit!"

The boy butts in and says he knows these people and he's sure it won't be a problem. Even so I object. He listens to my arguments almost dismissively as if he's bored. My husband says that after all it's a Samburu shop and he has to help his own people. Once again I'm left there like the evil greedy white woman when all I'm doing is struggling to make a living. My money from Switzerland will last another two years at most, and then what? Lketinga walks out of the shop because he can't bear it when I start getting worked up. And of course everyone stares at me when I, as a woman, dare to raise my voice.

All day there are endless arguments with customers who were

expecting to get credit. A few of the hardest-nosed decide simply to wait for my husband. Working with the boy is a lot less fun than with Anna. I scarcely dare go to the toilet because I don't trust him. Because my husband doesn't turn up again until the evening I've already worked more on the first day than I'm supposed to. My legs ache, and I've hardly eaten anything all day. Back home there's no water or wood for the fire. I think almost nostalgically how good the service was in the hospital: three meals a day without having to cook!

My legs get tired far more quickly now, and something is going to have to be done. One cup of chai in the morning and one in the evening are simply not enough to build up my strength. Mama agrees that I need to eat a lot more or the child won't be healthy. We decide to move into the back room of the shop as soon as possible. So after just four months we have to leave our lovely *manyatta*, but Mama will get it and she's very pleased about that.

When we order our next truckload we'll order a bed, a table, and chairs so we can move in properly. The thought of a bed cheers me up a lot because sleeping on the ground is gradually giving me a backache, although for the past year it didn't bother me.

For the past few days, clouds have started to appear in the otherwise perpetually blue sky, and everybody is expecting rain. The land is totally dry, the ground cracked and as hard as stone. More and more frequently we hear stories of lions attacking the animal herds in broad daylight. The children who look after them panic when they have to run home without the goats to fetch help. So my husband now regularly spends days out wandering with the herds, and there's nothing I can do but spend all my time in the shop, working alongside the boy and keeping tabs on him.

The Great Rains

On the fifth overcast day the first raindrops began to fall. A Sunday, our day off, and we rush to spread plastic sheeting over the *manyatta*, not an easy task in the rapidly rising wind. Mama is struggling with her hut just as we are with ours. Then the rain pours down, a rainstorm the likes of which I have never experienced before. Before long everything is under water, the wind blows damp into every crack, and we have to extinguish the fire to stop sparks from being blown everywhere. I put on every warm piece of clothing I have. Within an hour the first drops of water are already falling inside our hut, despite the plastic sheeting. I can only imagine what it must be like for Mama and Saguna!

The water is creeping in the door toward our sleeping space, and I use a cup to scoop the earth into a dam. The wind is tugging the plastic sheeting, and I imagine it being ripped off at any moment. It sounds as if there's a river raging outside. The water's coming in through the sides of the hut now, and I do my best to get things off the ground. I stuff our blankets into my travel bag so that at least they will remain dry.

Suddenly, after two hours, the torrent ceases. We crawl out of the hut, but I no longer recognize the landscape. A few huts have been all but swept away. The goats are running around in confusion. Mama is standing, soaked to the skin, outside her hut, which looks flooded, with Saguna standing in one corner shivering and crying. I bring her over and put one of my dry sweaters on her; at least she can wrap herself up in it. Everyone is coming out now to see the streams the water has carved rushing down toward the river. Suddenly we hear a loud bang. I turn to Lketinga in shock to ask what it is. Wrapped in his red blanket, he just laughs and says the floodwater in the river will have reached the edge of the cliffs, and indeed there's a roaring as if from a giant waterfall.

Lketinga and I are keen to go down to the big river, but Mama says no; it's far too dangerous, she insists. So we go down to the other side where the truck became stuck in the sand. This river is some seventy-five feet across; the other one maybe three times that. Lketinga has pulled his woolen blanket up to cover his head, and for the first time up here I've got my jeans, a pullover, and a jacket on. The few people we bump into stare at my appearance. They've never seen a woman in trousers before. I have to watch that they don't fall down, as I can no longer do them up across my stomach.

The roaring keeps getting louder to the point where we can hardly hear each other speak. Then all of a sudden I see the rolling river. It's impossible to believe how much it's changed! A brown mass of water carrying all before it, including bushes and stones. I'm left speechless by this demonstration of the power of nature. Then I think I hear a cry and ask Lketinga if he heard it too. He says no, but I can hear it quite clearly now, someone shouting out, and now he hears it too. Where can it be coming from? We run along the upper riverbank, taking care not to slip.

After just a few yards we see a terrible sight—two children up to their necks in water hanging on to a few rocks in the middle of the raging river. Lketinga doesn't waste a second: he shouts something to them as he clambers down the bank. It looks terrifying. Every other second their heads are submerged by the onrushing torrent, but their hands cling tightly to the rocks. I know my husband can't swim and is afraid of deep water. If he loses his footing in the rushing torrent, he's done for. Even so I can understand why he's trying to save these children, and I'm proud of him.

He grabs a long stick and uses it to fight his way through the river to the rocks, all the time shouting to the children. I'm just standing there, praying to my guardian angel. He reaches the rocks, throws the girl across his back and fights his way back. I watch in spellbound horror as the boy clings on, his head barely visible now. I rush down into the water to meet my husband and take the girl off him so he can go back straightaway. The child is heavy, and it's a real effort to carry her the seven feet back to the riverbank. I lay her down and immediately throw my jacket over her. She's cold as ice. My darling has saved the little boy too, who's now spitting out water as Lketinga massages him. I do the same for the girl, and slowly her stiff limbs begin to regain warmth. But the boy's gone listless and can't walk. Lketinga carries him home while I let the girl lean on me. I'm horrified to think how close both children came to dying.

Mama frowns when she hears the story and tells the children off. Apparently they were out with the goats and were crossing the riverbed when the flood struck. Many of the goats were washed away, although a few made it to the bank. My husband tells me the first wave's always taller than a man and comes over the cliff edge so suddenly and quickly that nobody who's at the river stands a chance. Every year several animals and people are drowned. The children stay with us awhile, but we've no hot tea because all the firewood is soaked.

We go to take a look at the shop. The veranda is covered in a thick layer of sludge; inside is dry except for a couple of puddles. Then we go down to the teahouse, but there's no tea to be had there either. The roaring of the big river is really loud, and we go to take a look. It's frightening to see. Fathers Roberto and Giuliani are there too, staring at the power of the water. I mention what happened at the other river, and Giuliani for the first time comes up to my husband and takes him by the hand in thanks.

On the way back we fetch the little stove and charcoal to bring home so that at least we can make hot tea for everybody. It's an uncomfortable night because everything is so damp, but in the morning the sun's out again, and we spread our clothes and blankets on the thornbushes to dry in the heat.

A day later the landscape changes once again, but this time it's soft and gentle: grass sprouting everywhere and flowers here and there springing up from the earth so quickly we can almost watch them grow. Thousands of tiny white butterflies cover the ground like snowflakes. It's a magnificent sight to watch life suddenly bloom in this harsh landscape. Within a week all of Barsaloi has become a sea of little purple flowers.

But there's a downside too. There are awful numbers of mosquitoes swarming around in the evening. Not only do we sleep under the mosquito net, but it's so bad I even light one of the repellent coils in the *manyatta*.

Ten days after the rains we're still cut off from the outside world by the two flooded rivers. It's already possible in some places to get across on foot, but it would be unwise to risk it in a car. Giuliani expressly warned me: several vehicles have already been caught in the river, and you could watch the quicksand swallow them up.

A few days later we risk a journey to Maralal, taking the long route because the jungle route is wet and slippery. This time there isn't a truck available right away, and we have to hang around for four days. We drop in on Sophia, who's well. She's already so fat she can hardly bend over. She hasn't heard from Jutta.

My husband and I spend a lot of time in the Tourist Lodge because, since we have the time, it's absolutely fascinating to watch the wild animals' watering hole. On the last day we buy a bed with a mattress, a table with four chairs, and a little cupboard. The furniture isn't as nice as the stuff in Mombasa, and it's more expensive. The truck driver is unimpressed when he hears he's supposed to pick this lot up too, but I'm paying the bill! We drive behind him, and this time the trip back to Barsaloi takes almost six hours but with no problems: not even a flat tire to change. First of all we put the furniture out in the back room, then we get on with the usual unloading.

Moving Out of the Manyatta

The next day we move into the shop. It's oppressively hot, and the flowers have vanished again—the goats have done a good job there. I arrange and rearrange the furniture, but I can't get it to feel as cozy as inside the *manyatta*. But I have promised myself less effort and more regular meals, both of which I desperately need. When the shop closes, my husband disappears off home to welcome his animals back, and I cook up a good stew with carrots, cabbage, and turnips.

The first night we both sleep badly, even though we're comfortable in the bed. There are continuous noises from the tin roof, and that keeps us awake. At seven A.M. there's someone knocking at the door. Lketinga goes to see who it is and finds a boy looking for sugar. Out of his good nature he hands him a pound and closes the door again.

It's much easier for me now to see to my morning toiletry needs: I have a basin to wash in, and the earth toilet is only one hundred and fifty feet away. Life has become a lot easier, if a lot less romantic.

The other thing is that when Lketinga is in the shop now, I can go lie down. While things are cooking I can also serve in the shop. For the first week it's all wonderful. I've got a girl who goes and fetches water from the Mission for me. I have to pay, but on the other hand I no longer have to go down to the river. Also, the water is clear and clean. However, word soon gets around that we're now living in the shop, and soon people are coming incessantly asking for drinking water. It's customary in the *manyattas* to give people some, but now I've nearly used up my whole four gallons by lunchtime. There are forever warriors sitting on our bed waiting to see Lketinga and to be offered tea and food. As long as the shop is full of food, he can hardly say we don't have anything.

After such visits the living space is a shambles: dirty pots or gnawed bones all over the floor, brown slime on the walls, and my woolen blanket and the mattress covered in red ochre from the warriors' body paint. I have more than a few arguments with my husband because I feel I'm being exploited. Sometimes he agrees with me and sends them to his mama's, but at other times he turns against me and goes off with them. We're going to have to find a way of fulfilling our duties of hospitality without being taken advantage of.

I've become friendly with the vet's wife and get invited around for tea occasionally. I try to explain my problem to her, and to my astonishment she understands what I'm saying straightaway. She says it's a custom of the *manyatta* people and that in "town" the number of guests has had to be seriously restricted. There the laws of hospitality apply only to family members and very good friends and not just anyone who's passing. That evening I pass this on to Lketinga, and he promises to follow suit.

During the next few weeks there are several marriages in the neighborhood. Mostly it's older men marrying their third or fourth wife: always young girls whose misery can be seen written on their faces. It's not unusual for the age difference to be thirty years or more. The happiest girls are those who become a warrior's first wife.

Our sugar goes quickly, not least because 224 pounds of sugar is part of the price paid for the bride, and several more pounds are needed for the celebration. Eventually we're left one day with a shop full of maize meal but no sugar. Two warriors who're due to be married in a few days' time are standing there with no idea what to do—even the Somalis have run out of sugar. Reluctantly I set out to Maralal, accompanied by the vet, which is pleasant at least. He wants to pick up his salary and come back with me. I get the sugar quickly and pick up the *miraa* I've promised Lketinga.

The vet is late, and it's nearly four in the afternoon before he turns up. He suggests we take the jungle route, but I'm not happy with the idea, as I haven't used it since the rain. But he thinks it should be dry now, so we set off. There are lots of mud puddles, but that's no problem with the four-wheel drive. At the "death drop," however, it's another story; the rain has washed away the earth to leave huge gullies. At the top we get out and walk down a bit to see how best we can manage it. Apart from one gully about a foot wide running right across the track, I see no real problem getting down, with a bit of luck.

We attempt it. I stick to the upper level, hoping not to slide into a gully where we might get stuck in sludge. We manage it and breathe a sigh of relief. At least it's relatively stable over the rocks. The car bumps and grinds its way over the boulders. The worst is behind us; now there's just sixty feet of scree.

Suddenly something underneath the car starts rattling. I keep going at first, then stop because the sound has grown louder. We climb out, but there's nothing obvious. I take a look under the vehicle and discover what's wrong—on one side the springs are broken in all but two places; there's practically no suspension left; and the broken bits are dragging along the ground, making the rattling.

Once more this car has let me down. I'm furious for allowing myself to be persuaded to come this way. The vet suggests we just continue as we are, but I rule that out. I try to work out what to do and fetch cables and pieces of wood out of the back. Then we bind everything up tight and shove the pieces of wood in between so that the cables don't get worn through. I drive like that slowly as far as the first *manyattas*, where we unload four of the five sacks and store them in the first hut. The vet warns the people there not to open the sacks, and we drive carefully on toward Barsaloi. I'm so annoyed by this damn car that I give myself stomach cramps.

Happily we get to the shop without further ado. Lketinga immediately crawls under the car to see if what we told him is true. He doesn't understand why we unloaded some of the sugar and lets me know that he's not going to be around later. I make my way into the living room and lie down, dog-tired.

The next morning I go to find Father Giuliani to show him my car. Rather crossly he tells me he's not running a car repair shop. He says he'd have to take half the car apart to weld the parts back together and he really doesn't have the time. Before he can say anything else, I turn around and leave in disappointment, feeling let down and left alone by everybody. Without Giuliani's help I'll never get this car back to Maralal. Lketinga asks me what Giuliani said, and when I tell him that he can't help us, his only reply is that he always knew the man was no good. I can't exactly agree: he's saved us more than once.

Lketinga and the boy work in the shop, and I sleep all morning. I'm not very well. By midday the sugar is sold out, and it's hard work preventing my husband from driving back in the faulty car to fetch the rest. In the early evening Giuliani sends his watchman to tell us to bring the car over to him. Relieved that he's changed his mind, I send Lketinga up with the car while I'm cooking. At seven P.M. we close up the shop, but Lketinga isn't back yet. Instead I've got two unknown warriors outside the front door. By the time he returns I've already eaten. He was back home with Mama looking after the animals. Laughing with pleasure, he brings me the first two eggs from my chicken, laid just yesterday. Now I can expand my menu. I make chai for the visitors and crawl exhausted under the mosquito net into bed.

The three of them eat, drink, and gossip while I fall asleep. In the middle of the night I wake up bathed in sweat and thirsty. My husband isn't next to me, and I don't know where the flashlight is. So I crawl out from under the blanket and the net to grope my way to the water canister when my foot bumps into something lying on the floor. Before I can think what it might be, I hear a grunt and exclaim in shock: "Darling?" In the light of the flashlight, which I've managed to find, I make out three figures lying asleep on the floor. One of them is Lketinga. I climb over them carefully to get to the water canister. Back in bed my heart is still pounding. I can hardly get back to sleep with these strange men in the room. The next morning I'm freezing so much I won't come out from under the blanket. Lketinga makes chai for everybody, and I'm glad to get something hot inside me. The three of them laugh at my nocturnal adventure.

Today the boy is in the shop on his own, because Lketinga and the two warriors have gone off to a ceremony, and I'm stuck in bed. At lunch Father Roberto drops in with the other four bags of sugar. I go into the shop to say thanks but find myself immediately feeling dizzy. I go to lie down again. I'm not happy leaving the boy on his own, but I'm too miserable to keep a watch over him. Half an hour after the arrival of the sugar there's the usual chaos. I lie there in bed, unable to sleep with all the noise and talking. In the evening we close up, and I'm on my own.

Actually I'd have liked to go down to Mama, but I'm feeling cold again. I can't be bothered to cook for myself, so I lie down beneath the mosquito net. There are still loads of the insects, and they're as aggressive as ever. During the night I get shivering fits, and my teeth chatter. Why doesn't Lketinga come home? The night drags on and on. At one stage I'm shivering horribly, only to break out in a sweat moments later. I need the toilet but don't dare go out. Out of necessity I pass water in an empty tin.

Early the next morning there's a knock on the door. I ask first who's there, because I'm not about to start selling, and then I recognize the familiar voice of my darling. He realizes immediately that there's something wrong, but I calm him down: I don't want to pester them up at the Mission again.

Full of high spirits, Lketinga starts telling me about the wedding ceremony of some warrior and then that there's going to be a Safari Rally passing through in two days' time. He's already seen a few cars. No doubt a few drivers will stop by to ask about the stretch as far as Wamba, he says. Somehow I doubt it, but despite how miserable I feel I let myself get carried away by his enthusiasm. Later on he goes to see how our car's getting on, but it's not finished yet.

At around two P.M. I hear an incredible roar, and when I get to the shop door, all I can see is a cloud of dust. The first test driver has just shot by. Before long half Barsaloi is out on the streets. About half an hour later a second roars through and then a third. It's a weird feeling to be here at the ends of the earth in a totally different time and suddenly grabbed by civilization like this. We wait and wait, but that's it for today. These were just the test cars. In two days' time there'll be thirty or more cars roaring past. It's a pleasant interruption to our routine, even if I am mostly lying in bed with a fever. Lketinga cooks for me, but I can't even look at food without feeling ill.

On the day of the rally itself, I feel awful. I keep losing consciousness for short periods, and for hours now I've no longer been able to feel the child inside me. I'm seized by panic and cry when I tell this to my husband. He leaves the house in a state of shock to fetch Mama, who talks to me while feeling my stomach. There's a grim look on her face, and I ask Lketinga in tears what's wrong with the child, but he just sits there uselessly and talks only to Mama. Eventually he tells me his mother believes someone must have put an evil curse on me that keeps making me sick. Somebody wants to kill me and the baby!

They want to know which people I've spoken to in the shop recently, if the old Somalis were here, if one of the old men grabbed me or spat at me, or if anyone showed me a black tongue. The questions weigh me down, and I'm getting hysterical with fear. Only one thing's going through my head: my baby is dead!

Mama goes off, promising to come back with good medicine. I don't know how long I lay there sobbing, but when I open my eyes I see six or eight old men and women gathered around me. Incessantly I hear "Enkai! Enkai!" Each one of these old people rubs my stomach and murmurs something. I couldn't care less. Mama holds a beaker to my lips containing a liquid I'm supposed to down in one swallow. Whatever it is, it's burning hot and so fiery that it shakes my whole body. At that very moment I feel something thrash and kick in my stomach and grab it in shock. Everything's going around in circles. All I can see is these old faces, and I wish I were dead. My last thought is that my child had been alive, but now it's surely dead. I call out: "You've killed my baby! Darling, they have now killed our baby." I feel my strength evaporate, and the will to live with it.

Once again ten or more hands are placed on my stomach, rubbing and pressing; there's loud singing and praying, and suddenly my stomach lifts a little, and I feel a little twitch inside. At first I hardly dare believe it, but then it happens again and again. The old folks seem to have felt it too, and their prayers grow softer. When I realize that my little baby is still alive, the will to live that I thought I'd lost flows back into me with new strength. "Darling, please go to Father Giuliani and tell him about me. I want to go to the hospital."

Flying Doctor

Giuliani turns up shortly afterward, and I can read pure horror in his face. He speaks curtly with the old folks and then asks me which month I'm in. "Beginning of the eighth month," I answer blankly. He says he's going to try to get hold of a flying doctor on the radio and leaves. The old folks go too, except for Mama. I'm left lying in sweat praying for myself and the baby—my whole happiness depends on this little entity's life.

Before I know it I can hear an engine, not a car's but an aircraft's: an aircraft landing here out in the bush in the middle of the night! I hear voices outside, and Lketinga comes in all excited. Giuliani appears and says I should grab just a few things and get on board because the landing strip won't stay lit up for long. They help me out of bed. Lketinga gets the essentials together, and they carry me to the plane.

I'm astounded by how bright it is. Giuliani has used his generator to power a giant floodlight. To the left and right oil lamps and flaming torches have been used to mark out a flat piece of road, with big white stones laid out beyond. The pilot, a white man, helps me into the plane and beckons Lketinga to get in with me. He wants to come but can't get over his fear.

My poor darling. I shout to him, telling him to stay here and look after the shop, and then the door closes. We take off, and for the first time in my life I feel safe in such a tiny aircraft. In twenty minutes we're over the hospital in Wamba. Here too there are lights everywhere, but at least there's a proper runway. When we land, I see two nurses coming out with a wheelchair. With some effort I clamber out, using one hand to support my stomach, which has dropped down low. As they push me in the wheelchair toward the hospital I'm once again overcome by self-pity, and the kind words of the nurses make things only worse and leave me sobbing all the more. At the hospital there's a female doctor waiting for me, a Swiss! I can see the worry in her face, but she reassures me everything will be okay.

In the exam room I lie back in the gynecological chair and wait for the head doctor. I'm only too aware of how dirty I am and feel deeply embarrassed. When I try to apologize to the doctor, he dismisses it and tells me that right now there are more important things. He gives me a thorough examination using only his hand, no instruments. I hang on his words to hear how my baby is.

At last he puts me out of my misery, telling me the baby is alive. But it's far too small for the eighth month, and we'll have to do everything possible to prevent a premature birth, although it's already positioned very low. Then the Swiss doctor comes back and gives her dispiriting diagnosis. I have serious anemia and malaria and am in immediate need of a blood transfusion. The doctor tells me how difficult it is to get blood supplies: they have only limited reserves, and I'll have to find a donor to replace it.

I'm panicky about receiving other people's blood here in Africa where there's an AIDS epidemic. I ask him worriedly if the blood has been tested. He tells me honestly that it's only partly checked out, as most patients with anemia have to bring in a donor from their own family before they're allowed a transfusion. Most people here die of malaria or the anemia that it causes. Only a small amount of blood comes from donors overseas.

I lie there in the chair, trying to put my thoughts in order. "Blood means AIDS" keeps going through my head. I try to protest that I don't want to risk this fatal disease, but the doctor gets serious and tells me in no uncertain words that my choice is between this blood and certain death. An African nurse appears who helps me back into the wheelchair and takes me into a room with three other women. She helps me out of my clothes and into a hospital gown like all the others.

First I'm given an injection, then the transfusion apparatus is attached to my left arm. The Swiss doctor comes in with a bag of blood and with a reassuring laugh tells me she's found the last Swiss batch with my blood group. It will last until the morning, and most of the white nurses in the Mission are willing to be donors for me if their blood group matches.

I'm moved by so much care and attention and try to hold back my tears and say thanks. When she plugs me into the transfusion apparatus, it hurts like mad because the needle is so thick, and she has to try several times before she can get the lifesaving blood to flow into my artery. Both my arms are taped to the bed to stop me pulling the needle out in my sleep. I must look a sorry sight, and I'm pleased my mother can't see the state I'm in. Even if it all comes out okay, I won't tell her any of this. With that thought I fall asleep.

All the patients are woken at six A.M. to have their temperatures taken. I'm half wrecked because I've had only four hours of sleep. At eight I get another injection and around midday another transfusion. I'm lucky in that this has come from the local nurses. At least I don't have to worry about AIDS.

The normal prenatal examination takes place in the afternoon—they feel my bump, listen to the baby's heartbeat, and measure my blood pressure. There's nothing more they can do here. I can't eat anything because the smell of cabbage turns my stomach here too. Nonetheless, by the end of the second day I'm feeling much better. A third transfusion makes me feel like a flower receiving the first drops of rain after a long drought; slowly but surely life is returning to my body. After the last transfusion I risk a look in the mirror, but I no longer recognize myself: my eyes look enormous and sunken, my cheekbones protrude, and my nose is long and pointed. My hair looks long and thin and sticks to my head with sweat. And this, I think to myself in shock, is when I feel a lot better. But then I've done nothing but lie there without getting out of bed once in three days, and now once again I've got an antimalarial drip.

The nurses are very nice and come by as often as possible, but they worry because I still won't eat. One of them is particularly nice, and I'm touched by the warmth and goodness she exudes. One day she brings me a cheese sandwich from the Mission. It's been so long since I've seen cheese like this that it takes no effort for me to eat it slowly. From that day on I start to manage solid food again. From now on it's uphill all the way, I tell myself. They use the radio to tell my husband that the baby and I are out of danger.

After a week the Swiss doctor tells me I should go back to Switzerland to have the baby. I look at her in horror and ask why. She says I'm still too thin and weak for the eighth month, and if I don't get proper nourishment, there's a real danger that I might die from the effort and loss of blood involved in giving birth. They don't have any oxygen equipment or incubators for the baby. Also they won't use any painkillers during the birth for the simple reason that they don't have any.

I'm terrified at the thought of getting on a plane to Switzerland in my condition. I tell the doctor I know I couldn't do it. We look for alternatives because she thinks that in the next few weeks I have to get my weight up to at least one hundred and fifty pounds. I can't go home because of the risk of recurring malaria. Then I remember Sophia in Maralal. She has a nice apartment and is a good cook. Even the doctor agrees with this suggestion and will allow me to leave the hospital in two weeks' time.

Because I'm no longer sleeping so much during the day the time drags. I'm only able to have the most basic conversations with my fellow patients, Samburu women who already have several children. Some of them have been referred by the Mission or have had complications that led to them being admitted. Visiting time is every afternoon, but there are not many visitors to the maternity wards because having children is regarded as "women's business." Meanwhile the men are probably enjoying themselves with their other wives.

Gradually I start to wonder where my darling is. Our car must have been fixed by now, and even if it hasn't, he could still get here on foot in seven hours, which is no big problem for a Masai. Of course the nurses bring news from him every day, sent via Father Giuliani. He's working in the shop, helping the boy. Right now I couldn't care less about the shop; I don't want to burden myself with any more worries. But how am I going to tell Lketinga I won't be home until after the baby's born? I can already see the suspicion on his face.

Then on the eighth day, suddenly he's standing there in the door: a bit unsure of himself, but still beaming as he sits on the edge of the bed. "Hello, Corinne, how are you and my baby? Are you okay?" Then he brings out some roast meat. I'm really touched. Father Giuliani is in the Mission too and brought Lketinga with him. We have no opportunity for much intimacy because the other women are either watching us or asking him questions. Even so, I'm pleased to see him and decide not to mention that I intend to spend the next few weeks in Maralal. He promises to come back again as soon as the car's fixed. Giuliani looks in briefly too, and then they're both off again.

Now the days ahead seem longer than ever. The only things to look forward to are the visits of the nurses or doctors. Occasionally someone gives me a newspaper. During the second week I spend a little of each day walking around the hospital, but seeing all the seriously ill people depresses me. What I enjoy is standing by the cots of the newborns and thinking of my own baby. With such a father it's bound to be beautiful. But there are also days when I fear that the baby won't be normal because of all the medicines I've taken.

At the end of the second week Lketinga comes to see me again. When he asks with some concern when I'm finally coming home again, I've no choice but to tell him my plan. He frowns for a moment and then asks pointedly: "Corinne, why do you not come home? Why you will stay in Maralal and not with Mama? You are okay now, and you get your baby in the house of Mama!" He won't listen to any of my explanations and finally comes out with: "Now I know, maybe you have a boyfriend in Maralal!"

It's worse than a slap in the face. I feel as if I've dropped off a cliff and can only burst into tears. That only proves to him that he's right. He charges up and down the room repeating endlessly: "I'm not crazy, Corinne. I'm really not crazy. I know the ladies!"

Suddenly one of the white nurses appears in the room and stares in shock at my husband and me. She demands to know what's going on. In tears I try to tell her. She then tries to talk to Lketinga, but it's no use until she fetches the doctor and he argues the point with him. Reluctantly Lketinga agrees, but there's no joy left—he's hurt me too much. He leaves the hospital, and I don't know whether I'll next see him here or in Maralal.

The nurse comes back, and we have a chat. She's very worried about my husband's attitude, and she too advises me to go back to Switzerland to have the baby, as then it would have my nationality. Here the child would be the property of my husband's family and I couldn't do anything without the father's permission. I dismiss the idea wearily. I'm in no state for a long journey. Besides, my husband would not give me written permission as his wife to leave Kenya five weeks before the birth of our child. In any case, deep down I believe that when the baby is born he'll calm down and be happier.

Throughout the third week I hear nothing from him. Disappointed, I leave the hospital when the opportunity arises for a lift to Maralal with one of the missionaries. The nurses bid me a hearty good-bye and promise to let my husband know, via Father Giuliani, that I've gone to Maralal.

Sophia

Sophia is at home and hugely pleased to see me. But when I tell her my situation, she says there's no problem about eating with her but I can't sleep there; the rear part of the apartment has been converted into a gym for her boyfriend. I'm left sitting there in a quandary, and we both try to find another solution. Her boyfriend goes off to see if he can find somewhere else for me, and after several hours he comes back and says he's found a room.

It's nearby and is a room like the ones in the boardinghouses but with a bigger, nicer bed. Apart from that, it's empty. When we go to see it, we're immediately surrounded by a group of women and children. I take it.

The days drag by slowly. Mealtimes are the only real pleasure. Sophia is a fantastic cook. I'm putting on weight by the day. The nights, however, are awful. There's music or chatter from every direction until early morning, and the room is so poorly soundproofed that you would think you were in the same room as the neighbors. It's torture getting to sleep every night.

Sometimes the noise is so bad I could scream myself, but I don't want to lose the room. Each morning I wash in the room and wash my clothes every other day, so that I have a clean change. Sophia argues so much with her boyfriend that I make myself scarce rapidly after each meal. But my belly is growing steadily, and I'm very proud.

By the end of a week my husband still hasn't been to see me once, which makes me sad. But I've met James with other boys in the village, and sometimes Sali, Sophia's boyfriend, brings work colleagues to dinner and then we play cards, which passes the time pleasantly.

One evening four of us are sitting there in the apartment playing cards—we usually leave the door open so as to have more light—and suddenly my husband's standing there in the doorway with his spears. But before I can get up to welcome him he's asking who the other man is. Everyone laughs except for me. Sophia tells him to come in, but he stays there in the doorway and asks me brusquely, "Corinne, is this your boyfriend?" I'm deeply embarrassed by his behavior. Sophia tries to defuse the situation, but my husband just turns on his heel and leaves. Slowly my astonishment gives way to anger. I'm sitting here, nine months pregnant, and see my husband for the first time in two and a half weeks, and he accuses me of having a lover!

Sali goes off to find him while Sophia tries to calm me down. Their friend has made his excuses. When nothing happens I go off to wait in my room. Lketinga turns up later—he's been drinking and he's chewing *miraa*. I'm lying flat on the bed worrying about our future. Then after an hour, he finally actually apologizes: "Corinne, my wife, no problem. Long time I have not seen you and the baby, so I become crazy. Please, Corinne, now I am okay, no problem!" I try to smile and forgive him. The next night he goes home once more, and for the next two weeks I get a few messages but don't see him again.

At last the day arrives when Sophia and I have to go into the hospital. She's due in a week's time, and I've less than two to go. We're advised to set off in plenty of time because of the bad state of the roads. We're excited as we get into the bus. Sophia's boyfriend comes with us.

In the hospital we get to share a room; it's wonderful. The nurses are relieved when they weigh me and find that indeed I've nearly reached one hundred and fifty pounds. I spend almost every day knitting for the baby while Sophia spends her time reading books about pregnancy and birth. I don't want to know anything about it; it can all come as a surprise. Sali fetches good food for us from the village.

Time drags again. Every day babies are coming into the world. We can hear the mothers even from our room, and Sophia's getting increasingly nervous. She must be due any day now. During the daily examinations they discover that my uterus has already begun to dilate, and so I'm ordered to stay in bed. But it doesn't get that far because no sooner has the doctor left the room than my water breaks. I look over at Sophia in surprise and delight and say: "I think my baby is coming!" She doesn't believe it because I'm not due for another week. Sophia calls the doctor back and when she sees what happened, she confirms, with a serious look on her face, that my baby will be born that night.

Napirai

Sophia is confused because nothing's happened with her. By eight P.M. I'm having my first contractions, and within two hours they've become vigorous. From now on I get an examination every half hour. By midnight it's almost unbearable. The pain makes me vomit repeatedly. Eventually I'm taken into the birthing room. It's the same room in which I sat in the gynecological stirrups for my earlier examination. The female doctor and two black nurses try to calm me down, but somehow I've lost all my English. In between contractions I stare at the women and see only their mouths opening and closing. I start to panic because I'm not sure if I'm doing everything properly. Breathe, breathe deep, keeps going through my head. Then they tie my legs to the stirrups. I feel helpless, out of control. Even when I want to cry out that I can't take it anymore, the nurse puts her hand over my mouth. I stare at the doctor in fear, and at that moment I hear them say they can already see the baby's head. With the next contraction it'll be out. I push with the last of my strength, and it's as if there's an explosion in my lower body. My little girl has been born. It's one-fifteen A.M., and a healthy six-and-a-half-pound girl has come into the world. I'm ecstatic. She is as beautiful as her father, and we'll call her Napirai.

While the doctor is still dealing with the afterbirth, the door opens and Sophia throws herself into my arms. She watched the birth through the window. They show my baby to me again and then take her off to be with the other newborns. I'm happy enough about that because right now I'm too weak to hold her. I can't even hold the cup of tea I'm offered. They put me in a wheelchair and bring me back to our room and give me a sleeping pill.

I wake up at five A.M. with terrible pains between my legs and wake Sophia, who gets up immediately and goes to fetch the night nurse. They calm me down with painkillers. At eight o'clock I drag myself to the nursery to see my baby. I'm relieved when I finally find her, but she's screaming with hunger. I have to do something to comfort her, but that's not so easy. My breasts may have grown enormous, but there's not a drop to be had from them. Trying to express milk doesn't work either, and by evening I can't stand it: my breasts are as hard as rocks and hurt; and the whole time Napirai is crying incessantly. One of the black nurses tells me I ought to work harder to get the milk glands to open, or I'll get an infection. In extreme pain I try everything. Two Samburu women come along and "milk" my breasts for nearly half an hour before at long last my milk starts to flow. And then it won't stop! There's far more than my baby can drink. Not until midafternoon does everything seem to work properly.

Meanwhile Sophia's contractions began hours ago, but there's no sign of the baby. She's screaming and crying and demanding a cesarean, but the doctor won't do one because it's not necessary. I've never seen or heard Sophia use language like she does then. The doctor finds it a bit too much and tells her to control herself or he won't carry out the delivery. The examination takes place in Italian because he's from Italy. After a terrible thirty-six hours and the use of a vacuum extractor, her daughter too is born.

The same evening, just as visiting time ends, my darling turns up. He had heard about the birth in the morning via the regular radio contact and immediately set out for Wamba on foot. He's painted himself specially and had his hair done and greets me with joy. He's brought meat and a wonderful dress for me and wants to see Napirai right away. But the nurses tell him that he's too late and he has to come back tomorrow. Although he's disappointed, he beams at me proudly and happily, which gives me some hope again. Because he has to leave the hospital he decides to spend the night in Wamba, and he is there for the first visiting time in the morning. He comes into the room laden with little presents, just as I'm feeding Napirai. He lifts his daughter devotedly in his arms and carries her into the sunshine. She looks at him with curiosity, and he can't let her go. It's been ages since I've seen him so happy, and it reassures me that everything will be fine again.

The first few days with the baby are tiring. I'm still very weak and don't weigh enough and I have stitches in my vagina, which hurt when I sit down. My little girl wakes up two or three times a night either because she wants the breast or needs to be changed. As soon as she goes to sleep Sophia's baby starts crying. They use cloth diapers here, and the babies are washed in little basins. I'm not very good at diaper changing, and I don't dare put the things I've knitted on her for fear of breaking her arm or leg. So she lies there on her baby blanket naked except for the diaper, while my husband looks at us and says with obvious satisfaction, "She is looking like me!"

He comes to see us every day, but he's starting to get impatient. He wants to take his family home. But I'm still too weak and am a bit worried about being on my own with the baby. Washing diapers, cooking, fetching wood, and maybe working in the shop again are unimaginable. The shop has been closed for three weeks now because there's only maize flour left, and, according to Lketinga, the boy no longer seems so reliable.

Apart from anything else there's no transport; he had to walk here because there are problems yet again with our car. This time Giuliani's worked out that it's the transmission. So first of all he'll have to get back home to see if the Land Rover has been fixed before he can come to fetch us.

That at least gives me a bit more time. The doctor is pleased too that I can stay for a few more days. Sophia, on the other hand, is leaving the hospital just five days after giving birth and on her way back to Maralal. After a further three days my husband comes back in the fixed car. I really don't know what we'd do without Father Giuliani. I'm ready to leave Wamba because since Sophia left, an old-looking, emaciated woman having her tenth child, and premature at that, died the same night from weakness and anemia. It simply wasn't possible to get in touch with her family to find a suitable blood donor. The events of that night took so much out of me that I'm now desperate to leave.

The new father stands proudly at reception with his new daughter in his arms while I settle the bill. The twenty-two days in the hospital, including the baby's delivery, cost a mere eighty Swiss francs—I can hardly believe it. On the other hand, I have to delve somewhat deeper into my pocket for the air ambulance, which costs eight hundred francs. But what's that, against both our lives!

For the first time in ages I'm back behind the wheel while my husband holds Napirai. But after barely a hundred yards the baby's screaming because of the awful noise the car makes. Lketinga tries to calm her down by singing, but it's no good. So he drives, and I hold Napirai to my breast as well as I can. One way or another we get to Maralal before evening. I need diapers, some clothes, and baby blankets. We want to buy food too, because there's been nothing in Barsaloi for weeks now. There's no alternative but to stay in the boardinghouse. Just to find a dozen diapers, I have to search the whole of Maralal, while Lketinga looks after our daughter.

The first night out of the hospital isn't very comfortable. I have difficulty in changing Napirai because it's so cold in Maralal at night, and I'm not so good at breast-feeding in the dark either. The next morning I'm tired and I've got a runny nose already. Half of the diapers are already used, so I wash them here. By midday the car is loaded up with food, and we set off. There's no question of taking the jungle route this time. But my husband believes it's raining up in the mountains toward Baragoi and there's a risk of the rivers filling up and becoming impassable. So we decide to take the road back via Wamba in order to approach Barsaloi from the other direction. We take turns at driving, as Lketinga can handle the car well now; he drives too fast into large potholes only occasionally. Napirai doesn't like the car at all. She cries continuously and only quiets down when the car stops, so we take frequent breaks.

Homecoming for Three

Along the road Lketinga picks up two warriors, and after more than five hours we get to the great Wamba River. It's notorious for quicksand that becomes active at the slightest drop of water. The Mission lost a car here years ago. I stop in stunned amazement at the steep slope down to the river—and there's water in it! Unperturbed, the Masai get out and stroll down to the river. The water's not deep, no more than an inch or so, and a few sandbanks protrude here and there. But Father Giuliani expressly warned me to avoid the river if there's any water at all. And it's nearly five hundred feet wide. I'm sitting at the wheel of the car, thinking disappointedly that we'll have to go back to Wamba. One of the warriors has already sunk in as far as his knees, although the other, just a yard away from him, has no problem. Lketinga tests it too, but he keeps sinking. I think the whole thing is awful, and I've no intention of risking it. I climb out to tell my husband just that. But he comes toward me with a mad sudden decisiveness, takes Napirai from me, and tells me to drive at full speed between the two warriors. I try desperately to put him off the idea, but he won't see my argument—he wants to go home, and if he can't go with the car, then he'll go on foot. But I can't drive back on my own with the baby.

The river is slowly building up, and I refuse to drive. Now he gets furious, pushes Napirai into my arms, and wants to drive himself. He insists I give him the ignition key, but I don't have it and think with some reason that it's in the car, seeing as the engine's running. "No, Corinne, please give me the key, you have driven the car, now you have taken it that we go back to Wamba!" he says angrily, his dark eyes sparkling maliciously.

I go to the car to show him, but ironically it turns out that the engine is running without the key in. Feverishly I search the seats and the ground but the key—the only one we have—is missing.

Lketinga blames me. Furiously he climbs into the car, engages the four-wheel drive, and roars into the river. It's all too crazy for me; I burst into tears, and Napirai starts crying at the top of her voice. The car is getting stuck in the river. The first few yards are fine, the tires sinking just a little, but the farther he drives the slower he goes, and the back wheels slowly sink under the heavy weight. Just a few yards from a dry sandbank the car threatens to come to a stop, the wheels spinning uselessly. I'm crying and praying and cursing all at once. The two warriors splash their way to the car, lift it and push, and actually do manage the last six feet. The wheels grip again, and with a flourish he shoots across the other half of the river. My husband has managed it brilliantly, but I'm anything but proud: he risked everything far too carelessly, and in any case we still don't have the key.

One of the warriors comes back and helps me across the river. I sink up to my knees in places. Lketinga's standing there proudly and defiantly next to the car and demands I now hand over the key. "I don't have it!" I shout at him in despair. I go over to the car and search all over again, in vain. Disbelievingly Lketinga shakes his head and goes to search himself. In a couple of seconds he has it in his hand—it had fallen between the seat and the backrest and got stuck. How it could have happened is a mystery to me. But he's convinced I hid it from him because I didn't want to drive across the river. We drive home in silence.

When we finally get to Barsaloi, it's already dark. Of course we go first of all to see Mama in the *manyatta*, and my God she's delighted to see us. Immediately she takes Napirai and blesses her—wiping spittle on her forehead, the palms of her hand, and the soles of her feet—and prays to Enkai. She says something to me too, but I don't understand. The smoke is causing me problems, and Napirai is coughing too. Even so we will spend the first night here with her.

The next morning several people come to see the baby, but Mama says that in the first weeks I shouldn't show the baby to anybody but those she permits. I don't understand this and ask her, "Why? She's so pretty!" Lketinga mutters and says I shouldn't say she's pretty because it'll bring bad luck. Strangers shouldn't be allowed to see her in case they wish evil on her. In Switzerland we show off our babies proudly; here I have to hide mine away or if I take her out I have to cover her head with a kanga. I find it hard.

I spend three days sitting with my baby in the dark *manyatta* while Mama keeps guard on the door. My husband is preparing a party to celebrate the birth of his daughter. An ox has to be slaughtered. Several of the elders come, eat the meat, and bless our daughter for it. I get the best pieces to build up my strength.

In the evening the warriors dance with my husband in his honor, and of course afterward they have to be fed and watered. Mama has brewed me up a horrid-smelling liquid that is supposed to protect me from any more illness. Everyone watches while I drink it, and they pray to Enkai for me. I feel ill after the first sip and try to tip away as much as I can when no one's looking.

The vet and his wife turn up at the party, which pleases me. To my surprise I find out that the wooden house next to theirs has become free, and I look forward to the possibility of having a new house with two rooms and a toilet inside. The next day we move out of the shop into the wooden house, just five hundred feet away. First I have to give it a good cleaning. In the meantime Mama watches the baby outside, keeping her covered with a kanga so cleverly that you'd hardly know she was there.

People keep coming into the shop, looking for things to buy. It looks empty and dilapidated. The credit book is almost full, but there's not enough cash in the till to pay for another truckload. But for now I can't work and don't want to, so it can stay closed.

Each day I'm busy until noon washing the previous day's diapers. My knuckles have become completely raw. I can't go on with this and look for a girl who can help me with the housework and above all the washing, so I have more time for Napirai and cooking. Lketinga fixes things with a former schoolgirl. For thirty Swiss francs a month plus food she's prepared to fetch water and do the washing. Now at last I can enjoy my daughter. She is so pretty and happy and hardly ever cries. Even my husband can spend hours lying on the ground with her under the tree outside the house.

Slowly I get my routine under control. The girl is a slow worker, and I don't easily get on with her. I notice that our washing powder is disappearing fast, and our stocks of rice and sugar too. When Napirai starts screaming every time her diaper is changed and I discover that she's red and raw between the legs, I've had enough. I tell the girl that she has to rinse the diapers until there's no trace of the Omo left. She pays no attention and then says that she's not paid enough to fetch water more than once a day. I send her home in annoyance; I'd rather do the washing myself.

Hunger

People get impatient when they're hungry. For more than a month the shops have been empty, but every day people come to our house to ask us when we're going to open up again. For the moment, however, I don't see how I can go back to work. I'd have to go to Maralal and organize a truck. I'm afraid that in our car I'd get stuck somewhere with the baby. The transmission has only been patched up, the ignition lock is wrecked, and there's a lot of other work that needs doing.

One day the little boss man comes to us complaining that people are hungry. He knows there are still a few sacks of maize meal in the shop and asks us at least to sell these. Reluctantly I go into the shop to count the sacks. My husband comes with me but when we open the first sack I'm almost sick. The top is covered with fat white maggots with little black beetles scurrying amid them. We open the other sacks, and it's the same story every time. The boss man roots around in the sack and says it's not so bad beneath the top layer. But I refuse to sell it in that state.

In the meantime, however, people seem to have got wind of the fact that we have meal, and there are more and more women in the shop willing to buy it. We talk it over, and I offer just to give it away. The boss man says no because before long we'd have people committing murder; the best thing is to sell it cheap. By now there are fifty or more people outside with cloth and plastic bags. I can't face putting my hands into these sacks and having the maggots crawl over them. And in any case, I'm holding Napirai. I set off to fetch Lketinga's big brother from Mama's. He's there and comes back with me. I give Napirai to Mama. We're just in time. Lketinga is serving, but the little boss has to stop people from storming

the shop. Each person is allowed a maximum of six and a half pounds. I
put the weights on the scales and take the money, while the two men dole
out the unappetizing maize meal. We work like mad and are glad that the
boss man somehow manages to keep order. By eight P.M. all the sacks have
been sold and we're exhausted, but at least there's some money in the till
again.

Selling the meal and realizing how necessary our shop has become
occupy my thoughts a lot that evening. But I don't have much time before
I've got to get back home to my baby. Worried, I hurry to the *manyattas*
in the dark. For more than six hours now my baby hasn't had any breast
milk, and I'm expecting to find her in total despair. But when I get closer
to the *manyatta* I don't hear a chirp from her, just the sound of Mama
singing. I creep in and am amazed to see my baby sucking on Mama's big,
long, black breast. I can only stare in astonishment. Mama laughs and holds
out my naked baby to me. When Napirai hears my voice she cries out
immediately, wanting my breast, but I'm amazed that Mama could keep
her quiet for so long with her empty breast.

A little later my husband turns up, and I tell him about it. He laughs
and says it's normal here. Even Saguna did the same thing as a little baby,
because it's usual. The sons' first baby is given to their mother as
housemaid. I look at my baby and, even though she's filthy and stinks of
smoke, I'm quite content, although I know that I'd never hand her over
to anyone.

We drink chai with Mama and then go back to our house. Lketinga
carries Napirai proudly. The little boss is waiting at the door. Of course I
have to make tea for him too, even though I don't want to. Suddenly
Lketinga gets up, takes two hundred shillings from our box of money, and
hands it to the chief. I don't know why but say nothing. After he leaves I
learn that he demanded the money for his crowd-control work. I'm
annoyed by that because he forced us into it all. He was determined we
should open the shop, and it was his duty to keep order; that's what the
government pays him for. I try gently to tell this to Lketinga and am
pleased to note that he agrees with me and is cross too.

After that the shop stays closed. The boy who Lketinga brought into
the shop comes by often. He doesn't pay any attention to me, which
annoys me, but from his conversations with Lketinga I gather he's after
something. My husband dismisses it, saying he's demanding his last lot of

wages, which he's already been paid. I keep out of it; I was in Maralal and at the hospital and know nothing about it.

Life goes on quietly, and Napirai grows into a proper little infant. I'm still not supposed to show her to strangers, and when anyone comes near, Lketinga hides her head under the baby blanket, which she hates.

One day we're on our way back from the river and are about to go to the teahouse when an old man comes up to Lketinga. There's the usual conversation, then Lketinga tells me to wait and he goes over to the little police post. There I see the proper chief officer, the game warden, and the boy from the shop. From a distance I watch the conversation with growing concern. Napirai is asleep in a kanga at my side. When Lketinga hasn't come back after fifteen minutes, I amble over to the men.

There's something up, I can tell from my husband's expression. He's furious, and there's an argument going on while the boy just looks off casually to one side. I keep hearing the words *"duka"* and "shop." I know the chief speaks English, and I ask him what's going on. I get no answer; instead, everyone shakes hands, and Lketinga steals away in a bad mood. In a couple of paces I'm alongside him and grab him by the shoulder to find out what's happened. He turns around to me wearily and says he has to give the boy five goats for his work in the shop or else the boy's father will report him to the police, and he doesn't want to go to jail. I've no idea what this is all about.

I ask my husband forcefully whether the boy got his pay every month or not. "Yes, Corinne, I don't know why they want five goats, but I don't want to go again in prison. I'm a good man. The father of this boy is a big man!" I believe Lketinga did pay the money. To threaten him with prison for absolutely nothing is really the last straw, particularly when this boy is the cause of it. In a furious temper I rush back to him and shout: "What do you want from me?" "From you nothing, only from your husband." He smiles at me stupidly. I can't take it anymore and lash out at him with hand and foot. He tries to dodge me, but I grab his shirt and pull him over, cursing at him in German and spitting.

The men standing around restrain me, and Napirai starts screaming her head off. Meanwhile Lketinga has come over and says angrily: "Corinne, you are crazy, go home." "I'm not crazy, really not crazy, but if you give goats to this boy, I don't open again this shop!" The boy's father has to restrain him to stop him attacking me. Furiously I tear myself free and run back to the house with Napirai howling all the way. I don't understand my husband, why he lets himself be cowed like this, and I don't understand the chief either. From now on I'm going to take the money myself for every handful we sell. Nobody will get a lift in the car unless they've paid first. People stare at me as I rush past, but I couldn't care less. I'm aware that I've deeply offended the boy and his father because here it's men who beat women, not the other way around.

Before long Lketinga and the chief appear at the house. They immediately demand to know why I did what I did. My man is upset and horrified, which makes me even angrier. I produce our credit book and lay it on the table so the chief can see how many thousands of shillings we're out because of the boy. And the boy himself owes us three hundred shillings. And now he's demanding five goats, the equivalent of half a year's pay. At this point even the chief frowns and apologizes for his ruling, but we'll have to sort it out with the old man because Lketinga has already accepted the verdict with his handshake.

Out of politeness I'm obliged to make chai for the chief. I light the charcoal in our little stove and set it outside so that the air can get the coals glowing more quickly. It's a clear starry night, and I'm just about to go back into the house when I see a figure holding something shiny. Immediately I sense danger and go back into the house to tell my husband. He goes out with me close behind him. The chief stays in our hut. I hear Lketinga ask who's there and shortly afterward recognize the voice and the figure of the boy with a machete in his hand. Angrily I ask him what he's doing here. He says brusquely he's here to settle accounts with the *"mzungu."* Immediately I rush into the house and ask the chief if he's heard. He nods and comes out too.

The boy is shocked and goes to run away, but Lketinga holds on to him and takes the dangerous machete away from him. I look at the chief triumphantly: now he's witnessed an attempted murder. He should arrest him, and tomorrow we'll all drive to Maralal. I don't want this idiot danger to the community around us anymore. The chief goes off with the boy. My husband disappears too, and for the first time I lock and bolt the house door.

A bit later there's a knock, and after cautious questioning I open it to see the vet. He'd heard the noise and wants to know what happened. I offer him chai and tell him. He says what I want is right and offers to help me. He says he never understood why we let this crazy kid work for us in the first place because his father's already had to get him out of more than one tight spot. While we're talking, my husband comes home. He's somewhat taken aback and looks at me and then the vet. The vet starts to talk to him, and I say good night and creep under the mosquito net to Napirai.

I can't get the incident out of my head and find it hard to get to sleep. A bit later Lketinga comes to bed too and tries to make love to me, but I'm not in the mood and Napirai is lying between us. He simply wants sex. We make an attempt, but it just hurts me, and in extreme pain I push him away and ask him to have a bit of patience. Lketinga doesn't understand me and accuses me angrily of having just done it with the vet. When he hurls that at me, I've really had enough for one day. After everything that's happened, for him to throw that one is too much, and right now I can't stand the sight of him. So he finds somewhere to sleep in the front room. During the night I have to feed Napirai two or three times and then change her diaper.

At six in the morning, when the baby's already demanding attention again, there's a knock on the door. It must be the chief, but after my row with Lketinga I'm not in the mood to drive to Maralal. Lketinga opens the door to find the boy's father standing there with the chief. While I'm putting on my skirt they start arguing. Half an hour later my husband and the chief come into the house. The men almost make me feel sorry for them. The chief gives me an apology from the boy and his father and says that if we don't go to Maralal, the father will give us five goats. I respond that that won't mean I'm out of danger; perhaps he'll try again tomorrow or the day after, whereas in Maralal he'll be put behind bars for two or three years.

The chief tells the old man my fears, and he promises to take the boy away to relatives for a while. He agrees to my insistence that his son never come closer than five hundred feet to our house. After the chief has given me this assurance in writing I agree, and Lketinga goes with the old men to fetch the goats before they leave the corral for the day.

I'm pleased he's gone, and in the afternoon I go up to the Mission to show them my daughter. Father Giuliani hasn't seen her since Wamba, and Father Roberto doesn't know her at all. Both of them are pleased to see me, and Father Giuliani is really entranced by my pretty little girl, who stares curiously at his white face. When he hears that my husband has gone off, he invites me to stay for lunch. They feed me homemade pasta and salad. How long has it been since I've had a salad? It's like being transported to heaven. Over the meal, Giuliani tells me that he's about to leave for three months' holiday in Italy. I'm happy for him but not so happy to lose him for three months, especially when I think how many times he's rescued me from the brink of disaster!

We've just finished eating when my husband turns up. Immediately there's tension in the air: "Corinne, why do you eat here and not wait for me at home?" He takes Napirai from me and leaves. I quickly thank the missionaries and hurry after Lketinga and the baby. Napirai is crying. When we get home, he gives me the baby and asks: "What do you have made with my baby, now she cries only when she comes to me!" Instead of answering, I ask him why he's back so quickly. "Because I know you go to other men if I'm not here!" Furious that he keeps making such allegations, I curse and call him crazy. "What do you tell me? I'm crazy? You tell your husband he is crazy? I don't want see you again." And with that he gathers up his spears and leaves the house. I'm left sitting there like a statue, incapable of understanding why he keeps suspecting me of having affairs. Just because we haven't had sex for a long time? I can't help that I was sick and then in Maralal for so long. In any case the Samburus don't have sex during pregnancy.

Our love has already taken a few knocks, and it can't go on like this. I pick up Napirai in despair and go off to Mama. I try as best I can to explain the situation to her, tears rolling down my face. She doesn't say much, just that it's normal for men to be jealous. I shouldn't pay any attention. This is hardly the advice I wanted to hear, and I sob even more. Now she gets cross with me and says there's no reason to cry, it's not as if he's beaten me. There's no sympathy for me here, and so I go back home again.

That evening my neighbor, the vet's wife, looks in. She seems to have got wind of our row. We make chai and chat hesitantly. The warriors are all very jealous, she says, but that doesn't mean I should call my husband crazy. That's dangerous.

When she leaves, I feel very alone with Napirai. I've eaten nothing since lunchtime yesterday, but at least I've an abundance of milk for the baby. I'm slowly beginning to worry that he really has left me. The next

morning I feel miserable and can hardly get out of bed. My neighbor
drops in again around lunch, and when she sees I'm in a bad way, she looks
after Napirai and washes all the diapers. Then she fetches meat and with
the last of my rice cooks me a meal. I'm moved by her gesture. This is the
first friendship in which it's not me, the *"mzungu,"* on the giving end, but
a friend helping me without being asked. She's already eaten, she says, and
won't have anything. When she's finished all my chores, she goes home to
start on her own.

Lketinga comes home in the evening and inspects all the rooms
without even saying hello. I try to behave as normally as possible and offer
him dinner, which he actually accepts: a sign that he's staying. I'm pleased
and build up my hopes again. But it's not to be.

Quarantine

Around nine P.M. I develop terrible stomach cramps. I lie in bed with my knees pulled up under my chin to make it just about bearable. But like that Napirai can't feed. She's with her papa, crying. This time he shows a bit of patience and walks up and down with her for hours singing, but she only quiets down for a bit and then starts up again. By midnight I feel so ill that I have to be sick. The whole meal comes up undigested. I vomit and vomit until there's nothing left, just yellow bile. The floor is covered in it, but I feel too bad to clean it up. I'm cold and sure I've got a temperature.

Lketinga starts worrying and goes to fetch our next-door neighbor, even though it's late. Before long she's with me and cleans up the whole mess as if it's no problem. She asks me worriedly if I might have malaria again. I don't know and hope I won't have to go back into the hospital so soon. The stomach pains ease off a bit, and I can stretch out my legs again. Now I can feed Napirai at least.

The neighbor goes home, and my husband sleeps next to our bed on a second mattress. The next morning I'm not so bad and drink chai, which Lketinga's made. But in less than half an hour the tea erupts uncontrollably from my mouth like a fountain. At the same time the stomach cramps start again, so fiercely that I have to squat down on the floor with my knees pulled up. After a while my stomach calms down again, and I start to wash the baby and her diapers. Before long I'm exhausted, even though for the moment I have neither a temperature nor cramps. Nor do I have the typical shivering fit, and I think it probably isn't malaria but some sort of tummy bug.

For the next two days every attempt to eat or drink anything is useless. The pains come more frequently and last longer. My breasts start to shrink because I can't keep any food down. The fourth day I'm totally exhausted and can't even get up. My friend from next door comes every day to help out, but I still have to breast-feed the baby.

Today Mama arrives because Lketinga's been to fetch her. She feels around my stomach, causing terrible pains. Then she looks into my eyes. They're yellow, and my face has gone a funny color. She wants to know what I've eaten. But I've hardly had anything but water for several days. Napirai's crying and wants to be fed, but I can't manage. I can't even hold her because I can't sit up. Mama holds her to my loose breast, but I doubt that I've got enough milk and worry about how else my little girl is going to get fed. Because Mama doesn't know what to make of my illness either, we decide to go to Wamba.

Lketinga drives, while my friend holds Napirai. I'm too weak. Of course we get a puncture en route. It's unbelievable; I hate this car. With enormous effort I find myself some shade and feed Napirai while the other two carry out the tire change. We get to Wamba late in the afternoon. I drag myself to the hospital reception and ask to see the Swiss doctor. An hour passes, and then the Italian doctor arrives. He asks what's wrong with me and takes a blood sample. After a while they tell us that it's not malaria. Tomorrow we'll know more. Napirai will stay with me, while my friend and Lketinga drive back to Barsaloi, somewhat relieved.

We're brought into the maternity unit again so that Napirai can sleep in a cot next to me. But because she's not used to sleeping apart from me, she cries continuously until a nurse comes and puts her in my arms. Immediately she suckles herself to sleep. The next morning the female Swiss doctor turns up at last, but she is not pleased to see me and the child back again in such a state.

After an examination she gives her diagnosis: hepatitis. At first I don't understand what that means. She explains it to me worriedly: a type of jaundice, or to be more precise a liver infection, which is also contagious. My liver can't process food anymore. The pains are brought on when I eat the tiniest amount of fat. From now on I'll have to follow a strict diet, have complete rest, and go into quarantine. Fighting back the tears, I ask her how long it'll last. She looks at Napirai and me with sympathy and says: "Six weeks at least." Then the contagious period will be over, but I'll still be far from cured. They'll also have to carry out tests on Napirai. I've almost certainly infected her. Now I can't hold back the tears. The good doctor tries to console me, saying it's not certain yet that Napirai's been infected. But my husband too will have to be tested as soon as possible.

My head is swimming with all this depressing news. Two black sisters bring a wheelchair, and I'm taken into a completely different section of the hospital. I'm given a room with a toilet that has a glass wall but no door. The room can't be opened from the inside. There's a slot in the door that is used for passing meals in and out. It's a new wing and the room looks nice, but I feel like a prisoner.

Our things are all taken away to be disinfected, and once again I'm dressed in a hospital gown. Then they examine Napirai, who squeals like a stuck pig when they take a blood sample. I feel desperately sorry for her; she's so small, barely six weeks old, and has to suffer so much. I'm attached to an IV and get a jug of water sweetened with a pound of sugar. I'm to drink lots of sugared water because that's the quickest way for the liver to heal itself. Then I need rest, absolute rest. That's all that can be done for me. They take my baby away, and I cry myself to sleep in misery.

I wake up to bright sunshine but with no idea what time it is. The deathly silence scares me. There's absolutely nothing to be heard, and if I want contact with the outside world I have to ring a bell. Then a sister appears on the other side of the glass wall and speaks to me through the perforated opening. I want to know how Napirai is. She goes to fetch the doctor. Minutes pass, but they seem like hours to me in this silence. Then the doctor comes into my room. I'm shocked and ask if she won't be infected. She laughs and says: "Hepatitis once, but never again!" She had the disease herself years ago.

Then at last I get good news. Napirai is completely healthy, but she won't drink either cow's milk or powdered milk. With a shaking voice I ask if I really won't be able to hold her for a whole six weeks. The doctor says that if she really won't take any other form of food, then for better or worse I'll have to feed her, although the risk of infection is enormous. It's a miracle as it is that she hasn't been infected.

Around five P.M. I get my first meal—rice with boiled cabbage and a tomato. I eat slowly and manage this time to hold down my little ration. The pains resume but not so strongly. They bring Napirai to the glass twice to see me. My little girl is crying, and her stomach is caved in.

At lunch the next day the despairing sisters bring me my little brown bundle. I'm enveloped by an aura of happiness I haven't known for ages. She reaches hungrily for my breast and soon calms down as she starts sucking. Looking at Napirai, I realize that I need her if I'm to have the rest I need and find the strength to withstand this long isolation. She looks up at me with her big dark eyes as she's feeding, and I have to pull myself away in case I hug her too tightly. When the doctor looks in later, she says: "I see you two need each other, whether it's to get healthy or to stay healthy!" At last I can smile again and promise to do my best.

Every day I have to force down three or four pints of extremely sweet water, which almost makes me throw up. Because I'm allowed salt now my food tastes better. For breakfast I get tea and a sort of crisp bread with a tomato or piece of fruit; for lunch and dinner it's always the same: rice with or without boiled cabbage. Every third day they take blood and urine samples, and after a week I feel a bit better although still very weak.

Two weeks later, though, the next blow comes. From the urine samples they've determined that my kidneys are no longer functioning properly. It's true that I had a backache, but I'd put that down to continually lying down. Now I no longer get salt in my bland food, and I have a catheter inserted to collect my urine, which is painful. Every day I have to write down how much I drink, and the nurse compares it with the collection bottle to see how much comes out again. I'd just got enough strength to take a few steps, and now I'm tied down to the bed again. At least Napirai is with me. Without her I'd have no will left to live. She must sense that I'm doing okay because since she's been back with me she hasn't been crying anymore.

Two days after I was brought in my husband came to be tested. He was healthy and hasn't been back in the past ten days. I wasn't exactly a pretty sight, and we couldn't talk to each other. He stood there sadly in front of the glass panel for half an hour and then left. From time to time he sends me his best wishes. He misses us a lot and to kill the time spends most of it out with his herds, they tell me. Since they've heard in Wamba that there's a *mzungu* in the hospital, strangers keep coming to see me, standing on the other side of the glass staring at me and the baby. It annoys me every time, and I pull the bedsheets over my head.

Time drags terribly, I either play with Napirai or read the paper. I've been here for two and a half weeks now and haven't felt the sun or a breath of wind the whole time. I even miss the chirping of the cicadas and the singing of the birds. I'm slowly falling into depression. I think over my life and am quite clear that I'm homesick for Barsaloi and its inhabitants.

It's nearly visiting time again, and I hide under the sheet when the nurse says I have visitors. I peer out and see my husband and another warrior in front of the glass. He's beaming happily at Napirai and me. For a moment his handsome, happy appearance gives me a high I haven't felt for ages. How I'd love to go over to him, touch him, and say, "Darling, no problem, everything becomes okay." Instead I hold Napirai so he can see his daughter from the front and point her papa out to her. She stamps up and down and waves her fat little arms and legs. When some strangers again try to peer through the glass, my husband shoos them all away. I have to laugh, and he and his friend laugh too. His painted face is glistening in the sunshine. Oh, despite everything, I still love him. Then visiting time is over, and we wave to each other. My husband's visit has given me the strength to get a grip on myself mentally.

At the end of the third week they remove the catheter for my urine, as the readings are now significantly better. At last I can wash properly, even take a shower. When the doctor comes around she's amazed how pretty I've made myself. I've tied my hair up in a ponytail with a red ribbon and put lipstick on. I feel like a new woman. When she reveals to me that in a week's time I'll be able to go outside for fifteen minutes, I'm delighted and start counting the days.

The fourth week is finally over, and I'm allowed out of my cage with my daughter in a kanga on my back. The tropical air almost takes my breath away, and I inhale it greedily. After a month away from it all I now realize more than ever how wonderful the birdsong is and how good the red bushes smell. I could shout aloud with joy.

Because I'm not allowed out of the section, I wander past the other glass windows. The scenes behind them are terrible. Almost all the children have deformities. Sometimes there are up to four beds in one room. There are misshapen heads and bodies, children with spina bifida or clubfeet, children missing arms or legs. The third window gives me a shock: lying there quite still is the body of a tiny baby with a huge head that looks ready to explode. Only the lips are moving; it's probably crying. I can't take the sight any longer and go back to my room. I'm distraught. I've never seen so many deformities before. I realize how lucky I am to have the baby I have.

When the doctor comes to me, I ask her why these children are still alive. She tells me that in a missionary hospital there is no such thing as euthanasia. These children have mostly been left outside the door and are simply waiting to die. The thought makes me miserable, and I wonder if I'll ever have a good night's sleep again. The doctor suggests that tomorrow I take a walk on the other side of the section, away from the windows, to avoid seeing them. As it happens there's a lawn and pretty trees there, and we're allowed to stay outside for half an hour. I walk through the greenery with Napirai, singing, which makes her happy because every now and then she joins in with a noise of her own.

But before long morbid curiosity draws me back to the abandoned children. Now that I'm prepared for the sight, it's not so shocking. A few of them are aware of someone looking at them. When I'm on my way back to my room, I notice the door to the room with four beds is open. The black nurse who's changing the children calls to me, and hesitantly I go up to the door. She shows me how the children react differently when she speaks to them or laughs. I'm astonished how happily these children can react. I'm relieved and at the same time ashamed that I was questioning these creatures' right to life. They experience thirst and hunger, are conscious of both pain and happiness.

From that day on I go to each door in turn and sing the three songs that I remember from school. Within a few days I'm overwhelmed how happy they appear to be when they hear or recognize me. Even the baby with water on the brain stops whimpering when I sing my songs to him. At last I've found something that can reinforce my newfound lust for life.

One day I put Napirai in a child seat with wheels and push her backward and forward in the sunshine. She laughs happily as the wheels crunch over the path and the little cart bumps along. By now she's become the darling of the nurses. They all keep coming over to lift up the little light-brown baby. She's very patient with all of them and seems to enjoy the attention. All of a sudden my husband and his brother James appear, and Lketinga rushes over and lifts Napirai out of the little cart. Then he greets me too. I'm hugely pleased by such a surprise visit.

Napirai, however, is not so sure about her father's painted face and long red hair and soon begins to cry. Straightaway James goes over and starts speaking softly to her. He's enthralled by our baby too. Lketinga tries singing to her, but it's no good; she wants to come back to me. James takes her from him and immediately she quiets down. I put my arm around Lketinga to console him and try to explain that Napirai will have to get used to him again after five weeks in here. He asks exasperatedly when we're finally going to come home, and I promise to ask the doctor that evening and tell him to come back again tonight at visiting time.

When the doctor makes his afternoon rounds, he assures me that I should be able to leave the hospital in a week as long as I don't go back to work and stick to my diet. In three or four months' time I can start trying to eat a little bit of fat again. I can't believe what I'm hearing: I've got to make do with this diet of rice or potatoes boiled in water for another three to four months. My craving for milk and meat is already ravenous. That evening Lketinga and James turn up and bring me some lean cooked meat. I can't resist and eat a few tiny pieces, slowly and chewing thoroughly. Reluctantly I tell them to take the rest away, and we agree that they'll come back to fetch me in a week's time.

That night I have a fearful stomachache. My insides are on fire, as if the wall of my stomach is burning up. After half an hour I can't bear it anymore and call for the nurse. When she sees me curled up in bed, she fetches the doctor. He gives me a stern look and asks what I've been eating. In deep embarrassment, I'm forced to admit to eating five pieces of lean meat. That sends him into a temper, and he starts calling me a stupid cow. Why on earth did I come here if I'm not going to do what I'm told? He's played savior too long; I'm not his responsibility.

If the woman doctor hadn't come into the room, no doubt I'd have gotten worse. Even so I'm taken aback by his attack on me when up until now he'd always been so nice. Napirai starts crying, and I join in. The male doctor leaves, and his Swiss female colleague calms me down, apologizing on his behalf, saying he's overworked, hasn't had any holidays for years, and spends every single day battling to save lives, usually in vain. Still bent over with pain, I apologize too; I feel like a criminal. She goes too, and I'm left to suffer for the rest of the night.

I long to be out now. Eventually the big day comes. Napirai and I have already said our good-byes to most of the nurses and are waiting for Lketinga. He doesn't turn up until after midday, in the company of James, but his beaming smile is everything I hoped for. They had problems with the car on the way, he explains. The transmission still isn't working properly. Several times he couldn't get into gear, and now the car is in the missionary workshop in Wamba.

Nairobi and a New Car

James carries Napirai, and Lketinga takes my bag. Freedom at last! I pay for my stay at reception, and we go over to the Mission building. There's a mechanic lying under the Land Rover fiddling with various bits. He crawls out, covered in oil, and tells us that the transmission has nearly had it and that we can't use second gear anymore.

That's it, I tell myself. Now that I've got my health back and my baby, I'm not taking any more risks. I suggest to my husband that we go back to Maralal today and on to Nairobi tomorrow to buy a new car. James is immediately thrilled at the idea of going to Nairobi. We get to Maralal before dusk. The gears crunched all the way, but we made it safely to the boardinghouse. We'll leave the car here.

Five of us set off for Nairobi—James insisted on bringing a friend along so that he wouldn't have to spend the night in a room on his own. We're carrying the equivalent of twelve thousand Swiss francs, everything that we could muster from the shop and my account at present. How we're going to find a new car, I don't know yet. Kenya doesn't have any secondhand-car dealers, where you can just go and pick one up. Cars are hard to come by.

We get to the city around four P.M., and all we plan for the day is to find somewhere for us all to stay. The Igbol is full, so we try some of the cheaper places because I figure it's for only a night or two. We're in luck and find two rooms. First I have to wash and change Napirai. A basin serves to get the dust and dirt off my little girl. Of course, half the diapers are used up already, and there's no way of washing them. We grab something to eat and have an early night.

The next morning the question is: Where do we start? I try the telephone book in the vain hope of finding a secondhand-car dealer, but with no luck. Then I stop a taxi and ask the driver. He immediately wants to know if we've got the money on us. Sensibly I say no, because I want to find a suitable car first. He promises he'll ask around for us, and we agree to meet at the same place tomorrow. Even so I don't want to sit around doing nothing, so I ask three more taxi drivers, who just give us funny looks. There's nothing for it but to go back to the taxi stand as agreed the next day.

The driver is waiting there for us and says he knows a man who might have a Land Rover. We drive halfway across Nairobi and stop outside a little shop. I talk to the African, who indeed has three cars for sale, but unfortunately none with four-wheel drive. We can't see the cars either because he'll ring the current owner only when he's found a potential buyer. He says there's no way we're going to find a secondhand car that isn't still being used. Disappointedly I turn him down; we absolutely need a four-by-four. I ask him with little hope if he knows someone else. He makes a couple of phone calls and gives the taxi driver an address.

We drive to another district and stop in the city center near a shop. An Indian in a turban comes out to greet us in amazement, asking if we're the people who want to buy a car. "Yes" is my short answer. He asks us in to his office, where tea is served, and he tells us he has two on offer.

The first, a Land Rover, is far too expensive, and I start to lose hope again. Then he tells us about a five-year-old Datsun with twin seating areas, which we could have for fourteen thousand Swiss francs. But even that's way more than I've got, and in any case I've no idea what the car even looks like. He keeps on telling us how hard it is to find cars, but nonetheless we leave.

When we're out on the street, he comes after us, telling us to come by again tomorrow and he'll show us the car with no obligation. We agree, even though I've no intention of spending that much.

Once again we've nothing to do for the rest of the day. I buy some more diapers because all the ones we brought have been used. The dirty ones are piling up in the hotel room, which isn't exactly doing wonders for the atmosphere.

We go back to the Indian, even though I've no intention of buying from him. He greets us jovially and shows us the Datsun. There on the spot I'm suddenly ready to buy it as long as it drives. It looks comfortable and well looked after. The Indian suggests we take it for a test drive, but I decline in horror at the idea of losing my concentration in three-lane traffic, driving on the left. So we just try the engine. Everyone is in love with the car, but I'm worried about the price. We go into his office. When I tell him I have a Land Rover in Maralal, he's prepared to buy that from me for the equivalent of two thousand francs, which is a good deal. Even so, I'm reluctant to hand over twelve thousand francs, which is all the money we have, and we still have to get home. We're thinking it all over again when he offers to send a driver with us, who'll come as far as Maralal and drive our Land Rover back. All I have to do is give him the ten thousand francs and then hand his driver a check for the rest. At this point I'm surprised how trusting he is and impressed by the generous offer, given that Maralal is two hundred and eighty miles away.

On the spur of the moment I accept, particularly as it solves the problem of driving out of Nairobi. My husband and the lads are delighted when they hear that I've decided to buy the car. I pay up, and we write out a proper contract. The Indian tells us we're very brave to drive around Nairobi with so much cash. By tomorrow evening he'll have the car ready, along with its registration, which will have to be transferred into my name. That means spending another two nights in Nairobi! But the thought of having such a nice car leaves me in no doubt. We've done it and can return home with a magnificent vehicle.

The driver turns up as agreed at our hotel early on the morning of the second day. I check the papers and find my name really is on them. We load up with our bags, including God knows how many pounds of unwashed diapers. In our good-looking quiet car with a driver we feel like kings; even Napirai seems to enjoy the ride. By evening we reach Maralal. The driver is taken aback by where he's ended up. Everyone in Maralal notices the arrival of a new car. We park outside the boardinghouse right behind the Land Rover. I explain the problem with the car to the driver, who's also a mechanic. "It's okay," he says, and goes off to bed. The next day I hand him his check and off he goes.

We spend another night in Maralal and drop in on Sophia. She and her daughter, Anika, are well. She wondered why she hadn't seen me for so long and is shocked when I tell her about my hepatitis. I admire her cat and its three kittens, tell her to keep one for me, and then we set off.

We go via Baragoi and get to Barsaloi almost an hour earlier than we would have done in the old Land Rover. Mama beams when she sees us; she had been getting worried, as she didn't know we had gone to Nairobi. We've barely arrived before there's a crowd gathered to admire the car. I'd sent a letter to my mother from Maralal asking her to send more money from my Swiss bank account.

After chai we go down to our house. That afternoon I pay a visit to Father Giuliani and proudly tell him about my new car. He congratulates me on the purchases and offers to reimburse me generously if I use it to take schoolchildren to Maralal or transport the sick. At least that's some income.

We get back to enjoying life; things are good. The only problem is sticking to my diet, which is not easy out here. The schoolchildren have a few more days before the end of the holidays. Then I take them to Maralal, leaving Napirai with "Gogo," her grandmother. On the way James and I discuss opening the shop again, but only in three months' time when school is over and then he'll be eager to work there.

In town I again go to see Sophia, who tells me she's going to Italy in two weeks to show her daughter to her parents. I'm pleased for her and at the same time feel a little homesick for Switzerland. I'd like to show off my daughter too. Even the first photographs were spoiled because someone opened the camera. I pick out a little orange-and-white tiger-striped kitten to take with me in a box. The journey back home is wonderfully easy, and despite going the long way I'm back before dark. Napirai has been drinking cow's milk all day off a teaspoon, but when she hears me she won't stop crying until she's back at my breast.

My husband has been out all day with the cattle. There's a cattle sickness going around in Sitedi, and valuable animals are dying daily. He comes home late thoroughly depressed: two of our cows have died, and another three can't stand up. I ask if there's no cure. He says there are only preventive measures for healthy animals; the infected ones just die. The medicine is expensive, and you're lucky to find any in Maralal. He goes to talk it over with the vet. The next day we set out again for Maralal, taking Napirai and the vet along, and at a high price get hold of the medicine and a syringe. We have to inoculate all the healthy animals in the next five days. Lketinga reckons he'll have to spend the whole time in Sitedi.

Rest and Recreation

After three days I start to feel lonely, even though each day we go to see Mama or my new friend. But it's very monotonous. I don't enjoy eating on my own, and I miss my family. Soon I decide to take a month in Switzerland. At least there it'll be easier to stick to my diet. The thought cheers me up more and more, and I wait impatiently for my husband to return.

I'm in the kitchen cooking on the floor under the open window when the door opens and Lketinga comes in. He doesn't say a word to us but stares at the open window and asks sarcastically who's just climbed out. After five lonely days waiting for him, it feels as if I've been punched by a fist, but I try to control myself because I want to discuss my travel plans with him. So all I say is: "Nobody, why do you ask me this?" Instead of answering he goes into the bedroom and examines the mattress and sheets. I'm embarrassed by his lack of trust in me, and my joy at seeing him again vanishes. All the time he keeps asking who I've been seeing. Of course warriors came by a couple of times, but I let nobody in.

Finally he manages to say a couple of words to his daughter and takes her out of the wicker-basket cot I bought on our last visit to Maralal. She spends most of the day in this portable infant bed outside under the tree while I'm washing her diapers and our clothes. He takes her in his arms and heads off to the *manyattas*. I assume he's going to Mama. My dinner's ready, but I just poke at it, asking myself all the time why he trusts me so little.

When he hasn't come back two hours later, I go down to Mama too. She's sitting with the other women under their tree with Napirai sleeping on the cowhide next to her. Lketinga is lying in the *manyatta*. I sit down next to Mama, and she asks me something but I understand only half of it. It appears she too thinks I have a boyfriend. Obviously Lketinga's been making things up and telling her. She laughs conspiratorially but warns me it's dangerous. Disappointed in her, I insist there's only Lketinga. Then I take my daughter and go home.

In these circumstances it's hard to bring up my plan to go to Switzerland, but it's clearer than ever to me that I need a vacation. Still, for the moment I keep it to myself and wait until things quiet down.

From time to time I try to eat a little bit of meat but pay for it immediately in stomach cramps. I'm better sticking to maize, rice, or potatoes. But because I'm not eating any fat and still breast-feeding every day, I'm losing more and more weight. I have to use belts, or my skirts would fall off me. Napirai is three months old now and we have to take her to the hospital in Wamba for a checkup and inoculations. In the new car this is an enjoyable break. Lketinga comes along, but now he thinks it's time for him to drive the new car too.

I'm less than enthusiastic about this, but since I can't go on my own with Napirai, I need him and reluctantly hand him the keys. Every time he crunches the gears I wince. He drives slowly, almost too slowly. When I hear a strange noise, I notice that he's been driving with the hand brake on. He's extremely embarrassed because now it doesn't work properly anymore, and I'm cross because the faulty hand brake on the Land Rover caused us enough problems. Now he doesn't want to drive anymore and sits sulking beside me holding Napirai. I feel sorry for him and assure him we can get the hand brake fixed.

At the hospital we have to wait nearly two hours before we're called. The Swiss doctor examines me and says I'm far too thin and don't have enough body weight. Unless I want to be readmitted as a patient I need to spend two months back home in Switzerland. I tell her that I've been planning such a trip but don't know how to tell my husband. She fetches the male doctor, who also tells me to go to Europe immediately, I'm totally undernourished, and Napirai is sucking the last strength from me. She, however, is the picture of health.

I ask the doctor if he'll speak to Lketinga. My husband looks as if he's been hit by a thunderbolt when he hears that I'm planning to go away for such a long time. After a lot of discussion he agrees to five weeks. The doctor gives me a letter to speed up the travel permission for Napirai. She gets her injections, and we drive back to Barsaloi. Lketinga is upset and keeps asking: "Corinne, why you are always sick? Why you go with my baby so far? I don't know, where is Switzerland. What shall I make without you such a long time?" My heart almost breaks when I realize how hard it is for him. Mama's sad too when we tell her I'm off to Switzerland. But I promise them all I'll come back fit and well and we can open up the shop again.

Just two days later we set off. Father Giuliani takes us to Maralal, and I leave my car with him. Lketinga comes with Napirai and me as far as Nairobi, another long journey during which the baby's diaper has to be changed again and again. I don't have much luggage.

In Nairobi we find a place to stay and go first of all to the German embassy to get a children's passport. Our problems begin at the gate. First of all they don't want to let Lketinga in wearing his Samburu clothing, until I prove to them that he's my husband. Immediately he gets nervous and suspicious.

There are lots of people waiting in the embassy. I start filling in the form and realize right away with the surname that there are going to be problems. I write down "Leparmorijo-Hofmann, Napirai," but my husband will not have the "Hofmann"—his daughter is a Leparmorijo. I try to explain as calmly as I can that we're only doing it to get a passport and otherwise Napirai can't go with me. We get into an endless debate with people staring at us in curiosity until at last he agrees to sign the form.

We still have to wait. At last I'm called up and asked into a back room. My husband wants to come too but is stopped. My heart's pounding because I'm waiting for him to explode again; I can see Lketinga pushing his way to the counter and starting to argue violently with the man.

I'm called in by the ambassador, who tells me in a friendly manner that they are happy to issue a child's passport but only in the name of Hofmann because our marriage certificate has not been legalized, and although I'm married in Kenyan law, I'm not according to German law. When he tells me my husband will have to sign a new form, I tell him he won't do it. I show him the letter from the doctor, but he says there's nothing he can do.

When I come back, Lketinga's sitting there angrily on his chair holding a crying Napirai: "What is wrong with you? Why you go there without me? I'm your husband." I feel terrible as I fill in the form again without Leparmorijo on it; he stands up and says he's not signing anything anymore.

I give him an angry look and tell him that if he doesn't sign here and now, one of these days I'll take Napirai to Switzerland anyhow and never come back. He ought to get it into his head that my health is at stake! Only when the man at the counter repeatedly reassures him that Napirai will still be his daughter does he sign. I go back in to see the ambassador. When he asks me uncertainly if everything is okay, I tell him that it's hard for a warrior to understand bureaucracy.

He hands over the child's passport and wishes me all the best. When I ask him if I can now leave the country, he points out to me that the Kenyan authorities have to give us an exit and reentry stamp and for that I also need the child's father's permission. I'm already imagining the next altercation. We leave the embassy in hardly the best of moods and go to the Nyayo Building, where once again it's a case of filling in forms and waiting.

Napirai's crying, and even the breast won't stop her. Once again people are looking at us. Eventually we're called up, and the woman behind the glass window asks my husband disparagingly why Napirai has a German passport when she was born in Kenya. It all starts again, and I have to hold back the tears. I tell this arrogant woman that my husband doesn't have a passport despite having applied for one two years ago, and so our daughter can't be put on it, and that I have to go to Switzerland because of my bad health. The next question nearly knocks me over: Why don't I leave the baby with its father? I tell her indignantly that it's normal for a mother to take a three-month-old child with her, apart from which my mother has the right to see her granddaughter. Eventually she stamps the passport and mine too. Relieved but exhausted, I collect the passports together and leave the office. Now I have to book a ticket. This time I can prove where the money came from. I present the passports, and we book a flight that leaves in two days' time. Before long the booking clerk comes back with the tickets, shows them to me, and reads aloud: "Hofmann, Corinne," and "Hofmann, Napirai." Lketinga breaks into a temper and wants to know why we bothered getting married at all if I'm still not his wife. Even his baby apparently isn't his. It's the last straw for my nerves, and I burst into tears again. I shove the tickets in my bag, and we leave the office to go back to the hotel.

Eventually my husband calms down but sits there on the bed upset and unhappy, and I sort of understand. In his world the family name is the most valuable present a man can bestow on his wife and children, and I reject it. For him, it as good as means that I don't want to belong to him. I take him by the hand and tell him earnestly that he really doesn't need to worry, that we'll be back. I'll send a telegram to the Mission so that he'll know which day. He explains to me that he feels lonely without us but that he really would like to have a healthy wife again. When we come back, he wants to come to meet us at the airport. That pleases me enormously because I know what an effort a journey like that is for him. Then he tells me that he's leaving Nairobi now to go home. I understand and accompany him to the bus station. Standing there, waiting for the bus to depart, he asks me once again worriedly: "Corinne, my wife, you are sure, you and Napirai come back to Kenya?" I answer with a smile, "Yes, darling, I'm sure." Then the bus leaves.

I'd only managed to call my mother the day before to tell her we are coming. She was obviously surprised but delighted that she was going to see her grandchild at last, so I want to make both of us pretty. But it's hard to leave such a tiny impetuous baby alone. The shower and toilets in the hotel are at the end of the corridor, and when I want to use the toilet I've no alternative but to take her with me. I go to the receptionist and ask her if she'd look after the baby for fifteen minutes while I take a shower. She says she'd be glad to but right now half of Nairobi has no water because of a burst pipe. She says maybe the shower will be working better this evening.

I wait until six, but nothing happens. On the contrary everything's started to stink. I decide not to wait any longer because I have to be at the airport by ten and go to a shop where I buy a bottle of mineral water with which I wash Napirai first, then my hair, and then what I can of the rest of me.

We take a taxi to the airport. We don't have much baggage, even though the temperatures in Europe at the end of November are going to be wintry. The flight attendants look after us well and keep stopping to admire the baby and exchange a few words. After we've eaten I get a baby bed for her, and she falls asleep. Tiredness overcomes me too, and when I'm woken again, it's for breakfast. The thought of being on Swiss soil once more fills me with apprehension.

White Faces

With my baby wrapped in her kanga on my back we pass through immigration without problems and to our mutual delight find my mother and her husband, Hans-Peter, waiting for us. Napirai is interested in all the white faces.

On the trip up into the Bernese Oberland I notice from my mother's face that she's worried by my appearance. When we get home, the first thing I do is take a bath: a hot bath at last! My mother has bought a little bathtub for Napirai and washes her. When I've been in the hot water for about ten minutes, all of a sudden my whole body starts to itch. The little cuts and scratches all over my body have opened up and started to ooze. These are mostly cuts from my Masai body decoration, and in this damp climate they don't heal well. I climb out of the bath to see my body covered with red blotches. Napirai is crying, and her grandmother is in despair—the baby too is covered with red spots that itch terribly. My mother is worried it might be something infectious and books us an appointment with a specialist for the next day.

He's amazed to diagnose our complaint: scabies, an extremely rare disease in Switzerland. There are little mites under our skin, and the extreme heat has set them to moving, which is what causes the itching. Obviously the doctor wants to know where we could have caught this. I tell him about Africa. When he discovers my other wounds, some of which have cut up to half an inch into my flesh, he suggests I should have an AIDS test. That's a bolt from the blue and knocks the wind out of me, but I'm prepared to do it. He gives me several bottles containing liquid that we should apply to the scabies three times a day and tells me to call back in three days' time for the results of the test. Those three days of not knowing are the worst thing of all.

The first day I sleep a lot and go to bed early with Napirai. The next day the phone rings, and it's the doctor for me personally. My pulse is racing as I take the receiver, waiting to hear what my fate is. The doctor apologizes for calling so late but tells me he just wanted to relieve my anxiety: the test is negative. I'm overwhelmed with thanks! I feel as if I've been given a new lease on life, and a feeling of strength returns to my body. Now I know I'll get over the aftereffects of the hepatitis. Each day I step up my consumption of fat and eat everything my mother puts on the table.

Time drags, though, as I no longer feel at home here. We go for lots of walks, visit my sister-in-law Jelly, and take Napirai out in the snow for the first time. She seems to like life here a lot, except for all the putting on and taking off of clothes.

After two and a half weeks I realize I don't want to stay beyond Christmas, but the first available flight is on January 1, 1990. By then I'll have been away from home for nearly six weeks. Nonetheless, parting is difficult because once again I'm thrown back on my own devices. I'm going back with nearly ninety pounds of luggage. I've bought or sewn presents for everybody. My family has given me lots too, and there are Napirai's Christmas presents to pack. My brother has bought me a baby carrier to go on my back.

A Fresh Beginning?

When we arrive in Nairobi, my nerves are stretched to breaking, not knowing whether or not Lketinga will have come to the airport to meet us. If not and I'm left on the street with Napirai and all the luggage, it won't be easy to find somewhere to stay in the middle of the night. We say good-bye to the flight attendants and make our way to passport control. We're barely through when I spot my darling with James and his friend. I'm overjoyed. My husband has painted himself magnificently and done his long hair beautifully, standing there wrapped in his red cloth. He throws his arms around both of us in delight, and we set off for the accommodation they've already booked. Now Napirai has problems with all the black faces and starts to cry. Lketinga is worried in case she no longer even recognizes him.

When we get to the hotel, they all want to see the presents straightaway, but I take out only the watches because we want to be on our way tomorrow and everything is carefully packed. The boys retire to their room, and we go to bed. We make love, and at last it no longer hurts. I'm happy and hope once again that everything will turn out for the best.

Amid all the chat on the way home I discover that they're going to build a proper big school in Barsaloi. A plane arrived from Nairobi with Indians on board, and they stayed a few days in the Mission. The school is going to be built on the other side of the big river, and lots of workers will come in from Nairobi—all Kikuyus—but nobody knows when they're going to start. I tell them all about Switzerland, and of course about the scabies, because my husband's going to have to be treated too or else he'll just infect us again.

Lketinga had brought the car as far as Nyahururu and left it at the Mission there—I'm astounded at his courage—so we get back to Maralal easily, although suddenly the distances seem vast to me. We return to Barsaloi the next day; Mama welcomes us happily and gives thanks to Enkai that we have returned healthy and well from the "iron bird," as she calls the aircraft. It's good to be back home.

There's a hearty welcome for me in the Mission too. When I ask Father Giuliani what all this is about a school, he confirms what the boys told me and that the building work is actually going to start in a few days' time. There are already people here putting up barracks for the workers to live in. The building material is coming on trucks via Nanyuki-Wamba. I'm astounded that such a major project is actually going to be realized, but Father Giuliani tells me it's part of a government plan to end the Masais' nomadic way of life and make them settle down. The area is suitable because there is always water in the river and enough sand to be mixed with stone to make cement. The presence of a modern Mission building also contributed to the government's decision. The days go by happily, and we take regular walks over on the other bank of the river to watch what's going on.

My cat has grown. It would seem Lketinga kept his promise to feed it, though apparently only with meat because it's as wild as a tiger. Only when she snuggles up next to Napirai in bed does she start purring softly.

After two weeks the first workers from outside arrive. The first Sunday most of them turn up in church as the mass is virtually the only entertainment for these townfolks. The Somalis have put up their prices for sugar and maize drastically, which has led to a lot of arguments and a village meeting with the elders and the little boss man. We take part too, and people keep asking me when the Samburu shop will finally open again. Some of the workers who've turned up ask me if I wouldn't consider using my car to fetch beer and soft drinks. They say they'd pay me well, as they get good wages and have nothing to spend them on. As Muslims, the Somalis won't sell beer.

When the workers keep coming by, I start thinking seriously about doing something to earn money again at last. I get the idea of opening a sort of disco with Kikuyu music, where we could grill meat and sell it along with beer and soft drinks. I talk it all over with Lketinga and the vet, with whom he's started spending a lot of time. Both think it's a great idea, and the vet believes we could sell *miraa* too, since people are always asking for it. In next to no time it's settled, and we decide to start up at the end of the month. I clean up the shop and knock out flyers, which we pin up around the place and distribute among the workers.

The feedback is huge. On the very first day a few people come to ask why we can't start that very weekend. But that's too little notice because, apart from everything else, sometimes there's no beer to be had in Maralal. We do our usual trip there and come back with a dozen cases of beer and soft drinks. My husband sorts out the *miraa*. The car is so packed that the journey home takes longer than normal.

When we get back, we store all the goods in the main part of the shop because our previous living space out back is going to be the dance floor. Before long the first customers are there looking for beer. Then the little boss man turns up and demands to see my disco license! Of course, I don't have one and ask him if I really need to. Lketinga has a chat with him, and he promises that the next day, for a consideration of course, he'll sort things out: for a handful of cash and a few free beers he'll grant us our license.

At last it's the day of the disco, and everyone is very worked up. Our shop assistant knows a bit about technology and has taken the battery out of the car to fix it up to a cassette recorder: we have sound! In the meantime a goat's been slaughtered, and two boys are butchering it. We have lots of volunteer helpers, and Lketinga is spending more time delegating tasks to other people than dealing with them himself. By half-past seven everything is ready: the music's playing, the meat is sizzling on the grill, and people are lined up outside the back door. Lketinga takes the entrance money from the men; women get in free, but most of them stay outside peeking in and giggling. Within half an hour the shop is full, and workers keep coming up and congratulating me on the idea. Even the foreman comes up to thank me for my efforts, saying his people needed a bit of entertainment, particularly because for some of them it's their first job far from home.

I enjoy being in the company of so many happy people, most of whom speak English. A few Samburus from the village turn up, even a couple of the elders who sit on upturned crates, wrapped in their blankets and watching the dancing Kikuyus with unfettered amazement. I don't dance myself even though I've left Napirai with Mama. A few people ask me to dance, but one glance at Lketinga is enough to persuade me against it. He sits there discreetly knocking back beer and chewing his *miraa*, all the rest of which is long gone.

At eleven P.M. the music is turned down, and some of the men say a few words of thanks, addressed in particular to me, the *mzungu*. An hour later the last beer is gone, and even the goat has almost vanished. Our guests are in a good mood, and the party goes on until four A.M. before everyone goes home. I fetch Napirai from Mama and stumble home with her, exhausted.

Counting up our takings the next day, I realize the profits were a lot more than we made from the shop. My good mood is soon ruined, however, when Father Giuliani roars up on his motorbike and asks what sort of a "hellish racket" was going on in our shop last night. Quietly I tell him about the disco. He says he doesn't mind if it's only twice a month, but he insists on getting to sleep after midnight. If I don't want to rub him the wrong way, that's something I'll have to bear in mind the next time.

A Failure of Trust

When a few men come over from the river and ask if there's still a beer to be had, I have to tell them no. Then my husband appears and asks the three of them what they want. I explain, but Lketinga goes up to them and says that if they want something in the future they're to ask him, not me. He's the man around here and decides what's to be done. His tone of voice is so harsh that they retreat docilely. I ask him why he has to talk to them like that, but he gives a nasty laugh and says: "I know why these people come here, not for beer. I know! If they want beer, why don't they ask me?" I had realized that sooner or later we were going to have a fit of jealousy, even though I haven't spoken to anyone for more than five minutes. But I restrain my rising temper; it's bad enough that these men have gone off with a bad impression when the whole of Barsaloi is talking about our disco.

Lketinga watches me all the time skeptically. From time to time he takes the Datsun and goes off to visit his half brother in Sitedi or some other relations. Of course I could go with him, but with Napirai I don't feel like squatting in the fly-infested *manyattas* next to the cows. Time goes by, and I wait until at last James will be done with school. We urgently need money to buy food and gas, and with all these people from outside here now we can easily be earning it.

Lketinga is off somewhere else nearly all the time because it seems there's always someone or other from his age group getting married. Every day warriors turn up with tales of some upcoming wedding or other. He sets off with them, and I don't know if he'll be back in two days, three, or maybe not for five.

When Father Giuliani asks me if I'm prepared to fetch schoolchildren again since it's the first day of the holidays, of course I agree. Even though my husband's not around I set off, leaving Napirai with Mama. James is glad to see me and asks how the disco went—news of it has reached even here. I've got five boys to bring back. We go shopping, and I drop in briefly on Sophia. She's back from Italy but is planning to move down to the coast as soon as possible. It's too much effort living here with Anika, and she can't see much of a future for her. I'm sad to hear it because now I'll have nobody to look forward to seeing in Maralal; we've been through some tough times together. But I understand and am even a little envious; I'd love to see the sea again myself. Since she's moving soon, we say our good-byes now; she'll send word of her new address.

We get back home just before eight P.M. My husband isn't back, so I cook for the boys after they've had chai with Mama. It's a jolly evening exchanging stories; Napirai is very fond of her uncle James, and I have to keep telling them about the disco. They sit there listening with sparkling eyes, imagining themselves there too, and in fact the next one is due to take place in two days' time, except that with Lketinga not here it can't happen. This weekend the workers are to be paid, and everyone keeps asking me to organize a disco, even though there's only one day left. I don't want to risk it without Lketinga around, but the boys persuade me, promising that they'll organize everything if I buy the beer and soft drinks.

I'm reluctant to go to Maralal, and so James and I go as far as Baragoi, the first time I've been to this Turkana tribe village. It's almost as big as Wamba and actually has a beer and soft drinks wholesaler, even though it's more expensive than in Maralal. But the whole thing takes us only three and a half hours. One of the boys writes out flyers, which they go out and distribute, and everyone starts to get excited about the disco. We haven't managed to sort out the meat, though, as there were no goats to be bought and I don't dare use one of our own, even though they belong partly to me. When I take Napirai down to Mama, I notice she's not as happy as usual because Lketinga isn't around. But I have to earn money, don't I? That's what we all live on.

Once again the disco is a great success. There are even more people because the schoolboys are home. Even three girls dare to come in. With the boys there and my husband not, the atmosphere is actually much more relaxed. Even one of the young Somalis comes in and has a Fanta. I'm pleased by that because Lketinga is always going on nastily about the Somalis. I feel as if I belong and can talk to lots of people. The boys take turns selling the drinks. There's a party mood, and everybody gets up to dance to the bouncy Kikuyu music. A lot of them have even brought their own cassettes. For the first time in two years, I even dance myself and feel as if I've let my hair down.

Unfortunately we have to turn the music down at midnight, but the party atmosphere lasts until two A.M., when we close up, and I hurry down to the *manyatta* with a flashlight to fetch Napirai. I have problems finding the gate in the thorn fence, and as I do my heart almost stops when I see Lketinga's spears planted in the earth outside the *manyatta*! My pulse is racing as I bend down to crawl in. Immediately I hear the grunt that tells me how ill tempered he is. Napirai is sleeping naked next to Mama. I say hello and ask him why he didn't come up to the shop. At first I don't even get an answer, then he starts shouting at me, cursing me, and looking deranged. He doesn't care what I say; he doesn't believe any of it. Mama tries to calm him down, telling him the whole of Barsaloi can hear him. Even Napirai starts crying. But when he calls me a whore who sleeps with Kikuyus and even schoolboys, I grab Napirai, wrap her naked in a blanket, and run home in tears. I'm starting to become afraid of my own husband.

Before long he flings open the door, pulls me out of bed, and demands to know the names of everyone I've "done it" with. Now he says that he knows Napirai isn't even his daughter and that I only told him she was premature because of my illness when really I'd got pregnant by someone else. Every sentence he utters rips away a part of my love for him. I don't even understand him anymore. In the end he storms out of the house, saying he's off to find a better wife and is not coming back. Right at this moment I couldn't care less. All I want is peace and quiet.

The next morning my eyes are so red with tears I can't bring myself to go out. Lots of people heard us arguing. Around ten o'clock Mama turns up with Saguna, wanting to know where Lketinga is. I have no idea. Then James turns up with a friend. He says he doesn't understand either, but his brother never went to school and warriors don't have any idea about running a business. James tells me what Mama thinks: she wants to talk to Lketinga, to tell him not to get so angry, and she thinks that he'll come back. She thinks I shouldn't keep crying; I should pay no attention to him; all men are like that, and that's why it's better for them to have more than one wife. James disagrees with her, but none of it's any help to me. Even the night watchman from the Mission has been sent down by Father Giuliani to find out what's up. I find it all very unpleasant.

Lketinga eventually turns up late in the day, but we hardly exchange any words. Life gets back to normal, and nobody says anything more about it. Then a week later he disappears again for another ceremony.

The girl who fetches water for me has become ever more unreliable, and so I have to drive down to the river myself to fetch a couple of canisters of water, leaving the boys to look after Napirai. But when I try to set off home again, I can't get into gear, the clutch keeps slipping. Depressed to find myself broken down again for the first time in two months, I walk up to the Mission for help; I can hardly leave the car down by the river. Giuliani is not exactly delighted but comes down anyway and takes a look at the car. He works out that the clutch has indeed gone and says he can't do anything about it. The only place I'll get spare parts is in Nairobi, and he has no plans to go there for at least another month. I burst into tears with no idea how I'm going to get food for Napirai or myself. Gradually I'm coming to the end of my rope.

He tows the car home for us and says he'll try to order the parts from Nairobi by telephone. If the Indians are coming back in the plane over the next few days, they might bring the parts with them, but he can't promise anything.

But four days later he roars up on his motorbike to say the plane will be landing today at eleven A.M.—the Indians are coming to inspect progress on the school construction—but he can't say whether or not they've got the parts.

And indeed the plane does land, at midday. Father Giuliani drives up to the temporary landing strip in his Land Cruiser, picks up the two Indians, and drives them down to the river. When I see Giuliani drive off, apparently toward Wamba, and don't know what's going on, I decide to walk down to the school and take Napirai to Mama.

The two Indians in their turbans look at me in surprise, greeting me with a handshake and offering me a Coke. They ask if I'm part of the Mission. I tell them no, that I live here and am married to a Samburu. That seems to make them even more curious, and they ask how a white woman can live out here in the bush. They had heard that even their workers find it difficult getting supplies. I tell them about my car and that it's broken down. They ask me sympathetically if the clutch was for me, then, rather than for the Mission. I say yes and ask hopefully if they managed to get it, only to have my hopes dashed when they say there are too many models and the only way to know which is correct is by looking at the vehicle. They see how deeply disappointed I am, and one of them asks where my car is. Then he tells the mechanic they've brought with them to take a look at the car and dismantle the faulty clutch. In an hour they're flying back to Nairobi.

The mechanic is a quick worker, and in less than an hour I learn that not only the clutch but the entire transmission is wrecked. He packs up the heavy parts, and we drive back. One of the Indians takes a look and thinks it ought to be possible to find the parts in Nairobi, but it won't be cheap. The two of them confer for a few minutes and then ask me if I want to come back with them. I'm completely taken aback and tell them my husband isn't here and in any case I have a six-month-old child at home. No problem, they say, they have space to take the baby too.

Put on the spot, I don't know what to do and tell them I don't know my way around Nairobi. "No problem," says the other Indian: their mechanic knows every spare-parts shop and will collect me from the hotel tomorrow morning and go with me to try to find the spares. In any case, if I tried to look on my own as a white woman, people would try to charge me far too much.

I'm dumbstruck by the overwhelming kindness of these two strangers, but before I can think any further they tell me to be ready in fifteen minutes at the aircraft. "Yes, thank you very much" is all I can stammer. The mechanic takes me home, and I hurry quickly to Mama's to tell her I'm flying to Nairobi. I grab Napirai, leaving Mama standing there in total confusion. Back home I throw together all the essentials for the baby and me, tell the vet's wife what I'm doing and that I'll be back as soon as possible with the spare parts. She should give my love to my husband and tell him why I couldn't wait for his permission.

Then I rush to the airstrip, with Napirai in a kanga sling and a travel bag in my hand. There's already a crowd of curious sightseers gathered around the plane, and they're dumbstruck when I turn up. The mzungu is flying off, the rumor soon runs, because her husband isn't here. I realize this is likely to cause problems, but then I think how happy he's going to be when his dearly beloved car is working again and he hasn't had to go to Nairobi.

The Indians arrive in one of the project's cars at the same time as Mama, who stumps up to me frowning and tells me I have to leave Napirai here. I tell her I'm doing no such thing and promise to be back, and she gives both of us Enkai's blessing. We get in, the engine screams, and the people standing around leap back in shock. I wave to them all, and already we're bumping down the runway.

The Indians have loads of questions about how I got to know my husband and how I manage to live in this wilderness. Their amazement makes me laugh, and I feel happier and freer than I have done in ages. In ninety minutes we're in Nairobi. It's like a miracle to me to have covered such a vast distance in such a short space of time. Now they ask where to take me. When I tell them the Igbol Hotel near the Odeon Cinema, they're horrified and tell me that part of town's far too dangerous for a lady like me. But it's an area I know, and I insist on being dropped there. One of the Indians, clearly the more important of the two, hands me his card and tells me I should ring at nine A.M. and his driver will pick me up. I don't know what to say and am effusive in my thanks.

Only in the Igbol do I start to wonder if I've actually got enough money; I've only the equivalent of one thousand Swiss francs. That was all the money I had at home, and even that was only because of the disco. I put a diaper on Napirai, and we go down to the restaurant. It's hard eating at a table with her; she either throws everything on the ground or tries to climb down herself. Since she's learned to crawl she can race along, and everything's so dirty here I don't want to put her down. But she screams and cries until I do. Within seconds she's covered in dirt, and the locals are looking at me wondering why I give in to her. A few white travelers, however, are delighted when she crawls under their tables. One way or another she's content, and so am I. When we get back to the room, I give her a thorough wash in the sink. I have to wait until she's asleep before I can have a shower myself.

The next day it's pouring with rain. At eight-thirty A.M. I'm standing in the line outside the telephone booth. We're soaked to the skin before eventually it's our turn. I get straight through to the Indian and tell him to pick me up at the Odeon Cinema. He says his driver will be there in twenty minutes. I dash back into the Igbol to change my clothes. My little girl is very brave and doesn't cry even though she's soaked through. When we get to the Odeon, the driver is waiting for us and takes us to an

industrial district. We're escorted into a grandiose office where the nice
Indian is sitting behind a big desk, wanting to know if we're all right. Then
he makes a call, and immediately the African mechanic from yesterday
appears. He gives him a few addresses to take me around to find the spare
parts. When he asks if I have enough money, I reply: "I hope so!"

We drive the length and breadth of Nairobi, and by midday we've
found a clutch for just one hundred and fifty Swiss francs. Napirai sits in
the back of the car; the rain has stopped, the sun is out, and soon it's hot,
but I'm not allowed to open the windows because we have to go through
some of the worst parts of Nairobi. The driver keeps doing his best, but
we can't find the rest. Napirai is sweating and screaming. She's had more
than enough when, after six hours of continuously sitting in the car, the
driver tells us it's hopeless: we're not going to find the other parts.
Tomorrow is Good Friday, and at five P.M. all the shops will shut. I had
completely forgotten about Easter. I ask him stupidly when things will
open again. He says the garages will be closed until Tuesday.

Suddenly I'm seized with pure horror at the idea of having to be on
my own with Napirai for so long in this city. Lketinga will go mad if I'm
away for a whole week. We decide to go back to the Indian's office.

The friendly Indian is very concerned by my problems and examines
the worn bearings in the transmission before asking the mechanic if
there's any way of repairing it. There isn't, he says, though I wonder if
that's just because it's time to go home. The Indian makes another phone
call, and another man wearing an apron and protective goggles appears at
the door. The Indian tells him to grind down the worn parts and reweld
them and makes a point of saying he wants it all done in half an hour
because that's as long as he can wait. Then he turns to me with a smile
and tells me I can go home in half an hour.

I thank him enormously and ask how much I owe. But he waves his
hand; it's his pleasure to be able to help. When I get back to Barsaloi, he
tells me to go to the foreman and he'll already know to see that
everything is fixed for me. I can hardly believe how much he's helped
me, and all for nothing! In next to no time I'm leaving his office. The
parts are heavy, but I'm proud that it's all worked. That very evening I
catch the bus to Nyahururu, and then I catch the bus the next morning
on to Maralal; but it's hard work carrying the spare parts and Napirai on
my back at the same time.

I have no idea, however, how to get from Maralal to Barsaloi. Exhausted, I drag myself into the boardinghouse for something to eat and drink after such a long, dusty, and tiring journey. Then I have to wash not just Napirai and myself but also a few dozen diapers, before I can fall into bed, dead to the world. The next morning I ask if there's anyone going to Barsaloi. My wholesaler tells me there's a truck going out for the Somalis. But after all our stress I don't think Napirai or I are up to a truck ride. I wait until I find a boy who's come in on foot from Barsaloi, and he tells me Father Roberto is due to pick up the post in Maralal tomorrow. Filled with relief, I pack up all my stuff in the boardinghouse the next day to be ready and waiting outside the post office. For four hard, long hours we stick it out by the side of the road until at last we see the second car from the Mission. Expectantly, I approach Roberto to ask if he can take us home. No problem, he says, he's going back in two hours' time.

The Downhill Path

In Barsaloi I climb out of the car to see my husband striding toward me. He says hello coldly and asks me why it's taken me so long to come back. So long? I've come as fast as I could, I tell him disappointedly. He doesn't even ask if everything went okay. Instead he wants to know why I had to spend another night in Maralal. Who was I meeting? One question after another, and not a word of praise.

I'm embarrassed at having to answer such distrustful questions in the presence of Father Roberto, and I walk off home with Napirai. At least Lketinga carries my bag, and even he finds himself almost having to drag it. He gives me a surly look and starts up again with his questions. I'm just about to explode in anger and disappointment when James and his friend come in happily. He at least asks how it went and says how brave it was to just fly off like that. Unfortunately he'd been down at the river washing his clothes when he heard about my expedition, or else he'd have loved to come with me. It's his one great wish to fly someday.

His words cheer me up, and I try to calm down. The boys make tea for me and keep talking while Lketinga just goes off into the dark. I ask James what my husband said when he came home and found I had gone. He smiles and tries to tell me that his brother's generation doesn't understand the concept of independent women and doesn't trust them. Lketinga thought I had gone off with Napirai and wasn't coming back. I find it incomprehensible, even though I was beginning to have good reason. But where would we go? Napirai needs her father, after all.

James takes me away from such morbid thoughts by asking me when we plan to open up the shop again. He would really like to work there and earn some money. And money is something we're definitely going to have to start thinking about if the car isn't to take all we have. As soon as the Datsun is fixed we'll open up the shop again, this time really properly, selling clothes and shoes along with beer and soft drinks. There's no question that there's money to be made as long as the workers from Nairobi are here, and after that there'll be teachers from outside with their families. With James as my sales assistant I can see it working. One way or another I make clear to him that this is my last chance and I'll be investing the last of my money. The boys' enthusiasm is infectious and makes me forget the problems I've had with Lketinga recently. When he comes back, the boys take off.

The next morning Lketinga goes over to the workers of his own accord and tells them the spare parts are ready. At the end of the working day one of the mechanics comes over and works on our car but doesn't manage to finish it all that day. In the end it takes three days before our luxury vehicle is back on the road. Now we can open up the shop again. We set off as a foursome, with James holding Napirai. He simply doesn't get tired of playing with her.

In Maralal I check to see if my last four thousand Swiss francs have arrived. The banker says no, but the next day the money does arrive, and we start our shopping. First of all, obviously, are 2,240 pounds of maize meal and sugar, then as much fruit and vegetables as I can find. The rest I plow into clothing, shoes, tobacco, plastic cups, water canisters: everything, in short, that can be sold at a decent profit. I even buy twenty loaves of bread, handing over my last shilling in the hopes of doubling it.

The reopening of the shop is a big event, and people come from near and far. Within two days we're sold out of kangas, clothing, and water canisters. The workers on the school buy up the vegetables, rice, and potatoes in lots of twenty or forty pounds. It's almost like a bush supermarket. In these first few days we find ourselves happy, proud, and content, even though we're tired. James is such an eager worker that he asks me if he can move into the shop in order to open up early.

We don't put the beer on the open shelves but keep it behind the counter so as not to have any trouble. The few cases we bring back are almost gone after two days. I don't like being without goods for more than a day or two and feel responsible therefore for ensuring supplies. With our profits I immediately buy more clothing because the workers on the school need lots of shirts and trousers. Every three weeks I make a special journey to Nanyuki to the big clothing market there. Clothes for the women and children sell like hot cakes, and I even take orders. It's amazing how suddenly everybody has money, partly because of the school project, on which many people have found jobs.

Business booms, and the shop has become a meeting place for many of the construction workers. In short, everything is going well until Lketinga starts getting his jealousy attacks again. I'm never in the shop in the morning because I do the housework first, and turn up only in the afternoon, strolling over with Napirai. It's usually fun with the boys, and even Napirai enjoys being the center of attention, since there are always children to play with her or carry her around. Only my husband dislikes it when he sees me happy because he says I never laugh or smile around him. It's all to do with his suspicions against anyone who spends five minutes with me. Primarily he's suspicious of the workers who turn up every day at the shop. He'll bar one or another of them from coming in or accuse them of coming just to see his wife. I find it embarrassing and leave the shop every time he does it. Even James can do nothing about his big brother and the unnecessary scenes he creates.

We argue more and more often, and it begins to occur to me that I don't want to spend the rest of my life like this. We do the work, and he stands there scowling at me or the customers; or else he's off with the other warriors slaughtering a goat, and I come home to find the floor covered with blood and bones.

Once or twice a week I drive in to Baragoi, which is much closer than Maralal, to stock up on food supplies. Yet again we're out of sugar because there's about to be a big wedding ceremony for a warrior. He wants to buy 675 pounds himself and will pay extra to have it delivered to an encampment some distance away. Just after midday I set off in a hurry—it's only an hour and a half each way—and reach Baragoi without any problems. I buy only 1,350 pounds of sugar, though, because I have to get across two rivers and I don't want to put unnecessary strain on the car.

With the car loaded up I turn the key in the ignition, but the engine won't start, and after a couple more tries it's completely dead. Before long I'm surrounded by Turkana tribespeople staring into the car. The shop owner comes out to ask what's up, and a few of them try to bump start me but with no luck. The shop owner suggests I check out a tent some three hundred yards down the road where there are other *mzungus* who have a car.

It turns out there is a young English couple there, and I explain my problem to them. The husband takes his toolbox out and has a look at my car. In next to no time he's able to tell me that my battery is flat and empty. He tries a couple of things but without success. When I tell them I need to get back to Barsaloi today because I have a baby at home, he offers to lend me the battery from their car, but I have to promise to bring it back because they need to set off for Nairobi in two days' time. I'm impressed by his good faith, leave my dud battery behind, and promise to be back in time.

Back home I tell my husband what happened, as yet again he wants to know what took me so long. I'm obviously upset too because once again we need to spend money and the car keeps eating up everything we earn. Very soon I'm going to need four new tires. It drives me mad that we never seem to get anywhere, and I can't bear the thought of having to go to Maralal again tomorrow.

Then we have a stroke of luck: the builders are sending a car down to fetch food and beer. I ask Lketinga to go with them, take the battery, buy a new one for us and then take the public *matatu* to Baragoi and give it to the English people, who'll be bound to give him a lift back to Barsaloi.

I stress to him how important it is that these people get their battery back tomorrow. He assures me it's no problem and sets off with the workers in their Land Rover to Maralal via the jungle route. I'm worried that things won't work out, but he promised me and was proud to be asked to do something important. He'll have to spend the night in Maralal and make sure he's up in time to catch the only *matatu* to Baragoi.

I spend the time at home and in the shop, helping James sell the sugar and expecting Lketinga back at any moment. But it's nine in the evening before we finally spot a light in the distance. I settle down to make some chai so that he'll have something to drink as soon as he gets in. Half an hour later the English pair's Land Rover stops in front of the shop, and I hurry over to them and ask where my husband is. The young man looks at me crossly and says he has no idea where my husband might be but he needs his battery back because he has to set off tonight to Nairobi to catch a flight back to England the next day. I feel wretched and deeply ashamed that I've let them down and broken my promise.

It's even worse when I have to tell them that my husband has their battery and was supposed to bring it to them today in Baragoi. Unsurprisingly the young Englishman starts to get annoyed. He's put our old battery in his car but it will last only until it drains and then there'll be no way to recharge it. I don't know what to do and am furious with Lketinga. They tell me the *matatu* arrived in Baragoi, but there was no Masai warrior on it. By now it's ten-thirty, and I offer them a cup of chai while we try to work out what to do.

As we're drinking our chai I hear the sound of a truck engine stopping near our house. Immediately Lketinga turns up and gasping for breath dumps the two batteries on the ground. I shout at him, asking him where on earth he's been since these people wanted to leave ages ago. Dubiously the Englishman switches the batteries, and immediately they set off. I'm fed up at having been let down so badly by Lketinga. He claims he simply missed the *matatu*, but I can smell alcohol on his breath. Also he has no money left and on top of that needs one hundred and fifty Swiss francs to pay the truck driver. I'm left speechless by his empty-headedness. The battery cost us three hundred and fifty francs, and now there's this to pay out on top, all because he was drinking beer in the bars and missed the cheap public bus. That means our whole profit for the last month and the next has gone.

I go to bed in a bad mood, but despite all my frustration and anger my husband decides he wants to make love to me. When I make it clear to him that right now he shouldn't even think of trying his luck, he starts to get appallingly angry again. It's midnight by now and as quiet as the grave except for the sound of us shouting at each other. Once again he accuses me of having a lover and meeting up with him last night, which was why I sent him off to Maralal. I can't stand it anymore and spend my time trying to console Napirai, who's woken up and started crying.

Desperate Stakes

I've made up my mind: I'm getting out of here. One way or another, we can't go on like this. My money is disappearing. My husband is making me into a laughingstock, and people keep away from us because he suspects every man of being my lover. On the other hand, I realize that if I leave him he'll take my daughter away from me. He loves her, and legally she belongs to him or to his mother. I have no chance of getting away with her. In despair I try to work out what can be done to save our marriage because I can't leave without Napirai.

He never leaves us alone now, as if he suspects something. If I think of my home back in Switzerland he senses it immediately, as if he can read my mind. He makes a big effort with Napirai, playing with her all day long. I'm torn apart—I long for nothing more than to bring up a family together with the great love of my life; but at the same time, I feel that love slowly dying because of his lack of trust in me. I'm tired of perpetually having to rebuild that trust and at the same time bear the whole burden of making a living for us, while he hangs out with his friends.

It makes me furious when men drop in, look at my little, eight-month-old daughter, and talk over potential marriage propositions with Lketinga, who listens to their proposals with interest. One way or another, I am not having this. Our daughter will choose her own husband and for love. I am not going to sell her off to some old man as a second or third wife. Also we argue about female circumcision—my husband just doesn't understand my point of view on this, even though for Napirai it's still far away.

All this time the battery is still sitting there in the house. I'm about to go and ask one of the missionaries to put it in the car for me when Lketinga declares he can do it. He won't listen to anything I say, and so to avoid another fight I leave him to it. And to my surprise, the car starts straightaway. However, an hour and a half later we're out in the bush and the car won't start anymore. At first I figure it's not such a disaster: maybe a cable's-just come loose. But when I open the hood my heart skips a beat. Lketinga didn't screw the battery down properly and with all the jogging up and down on the uneven roads it's come adrift and the battery fluid is pouring out down one side. I'm getting hysterical now. Our new, expensive battery is ruined already just because it wasn't installed properly. I try to use chewing gum to keep in what liquid was left, but it's no good; in next to no time the battery acid has dissolved it all. I burst into tears, furious with my husband. We're stuck out here in searing heat with a baby and have no choice but for him to go to the Mission on foot to ask for help while I wait here with Napirai. It'll take hours.

Thank God I can still breast-feed Napirai, or we'd be in a total mess. At least I have drinking water. The time drags, and the only entertainment is a couple of passing zebras and a family of ostriches. My thoughts are running wild, and I've made up my mind to invest no more money in the shop. I'm going to get out of here, go down to Mombasa like Sophia. We can open up a souvenir shop down there, which will bring in more money for a lot less effort. But how am I going to get my husband to agree? I have to convince him, or I'll never be able to take Napirai. Apart from anything else, I couldn't get there on my own. Who would hold Napirai for the long journey?

After a good three hours I see a distant cloud of dust and assume it must be Father Giuliani. He soon comes to a halt beside us, looks at the car, and shakes his head. Why didn't I get him to put the battery in, he asks—it's unusable now! My tears start up again as I try to tell him we've only had it a week. He'll have a go at fixing it, he says, but he can't promise anything and in two days' time he's off to Italy. He lends me a spare battery, and we drive back to Barsaloi, where he patches up the casing with tar, but it won't last long. Father Giuliani's departure fills me with apprehension because for three months I'll no longer have my guardian angel. Father Roberto is not much use.

That evening as usual the boys drop in and hand over the money from the shop. Usually I make chai and when Lketinga isn't there even offer something to eat. The boys always cheer me up because I can have a proper conversation with them. James is disappointed, though, that I'm not about to organize another truck.

For the first time I mention in front of everyone that I'm thinking of getting away from here because otherwise our money is going to run out totally. The room is deathly quiet as I explain to them that I simply don't have the money to continue. The car is ruining us. Lketinga immediately jumps in to say that we've only just reopened the shop and we should keep on with it. This is home and he's not leaving his family. I ask him what he's going to use for money to buy new supplies, and offhandedly he says I can write to my mother and she can send more money as usual. He doesn't understand that this was my own money. The boys understand, but they don't dare say much because my husband dismisses all their suggestions. I try sweet words and try to present Mombasa as a great place to do business. James would be ready immediately to go to Mombasa, as he'd like to see the sea too, but my husband doesn't want us to leave.

We let the conversation drop for today and play a round of cards. There's lots of laughter, but Lketinga, who refuses to learn the game, looks on dubiously. He still doesn't like the boys coming around and usually sits ostentatiously apart chewing *miraa* or teasing the boys until they get annoyed and leave. But they're the only people who do come to see us anymore. Day by day now I start mentioning Mombasa, and with no basic foodstuffs in the shop there's really not much to do there. Lketinga can see that too, but he still won't give in.

Yet again we're sitting there, the three of us playing cards with just an oil lamp to light the table and Lketinga stalking up and down the room like a tiger. Outside it's bright with almost a full moon in the sky. I decide to stretch my legs for a bit and put my bare feet on the floor, only to step on something slimy. I shout out in horror.

Everybody but Lketinga laughs. He grabs the lamp from the table and looks at the strange something on the ground. It looks like a squashed animal, maybe even a goat embryo. The boys think so too, but it's no more than four inches long, and it's hard to be sure. Lketinga looks at me and suggests it's something I've lost. For a minute I don't know what he's talking about.

Then angrily he demands to know who got me pregnant. Now he says he knows why the boys come around every day. I've been having an affair with one of them. James sees that I'm totally shocked and tries to calm him down, but Lketinga pushes his arms away and goes to grab James's friend. But the two boys are quicker and run out of the house. Lketinga turns and grabs me, shaking me and ordering me to tell him the name of my lover. I pull myself free and scream at him furiously: "You are completely crazy! Go out of my house; you are crazy!" I'm convinced that he's now about to hit me for the first time, but he simply says he will avenge this dishonor by finding the boy and killing him. And with that he storms out of the house.

Outside everyone is standing at their doors staring at us. When my husband is out of sight, I grab together some money and our passports and run to the Mission with Napirai. I knock on the door like a lunatic and pray that Father Roberto will open up. In a few seconds he's standing there staring at us. In as few words as possible I tell him what's happened and ask him to take us to Maralal immediately; it's a matter of life and death. Roberto wrings his hands and says he's sorry, but he can't. He has another two months on his own here before Father Giuliani comes back, and he can't afford to fall out with the local people. He tells me to go home, it can't be that bad. But he's clearly worried. At the very least I entrust our money and passports to him so that my husband can't find them and destroy them.

When I get back home, he's already there with Mama. He wants to know what I was up to at the Mission, but I refuse to reply. Then he asks angrily what happened to the embryo. I tell him the truth—that our cat dragged it out—but of course he doesn't believe me and says I must have flushed it down the toilet. He tells Mama that now he knows I've been having an affair with this boy and spent the night with him in the boardinghouse in Maralal before I went off for Switzerland the first time. How on earth did he find that out? My efforts to be helpful have rebounded in my face! Mama asks me if this is true. Of course I can't deny it, but they simply won't believe that nothing happened. I sit there sobbing, which just makes me look all the guiltier.

Thoroughly disappointed in both of them, I now just want to get out of here as soon as possible. After a long discussion Mama decides that Lketinga should spend the night in the *manyatta* and we should talk it all over tomorrow. But my husband refuses to leave without Napirai. I scream at him that he should leave my baby alone, particularly as he doesn't even believe it's his. But he grabs her and stalks off into the dark.

I'm left sitting alone on the bed and curl up in a ball sobbing. Of course I could just take the car and drive out of the village, but without my child that's not something I'm even willing to contemplate. I hear people talking and laughing outside; it seems a few people find it all funny. After a while the vet and his wife look in to see if I'm all right. They've heard everything and want to console me. I don't sleep a wink that night and just pray that someday we'll get out of here. My love has turned into pure hatred. How it could all go so sour in such a short time, I simply don't understand.

Early the next morning I go around to the back of the shop to tell the boys that Lketinga plans to take his revenge on one of them. Then I hurry down to Mama because I still need to breast-feed Napirai. Mama is sitting outside the hut with her. My husband is still asleep. I take the child, feed her, and Mama asks me if Lketinga really is the father. With tears in my eyes, I say: "Yes."

Anger and Impotence

My husband crawls out of the *manyatta* and orders me to come with him back to our house. He fetches the boys too. As ever, a crowd of onlookers has gathered. My heart is pounding. I don't know what's going to happen next. Angrily Lketinga turns to me and in front of everybody asks me if I've slept with this boy. He wants to know here and now. I'm deeply hurt and at the same time furiously angry. He's acting like a prosecution lawyer and doesn't even see how ridiculous he makes us look. "No!" I shout at him. "You are crazy!" But before I can say another word I get my first clip around the ear. Furiously I hurl my cigarette packet at his head. He spins around and lifts his *rungu* club at me. But before he can use it the boys and the vet intervene to hold him back. They talk to him angrily and tell him he needs to go off into the bush for a bit and not come back until he has a clear head. With that he takes his spears and stalks off. I rush back into the house and refuse to talk to anybody.

He's gone for two days, during which I refuse to leave the house. I couldn't leave if I wanted to because nobody would help me without payment. I spend the time listening to German music or reading poems to help me gather my thoughts together. I'm just in the middle of writing a letter home when my husband turns up unannounced. He turns the music off and asks why there's singing going on and where I got this cassette from? I've always had it of course, and I tell him that as calmly as possible, but he doesn't believe it. Then he finds the letter to my mother. He insists that I read it to him but refuses to believe I'm not making it up. So I rip the letter up and burn it. He doesn't say a word to Napirai, as if she weren't even there, but he's relatively calm, so I try not to agitate him.

In the end I'm going to have to make my peace with him if I want to get out of here someday.

The next few days pass quietly, as the boy has left Barsaloi. James tells me he's moved in with relatives. The shop remains closed, and after two weeks we've nothing more to eat. I want to go to Maralal, but my husband forbids it, telling me other women can get by on milk and meat.

Again and again I mention Mombasa. I tell him that if we were to move there, my family would be sure to send some money, but up here they won't send any more. We could always come back here at any time if the shop didn't work out. When one day even James says he has to leave Barsaloi to find a job, Lketinga asks me for the first time what we would do in Mombasa. His resistance may be wearing down. I've also done everything I can: I've got rid of my books and my music, I've stopped writing letters. I've even consented to intimacy again, albeit reluctantly. I have only one goal: to get out of here. With Napirai!

I conjure up pictures of a Masai Shop with lots of souvenirs. To get money for the journey to Mombasa we can sell everything that's left in the shop to the Somalis. Even our furniture will fetch a price; there's no other way of getting hold of a bed, chairs, or a table here. We can put on a farewell disco to make money and say good-bye to people at the same time. James can come with us and help get the shop up and running. I talk and talk and try not to show how nervous I am. He mustn't know how important it is for me to get him to agree.

Eventually he relaxes and says, "Corinne, maybe we go to Mombasa in two or three months." Taken aback, I ask him why wait so long. He says because then Napirai will be a year old and won't need me, so she can stay here with Mama. This knocks me back to say the least, and I tell him calmly that there's no question of my going away without Napirai. I need my daughter with me or else I will take no pleasure in working. Then James joins in: he can look after Napirai, and if we want to go, we ought to go now, he adds, because in three months' time he'll have his circumcision ceremony. The festival lasts a couple of days, and for a long time after that he'll only be allowed to be in the company of the other newly circumcised men. We talk it over and decide to set off in three weeks' time. June 4 will be my thirtieth birthday, and I want to celebrate it in Mombasa. I'm impatient now and live only for the day when we can leave Barsaloi.

As it's the beginning of the month we want to have the disco as soon as possible. For one last time we drive down to Maralal to fetch beer and other drinks. While we're there my husband insists that I phone Switzerland to make sure we'll have money in Mombasa. I fake the phone call and tell him everything's fixed up and as soon as we're in Mombasa I'm to get in touch again.

Once again the disco is a huge success. I've agreed with Lketinga that at midnight we'll make a short speech to say good-bye, as nobody has any idea we're leaving. But after a while my husband disappears and by midnight I'm on my own, so I ask the vet to translate the speech—which I've written down in English—into Swahili for the workers and Masai for the locals.

James turns the music off, and everybody stops what they're doing to see what's happening. Nervously I walk into the middle of the room and ask for their attention. First of all I apologize for my husband's absence, then I announce that this will be our last disco and that in two weeks' time we'll be leaving Barsaloi to start up a new business in Mombasa. It just isn't possible for us to continue up here with the high costs of keeping a car and also the constant risks to my own and my daughter's health. I thank everybody for their loyal support in the shop and wish them the best of luck with the new school.

No sooner have I finished than a great commotion breaks out with everybody talking at once. Even the little local boss man is depressed and tells me that I can't just pick up and leave when everybody has accepted me. A couple of others stand up to say nice things about us and how much everyone will miss us, how we've provided so much quality of life and entertainment, not to mention the good turns we've done for people with the car. Everybody applauds. I'm deeply moved and ask for the music to be turned on to get the atmosphere going again.

In the midst of all this the young Somali comes up to me and says he's sorry to hear we're going too. He says he's always been amazed by what I've achieved. I'm touched and buy him a soft drink and suggest he might like to buy the rest of our stock. He agrees immediately. He says I should just make an inventory and we'll settle on a price; he's even interested in buying our expensive weighing scales. I have a long chat with the vet, who didn't know our departure plans either. But after everything that's happened he can understand, and he just hopes that in Mombasa my husband will come back to his senses. He's probably the only one who understands the real reason we're leaving.

We close the doors at two A.M., and Lketinga still isn't back. I hurry down to the *manyatta* to fetch Napirai. My husband is sitting in the hut talking to Mama. When I ask him why he wasn't there, he says it was my party because I'm the one who wants to leave. This time I don't get involved in an argument but simply stay with him in the *manyatta*. Who knows, I'm thinking, maybe this is the last time I'll spend the night in one?

When the opportunity arises, I tell Lketinga about my deal with the Somali. At first he's cross and doesn't want to talk about it. He won't bargain with the likes of them, he says arrogantly. So instead I work out the inventory with James. The Somali asks us to bring the stuff down to him in two days' time and he'll have the money ready. The scales alone come to a third of the total.

People keep turning up at our house wanting to buy things; and everything, down to the last cup, is reserved for someone. I've asked everyone to bring their money on May 20 and they can pick up their goods on May 21. When we go to take all our stock down to the Somali, my husband comes along after all, to give his agreement on the price of every last item. When I include the scales, he takes them out and insists we should bring them with us to Mombasa. He simply can't see that we don't need them anymore and will get much more for them here. No, he insists, we have to take them, even though it infuriates me to have to give so much money back to the Somali, but I say nothing. Let's not have another argument before we leave. There's a whole week to go before May 21.

The days before we go simply crawl by, and I get more and more tense inside as the day of our departure approaches. I don't want to spend an hour longer here than we need to. Suddenly it's our final night. Almost everybody has brought their money, and anything we no longer need we've simply given away. The car is packed full, and the only things left in the house are the bed with the mosquito net, the table, and chairs. Mama spent the whole day with us looking after Napirai. She's upset about our leaving.

That evening a car stops in the village at the Somali's, and my husband goes down to see if there's any *miraa* to buy. In the meantime James and I are working out our itinerary, both of us excited at the prospect of such a long journey. It's over nine hundred miles to the south coast.

When my husband still hasn't come back an hour later, I start to get worried. Eventually he turns up, and I can tell at once that there's something wrong. "We cannot go tomorrow," he announces. He's chewing *miraa,* of course, but the look on his face is extremely serious. I'm starting to simmer and demand to know where he's been such a long time and why we can't set off tomorrow. With wild eyes he tells us the elders aren't happy that we should set off without their blessing. And in those circumstances it's impossible for him to leave.

I get worked up and ask why they can't give us their blessing first thing in the morning, but James tells me for a ceremony like that we need to slaughter at least two goats and brew beer. Only when they're in a good mood will they pronounce the will of Enkai. He can understand why Lketinga won't go without this blessing.

At that point my nerves give in and I shout at Lketinga, asking why this didn't occur to the elders before. They've all known for three weeks now when we were due to leave: we had a party, sold everything we didn't need, and packed up the rest. I refuse to stay one day longer. I'm going even if I have to drive all the way with Napirai on my own. I sob and rage because I know that this so-called surprise will delay us for at least another week because that's how long it takes to brew their beer.

Lketinga simply says that he's not going and chews his weed, while James goes off to ask for advice from Mama. I throw myself on the bed and wish I were dead. There's just one thought going around in my head: I'm leaving tomorrow; I'm leaving tomorrow. As a result I've hardly had any sleep when James turns up at dawn with Mama. There's more palaver, but I pay not the slightest bit of attention, blindly continuing to pack up our stuff. I barely notice what's going on through my puffy eyes. James is talking to Mama, and lots of other people keep turning up to collect things or say good-bye. I ignore them all.

Then James comes up to me and asks on Mama's behalf if I'm determined to leave. "Yes," I reply, and grab Napirai by my side. Mama stares silently at me and her grandchild. Then she says something to James that makes his face light up. He turns to me happily and says Mama will go off and fetch four Barsaloi elders who'll give us the blessing then and there. She doesn't want us to leave without it, because she's convinced she'll never see us again. Thankfully I ask James to translate for her that wherever I am I will always see that she is all right.

Mud in Your Eye!

We hang around for an hour with ever more people turning up. I hide myself back in the house until eventually Mama turns up with three elderly men. The three of us go and stand in front of the car, and Mama gives a little speech during which the others repeat "Enkai" in chorus. It takes about ten minutes before we get a gob of spittle pressed against each of our foreheads as a good-luck charm. With that, to my relief, the ceremony is over. I press some utensil or other into the hand of each of the elders, although Mama just points at Napirai and says all she wants is our baby.

But thanks to her help I've won the day, and she's the only one I embrace again before I climb behind the steering wheel. Lketinga hesitates until I start up the engine, and then he gets in sulkily. I drive off immediately without once looking back; it's a long journey but it leads to freedom.

With every mile I put behind me I feel strength returning. I intend to drive all the way to Nyahururu, and only then will I breathe freely. But an hour before we even get to Maralal we have to stop because of a puncture. We're laden to the roof, and the spare wheel is underneath everything, but I don't let myself get flustered: this will be the last time we change a wheel in Samburu country.

Our next stop is just outside Nyahururu, at Rumuruti, where the tarmac road begins. A police checkpoint stops us, demanding to see my registration and my international driver's license. The license expired long ago, but they don't notice and instead tell me I'll have to get a new sticker with our address for the windshield because that's the regulation. I'm amazed; in Maralal nobody's heard of such a sticker.

We spend the night in Nyahururu and the next day ask where we have
to get the sticker from. Once again the stress of Kenyan bureaucracy kicks
in. First of all we have to take the car to a garage to get all its faults fixed,
then we have to pay for a technical test. The car is in the garage all day,
which costs even more money. On the second day it's ready, and I'm
convinced it'll all work out, but when we get to the test, the inspector
immediately fails us for the patched battery and the lack of a sticker. I
explain to him that we're in the process of moving and don't yet have an
address in Mombasa, but he's not interested: without an address, we can't
have a sticker. I drive off, astounded by the stupidity of it all. We've spent
two days hanging around spending money, all for nothing. But I'm
determined to get to Mombasa, and we drive for several more hours until
we find a place to stay in a village on the other side of Nairobi. I'm tired
from so much driving, especially because I have to concentrate on driving
on the left, but I still have to wash diapers and feed Napirai. Happily with
the level roads we're not used to, she's slept a lot.

The next day we reach Mombasa after another seven hours on the
road. The climate down here is tropical heat, and we're exhausted as we
join the line of cars waiting for the ferry to the south bank. I fish out the
letter I received a couple of months ago from Sophia shortly after she
arrived in Mombasa. Her address is near Ukunda, and I hope she'll
provide us with a roof over our heads for the night.

It takes us another hour to find the new building where Sophia lives,
but nobody seems to be home at this grand address. I knock next door,
and a white woman opens the door and tells me Sophia's gone to Italy for
two weeks. I'm hugely disappointed and can't think where we'll find a
place to stay, until I remember Priscilla. My husband's not enthusiastic
about this idea, however, and says he'd rather stay on the north bank. I'm
not happy with that because I had such bad experiences over there. We're
starting to get irritable, and so I decide just to drive to our own village.
But when we get there only one of the five houses is still in a habitable
condition. At least we find out, however, that Priscilla has moved to the
adjacent village, just five minutes' drive away.

In next to no time we're in Kamau village, which is laid out in the
shape of a horseshoe with the buildings all a series of joined-together
rooms like the boardinghouses in Maralal, but with a big shop in the
middle. I'm immediately taken with this village. The minute we stop the

car children come out to look, and the shop owner's peering from his window. All of a sudden Priscilla appears, hardly able to believe her eyes. She's delighted, particularly when she sees Napirai. In the meantime she's had another boy too, a little older than Napirai. Straightaway she takes us into her room, makes tea, and demands that we tell her everything. When she hears that we're planning to stay in Mombasa, she's thrilled, and for the first time since we left Barsaloi even Lketinga seems to cheer up. She offers to let us stay in her room and use her water, which even here has to be fetched in canisters from a spring. She can spend the night with a friend, and tomorrow she'll fix up somewhere of our own for us. Yet again I'm overwhelmed by her simple friendliness and hospitality.

After such a tiring day we go to bed early. The next morning Priscilla has already found us a room at the end of the row, and we can park the car beside it. The room is just ten feet square, and everything is made of concrete except for the straw roof. During the day we see some of the other inhabitants, all of them Samburu warriors, some of whom we recognize. Before long Lketinga is sitting talking and laughing with them, showing Napirai off proudly.

Fresh Hope

When I go into the shop for the first time I feel as if I'm in paradise. There's everything here—even bread, milk, butter, eggs, fruit—all just two hundred yards from our door. My hope of starting again in Mombasa begins to grow.

James wants to see the sea at last, and so we set off together on foot. It's barely half an hour to the beach. The sight of the ocean fills me with happiness and a feeling of freedom. The only thing I can't get used to again is the sight of white tourists in swimming costumes. James, who's never seen anything of the sort, looks away in embarrassment and instead stares at the sea in astonishment. Just like his older brother, he finds it hard to deal with. Napirai, on the other hand, plays happily in the sand in the shadow of the palm trees. Here I can start to imagine my life in Kenya starting anew.

We go into one of the beach bars designed for the Europeans to quench our thirst. Everybody stares at us, and I don't know where to look standing there in my patched-up skirt, even though it's clean. When a German woman speaks to me, asking if Napirai is my baby, I can't even find the words to reply. It's been so long since I've spoken German, let alone Swiss German, that I feel like an idiot having to answer her in English.

The next day Lketinga goes off to the north bank to buy some trinkets so that he can join in the Masai dances where they sell them afterward. I'm pleased to see he's interested in earning money. Back home I'm washing diapers while James plays with Napirai, and Priscilla and I make plans for the future. She's thrilled when I tell her I want to find a shop to sell things to the tourists. Since James can stay for only a month before he has to go home for his big circumcision ceremony, I decide to go around to the hotels with Priscilla to see if there's a shop available.

In the grandiose hotels the managers look at us skeptically before quickly sending us away. By the fifth hotel my minimal self-confidence has evaporated, and I feel like a beggar. Obviously I don't look like the average businesswoman with my red-checked skirt and a baby on my back. By chance an Indian at the reception overhears us talking and gives me the telephone number of his brother. The next day James, Lketinga, and I drive into Mombasa to meet him. He has something available next to a supermarket in a newly built residence, but it costs seven hundred Swiss francs a month. My first reaction is to turn it down because the rent seems far too expensive, but then I agree to let him show us the building.

The shop has a regal position just off the main road to Diani Beach, only fifteen minutes' drive from us. The building already contains a huge Indian souvenir shop, and there's a newly opened Chinese restaurant opposite, but everything else is vacant. Because the whole building is stepped, the shop wouldn't be immediately visible from the street, but even so, and despite the fact that it's just two hundred feet square, I decide to take it. The room is completely bare, and Lketinga doesn't understand why I want to spend so much on a completely empty shop. He goes off to the tourist shows but spends the money he makes on beer or *miraa*, which causes a few more arguments.

While local workers assemble the wooden shelving to my instructions, James and I get wooden beams in Ukunda and transport them to the shop in the car. We work like lunatics all day while my husband hangs around with the other warriors in Ukunda.

I spend the evenings mostly washing and cooking and then, when Napirai is asleep, chatting with Priscilla. In early evening Lketinga uses the car to transport groups of warriors to their dance shows. I'm not happy about it because he doesn't have a driver's license and he drinks beer. When he turns up late at night, he wakes me up to ask me who I've been talking to. If any of the warriors living nearby are already home, he's convinced I've been talking to them. I warn him in no uncertain terms that he's going to ruin everything again with his jealousy. James tries to tell him the same thing.

At last Sophia has returned, and we're delighted to see each other. She can hardly believe that we're already working on a shop. She's been here for five months and still hasn't opened her café. But she soon puts a damper on my enthusiasm when she tells me how much bureaucracy I'm going to have to deal with. Unlike us she has a comfortable home. We see each other almost every day, which eventually starts to annoy my husband, who doesn't understand what we have to talk about and assumes it must be him. Sophia tries to calm him down and tells him he shouldn't drink so much beer.

It's just two weeks since I signed the rental agreement and already the shop is fitted out. I want to open at the end of the month, but we need to get a license for the shop and a work permit for me. Sophia tells me we can get the license in Kwale, and she and her boyfriend come with us. Once again we have to fill out forms and stand in lines. Sophia is called in first and disappears into the office with her companion. She comes out five minutes later to say it's no good because they're not married. We don't seem to do any better, which I can hardly believe. The official says we can't have the license without a work permit unless I go to a lawyer and sign over everything to my husband. And in any case first of all the shop name has to be registered in Nairobi.

How I've come to hate that city! And now we have to go back again. As we're plodding out to the car, disappointed and depressed, the official comes hurrying after us and says there might be a way to avoid Nairobi if he works on it. He'll be in Ukunda at four P.M., and we could meet up at Sophia's. Now of course we understand what it's all about: bribery! My gall is rising, but Sophia immediately agrees. We sit at her house, waiting, and I'm furious that Lketinga and I didn't go to Kwale alone. Then this character turns up and slimes his way into the house, comes straight out with it, and says we can have the licenses tomorrow if each of us brings five thousand shillings in an envelope. Sophia agrees immediately, and I have no alternative but to nod my agreement too.

So we get the licenses without further ado. That's the first step. My husband can now sell, but I'm not allowed to be in the shop or even to discuss a purchase with a customer. I know that this isn't going to work and persuade my husband to come with me to Nairobi to get me a work permit and register the shop name. We decide to call it "Sidai's Masai Shop," which leads to long arguments with Lketinga. Sidai is his middle name, but he doesn't want to use the word "Masai." But now that we've got the license, there's no going back.

When we get to the competent office in Nairobi, we have to wait for several hours before we're seen. I know how important this is and try to make sure my husband understands too. If they say no, there's no changing it. They ask us why and for what reason I need to be able to work. I take pains to tell the woman in charge that we are a family and that because my husband has never been to school, I have no choice but to work. She agrees with this, but to be certain of getting a permit, apart from the license, I need to have brought some hundred thousand Swiss francs into the country, and so far I'm still twenty thousand short. I promise to have the money sent from Switzerland and come back, and I leave the office with high hopes. I'm going to need money anyhow to buy stock. We set off for home exhausted.

When we get back, dog-tired, there are already a few warriors waiting for us making spears for sale. Edy is one of them, and we're delighted to see him again after such a long time. While we're talking about old times, Napirai crawls over to him happily. As it's late and I'm tired, I invite Edy to come over for tea tomorrow. After all, he was the one who helped me back when I had no idea how to find Lketinga.

No sooner have the warriors gone than my husband starts berating me with allegations about Edy and me. Now he knows why I spent three months in Mombasa on my own and didn't come looking for him sooner. I can't believe what he's suggesting and simply want to get away from him so I don't have to listen to his horrible allegations. I take Napirai, put her on my back, and charge off into the night.

I'm wandering around aimlessly when all of a sudden I find myself in front of the Africana Sea Lodge. I'm immediately overcome by the need to phone my mother and tell her what's happening to my marriage. I sob into the phone, telling my surprised mother how miserable I am. It's hard for her to advise me just like that, so I ask her to see if someone from our family could come out to Kenya. I need some sensible advice and moral support, and perhaps it would help Lketinga to start trusting me. We agree to talk again the next day at the same time. I feel better after our conversation and make my way back to our little home.

My husband of course is more ready for a fight than ever and demands to know where I've been. When I tell him I've been talking to my mother and that someone from my family is coming out, he immediately quiets down.

The next evening I'm relieved to hear that my older brother is prepared to come out and will be here in a week with the money I need. Lketinga is curious to meet someone new from my family, and because it's my oldest brother he's already respectful and in a better mood. He starts making him a Masai armband with his first name embroidered in glass beads. I'm impressed by how important James and he consider this visit.

My brother Marc checks in at the Two Fishes Hotel. We're all delighted, although he can stay only a week. He asks us over to the hotel for dinner often, and it's wonderful, although I don't dare think about his bill. Of course he sees my husband at his best; the whole week long he touches neither beer nor *miraa* and never leaves my brother's side. When Marc comes to see us, he's amazed to see where his sister, who was once so elegant, is living. But he's impressed by the shop and gives me a few good tips. The week passes far too quickly, and on the last evening he has a long talk with Lketinga. James translates every word. When Lketinga promises earnestly and solemnly not to plague me with his jealousy again, we're convinced that the visit has been a complete success.

Two days later James has to leave too. So we take him as far as Nairobi and go back to the Nyayo Building to see about the work permit. The atmosphere between us is good, and I'm certain everything will work out. The name has been registered; we have all our paperwork. We find ourselves back in the same office with the same woman from two and a half weeks ago, and when she sees the money everything is fine. I get my work permit, and she absolves me from the need to renew it for the next two years. During that time I have to get my husband's name on my passport and a Kenyan identity card for my daughter. I don't mind. The main thing is that I have a work permit for two years, something that lots of people wait years for, but despite having now brought enough hard currency into the country, we have to pay two thousand Swiss francs out of it as a fee.

In Nairobi we go down to the Masai market and buy lots of stuff. Now we can start up the business properly. In Mombasa I seek out factories where I can buy jewelry, masks, T-shirts, kangas, bags, and other goods at decent prices. My husband mostly comes with me and looks after Napirai, but he rarely agrees with the prices. Sophia is surprised when she comes to see the shop. After just five weeks back at the coast we've got everything, including the work permit. She hasn't got anywhere yet.

I get five thousand flyers printed up, introducing the shop and showing how to get there. They're aimed primarily at Germans and Swiss, and most hotels allow me to leave them at the reception desk. In two of the biggest hotels I rent window cases to display some of our goods and one of our unusual wedding photos. Now we're ready.

The next morning at nine we open the shop. I take an omelette and bananas along for Napirai. It's very quiet. Only two people show up briefly in the shop. By midday it's very hot, and there are no tourists to be seen on the street. We go off to eat in Ukunda and open up again at two P.M. Every now and then a few tourists wander along the street to the supermarket, but they don't notice our shop.

Eventually during the afternoon a group of Swiss turn up holding some of our flyers. I chat with them happily, and they all want to hear my story. Almost all of them buy something. I'm pleased enough with our first day, although I realize we're going to have to do something to make ourselves more noticeable. The next day I suggest to Lketinga that he go out and stick a flyer in the hand of every white person he comes across. He's the sort of person people notice. It works. The Indian next door is mystified when he finds all the tourists going past his shop to get to ours.

Today, day two, business is good. That said: it's been hard with Napirai sometimes when she's not asleep. I've laid out a little mattress for her underneath the T-shirt rail. Because I'm still breast-feeding it's inevitable, of course, that that's what I'm doing when tourists show up. Napirai doesn't like being interrupted and makes it clear and loud. We decide, therefore, to get a babysitter in the shop. Lketinga finds a young girl of about seventeen, the wife of one of the warriors. I like her right away, particularly as she turns up in traditional Masai clothing and pretty jewelry. She gets on with Napirai and fits in with the shop. We bring her with us in the car each morning and leave her off at her husband's in the evening.

By now the shop's been open for a week, and we're making more money every day. But that means we'll soon need to replenish our supplies from Mombasa. That's a problem in itself because Lketinga can't wait on customers on his own all day—sometimes there are up to ten people in the shop at once—and that means we'll need another shop assistant to fill in when neither of us is there. It will have to be someone from our village because in three weeks' time my husband is off home for James's circumcision ceremony. As a member of the family I ought to go too, and I have great difficulty convincing him that we shouldn't shut the shop down so soon after opening it. He accepts that I should stay only when my younger sister Sabine announces she wants to come to visit at exactly the same time. I'm thoroughly relieved by the news of her visit because wild horses wouldn't drag me back to Barsaloi.

Lketinga has no objections anymore and on the contrary will make the effort to be back in time to see her before she leaves. But we're not there yet. First we have to find someone to help out in the shop. I suggest Priscilla, but he is immediately against that idea; he doesn't trust her at all. I'm horrified and point out everything she's done for us. But he won't agree and instead brings a Masai boy back one evening. He's from the Masai-Mara and has been to school, as a result of which he's wearing jeans and a T-shirt. I don't mind, though, as he seems honest, so I agree that William will be our new assistant.

At last I can sort out replacement stocks of T-shirts and carvings and leave the pair of them to run the shop. The babysitter comes with me, bringing Napirai. It's hard work, going from one dealer to the next, looking at their goods and bargaining. I'm back around midday to find Lketinga at the bar of the Chinese restaurant drinking expensive beer, leaving William alone in the shop. I ask how many people have been in. Not many and they've sold only a Masai trinket. There are lots of tourists walking up and down the main street, and I ask somewhat irritably if Lketinga's been handing out our flyers. William shakes his head and says he's been drinking beer in the bar all the time and took the float from the cash till. That makes me angry, and when he strolls into the shop I can smell the beer on his breath. Of course we have an argument, which ends up with him taking the car and disappearing. I'm feeling let down again: now we have a babysitter and an employee, and my husband's drinking the profits.

William and I set out the new stock. As soon as we see white people he runs out onto the street and hands them a flyer. Almost everyone he approaches comes into the shop, and by five-thirty, when Lketinga comes back, the shop's full and we're talking up our wares to all sorts of customers. Of course people are asking about my husband, so I introduce him, but he just stares through the tourists and instead demands to know what we've sold and for how much. His behavior is worse than rude.

A Swiss man buys some trinkets and a carved mask for his two daughters—good business—but before he leaves he asks if he can take a picture of me and my husband and Napirai. Of course I agree because he's just spent a lot of money, but my husband says he'll agree to be photographed only if he gets paid. The pleasant Swiss man is annoyed, and I'm embarrassed. He takes two photographs and actually gives Lketinga ten shillings. When he's out of hearing, I try to impress on Lketinga just why you don't ask customers to pay to take photographs. He doesn't understand and accuses me of getting in his way whenever he tries to earn money. All the Masais demand money when they have their photograph taken, he says, why shouldn't he, and his eyes twinkle nastily. I tell him again wearily that the others don't have a shop like we do.

As new customers turn up I try to pull myself together and be pleasant, but my husband glowers at them suspiciously, and if one of them so much as touches something, he insists that they've bought it. William, cleverly and smoothly, tries to steer the customers away from Lketinga to save something of the situation.

Within ten days of our opening we've earned the month's rent. I'm proud of myself and of William. Most tourists come back the next day with other people from their hotel, and word about the shop gets around, not least because our prices are cheaper than the hotel boutiques'. I have to go into Mombasa every three or four days to get more stock.

Because lots of people ask for gold jewelry I see if I can find a suitable glass cabinet to display it. It's not that easy, but eventually I find a workshop that'll make it to order. A week later it's ready to be picked up. I take all our woolen blankets along and park right outside the workshop. Four men carry the heavy glass cabinet out to the car, but in the ten minutes that I'd left it—locked!—the woolen blankets have been stolen. The lock on the driver's side has been broken. The shop owner gives me old sacks and cartons so I can at least provide some protection, but I'm annoyed to have lost my Swiss blankets. Lketinga will be cross too to have lost his red blanket, and I'm in a bad mood as I drive back south.

There's just William in the shop, but he comes up to me proudly to say he's sold goods worth eight hundred shillings. I tell him how pleased

I am. There's no way we can unload the cabinet on our own, so he goes down to the beach to find friends to help and comes back after half an hour with three Masai who take the cabinet out carefully and set it upright. I give them all a soft drink and ten shillings each as thanks. Then I start displaying the fashion jewelry in the cabinet while they sit outside drinking their sodas with the babysitter and Napirai.

As ever my husband turns up when all the work's been done. With him is the babysitter's husband. He calls his young wife over angrily, and I see the other Masai slope away. Somewhat taken aback, I ask William what the matter is, and he says the husband doesn't like his wife sitting with other men. If he finds it happening again, he'll stop her working here. I'd like to get involved but know better and have to just content myself that Lketinga doesn't start up again. I'm appalled at the husband's attitude and feel sorry for the babysitter, who's gone to sit farther away with her head down.

Thank God some customers turn up, and William rushes off to deal with them. When I hear from their speech that they're Swiss, I go to talk to them. They're from Biel! I'm curious to hear the latest from my hometown, and we start chatting. Then one of them invites me over for a beer in the Chinese restaurant. I ask Lketinga if he minds, and he says generously: "Why not, Corinne, no problem if you know these people." Of course I don't know the couple at all, although they are about my age and may know some of my old friends.

We spend an hour in the restaurant bar before we say good-bye, but when I get back, the same old interrogation starts up. Where do I know these people from? Why did I laugh such a lot with the man? Is he a friend of Marco's or maybe an old boyfriend of mine? Questions and more questions and all the time it's: "Corinne, you can tell me. I know, no problem, now this man has another lady. Please tell me, before you come to Kenya, maybe you sleep with him?" I can't listen to it anymore and put my hands over my ears while the tears stream down my cheeks. I could scream with rage.

At last it's closing time, and we go home. Naturally William heard everything and tells Priscilla. At any rate she comes over to us and asks if we've got problems. I can't keep it in and tell her what happened. She tries to bring Lketinga to his senses, and I take Napirai to bed. In two weeks my sister will be here, and if I'm lucky my husband'll be gone. Our quarrels keep getting more frequent, and all his promises and good intentions after my brother's visit have come to nothing.

I get up at seven o'clock every morning in order to be in the shop by nine. Traveling salesmen now turn up almost every day offering carvings or gold jewelry, which makes it much easier to renew our stock. I can deal with them only when Lketinga isn't in the shop, however, because he behaves so appallingly. The salesmen speak to me first, and my husband finds that insupportable. He throws them out and says they should come back when they find out who the shop belongs to: it does, after all, say Sidai's Masai Shop above the door.

William, on the other hand, is a real help. He slips out after the salesmen and tells them to come back in the afternoon when my husband is in Ukunda. A whole week goes by like this until eventually Lketinga heads off home, saying he'll be back in three weeks' time so he can meet Sabine in the last week of her holiday.

Every day William and I drive to the shop together. Usually the babysitter is already there or we meet her on the way. Even in the mornings now we get several tourists turning up: often Italians, Americans, English, or Germans. I enjoy being able to talk to everybody so easily. William goes out onto the street to tout for trade without having to be asked, and he gets better and better at it. There are days when, among other things, we sell up to three gold chains with the Kenyan coat of arms. A dealer comes to see us twice a week so I can even place orders for customers.

We close regularly at lunchtime for an hour and a half and go to see Sophia. Now I can eat spaghetti and salad at her house with no problems. Her restaurant has just opened, although she still isn't allowed to work there herself. I pay for William's meal of course because it would cost half his monthly wages. The first time he realizes that he says he won't come anymore, but without him I couldn't take Napirai along, and as he works so hard I'm happy to treat him. The babysitter goes home to eat.

In the meantime I've been making so much money that I have to take it to the bank at lunchtime. We have no more problems with the car either. Once a week I go shopping in Mombasa, and anything else I need we get from itinerant food sellers. I feel like a proper businesswoman again. For the first time everything to do with the shop is working well.

In the second week of August Sabine arrives to stay at the Africana Sea

Lodge. On the day of her arrival I go to the hotel with Priscilla and Napirai, leaving William in the shop. It's great to see her again. This is the first time she's been on vacation to another continent. Unfortunately I don't have much time to spare, as I have to get back to the shop. In any case she wants to spend the day sunbathing, so we agree to meet in the hotel bar in the evening. I bring her straight back to our village, and she's amazed too at our living conditions, although she says she likes it.

There are a few warriors at home nearby, and they ask who the girl is. Before long they're all in love with my sister. She seems fascinated by them too, but I warn her off with some sound advice and start to tell her how badly things are going with Lketinga. She can't believe it and is sorry that he's not here.

She's eager to get back to the hotel for dinner, and I take her in the car. A few warriors take the opportunity for a lift. I leave them all in front of the hotel and agree to meet Sabine again the next evening in the bar. As I drive off she's still talking to the warriors. I go over to Priscilla's to eat when Lketinga isn't there, and we take turns at cooking.

To my surprise, Sabine turns up in the shop the next afternoon with Edy, whom she's met in the Bush Baby Disco. She's only just eighteen and wants to enjoy the nightlife. I'm not happy to see them together, even though I like Edy.

They spend most of the time hanging around the pool while I work in the shop and seldom see my sister. She spends a lot of time with Edy. Now and then we meet up in our village for chai. Obviously she'd like me to come with her to the disco, but I tell her I can't because of Napirai, and then there'd be problems when Lketinga gets back. My sister doesn't understand because I was always such an independent person. But she doesn't know my husband.

A Bitter Blow

Eight days later he's back. William and I are in the shop, it's boiling hot, and there are few customers. Even so we can be happy with our turnover, which for the moment is something Sophia can only dream of. I'm sitting on the step in the doorway with Napirai, still guzzling away at my breast despite her thirteen months, when suddenly a tall man appears from behind the Indian shop and comes toward us.

It takes me a couple of seconds to recognize Lketinga. I wait for my usual feeling of happiness to see him, but instead I'm still in shock. The way he looks throws me: he's cut his long red hair short and got rid of some of the decorations he usually wears on his head. I can accept that, but his clothes look ridiculous: he's wearing an old-fashioned shirt and dark red jeans that are far too tight and too short. His feet are in cheap plastic sandals and instead of his normal languid stroll he's walking stiffly. "Corinne, why you not tell me hello? You are not happy I'm here?" Only then do I realize the way I must have stared at him. I grab hold of Napirai to compose myself and point out her papa to her. He takes her in his arms happily, but she seems uncertain too because she immediately wants to get down and come back to me.

He comes into the shop and starts examining everything, wanting to know who I've got the new Masai belts from. "From Priscilla," I tell him. He puts them all on one side and says he'll give them back to her because he doesn't want to pay her for anything. I start to get angry and for a moment even get stomach cramps. "Corinne, where is your sister?" "I don't know. Maybe in the hotel," I answer curtly. He demands the car keys so he can go and visit her, although he doesn't even know what she looks like.

An hour later he's back. Of course he hasn't found her. Instead he's been to Ukunda to buy *miraa*. He sits down in front of the shop and starts chewing. Before long there are leaves and gnawed stems all over the place. I suggest he takes his weed somewhere else, which he takes to mean I want to get rid of him. He starts interrogating William.

He doesn't tell me much about James and things at home. He just waited for the circumcision and left the celebrations early. Cautiously I ask him where his kangas are and why he's cut his hair. His kangas, he says, are in his bag and his hair ornaments too. He's not a warrior anymore, so he doesn't need them.

I put it to him that most of the Masai in Mombasa still wear their traditional clothing, jewelry, and long hair, and that it might be better for our shop. From that he deduces that I like all the others better. In reality I just wish he'd get rid of his jeans and shirt for the kangas that suit him much better, but for the moment at least I let it be.

When we get home, Sabine is sitting with Edy and the other warriors from next door in front of the hut. I introduce my husband to her, and he greets her warmly. Sabine gives me a surprised look—obviously puzzled at the way he's dressed. For his part, Lketinga still hasn't asked himself why Sabine's sitting here.

Half an hour later she wants to go back to the hotel for dinner. It's a rare chance for me to exchange a few words with her in private so I suggest to Lketinga that I drive her back to the hotel quickly while he looks after Napirai. He says it's out of the question: he wants to drive her. My sister gives me a startled look and lets me know in broad Swiss German dialect that there's no way she's getting into the car if he's driving. She doesn't know him, and he doesn't look as if he's capable of driving a car. I don't know what to do and tell her so. She turns to Lketinga and says: "Thank you, but it's better I walk with Edy to the hotel." I hold my breath for a moment to see what will happen. Lketinga laughs and says: "Why you go with him? You are sister from Corinne. So you are like my sister."

When she still won't have him drive, he tries to arrange to meet her later in the Bush Baby Disco, saying he can't let her go there on her own. Sabine, who's starting to get cross, says: "No problem, I go with Edy and you stay with Corinne or come together with her." I can see from his face that he's starting to get the picture. Sabine takes the opportunity to disappear with Edy. I make myself busy with Napirai. For ages he says absolutely nothing and just sits chewing *miraa*. Then he demands to know what I've done every evening. I tell him I've been with Priscilla, who lives only a hundred feet away. And who did I spend the night with? he then demands to know. I know what he's getting at and respond sharply: "Just Napirai!" He laughs and keeps on chewing.

I go to bed hoping that he'll stay out there all night, for I feel not the slightest desire to have him touch me. Only now do I realize how my feelings for this man have changed completely. After two and a half weeks without any complications, living with him under this pressure is almost unbearable.

A little later he comes to bed too, but I pretend to be asleep and lie against the wall with Napirai. He speaks to me, but I don't reply. When he tries to make love to me, which after a long separation like this would otherwise be normal, I'm almost sick with fear. I can't and won't. My disappointment in his behavior is just too much. I push him away and say, "Maybe tomorrow." "Corinne, you are my wife, now I have not seen you for such a long time. I want love from you! Maybe you got enough love from other men!" "No, I have not got love, I don't want love," I shout at him angrily.

Of course everybody else can hear us arguing, but I can't control myself. We end up physically tussling, which wakes Napirai, who starts crying. Lketinga climbs out of bed, furiously puts on his kangas and ornaments, and stalks off. Napirai is inconsolable. All of a sudden Priscilla appears and takes Napirai. I'm too exhausted even to start talking about our problems. All I can tell her is that Lketinga is completely crazy. She tells me calmly that all men are like that but we shouldn't shout at each other or we'll have problems with the landlord. Then she disappears.

When I go into the shop the next day with William, I still don't know where my husband spent the night. I'm in a depressed mood, and neither William nor the babysitter says much. We're glad to see tourists come in, if only to lift the atmosphere, but I leave the sales talk to William.

Lketinga doesn't turn up until nearly midday, and then he makes William's life a misery. He no longer goes out onto the street to hand out flyers but sends William instead, and at lunchtime he refuses to take him with us even though we're going to Ukunda. I'm not allowed to go to Sophia's anymore because he doesn't see what we've got to talk about.

For the past few days there doesn't seem to be enough money in the till. I can't be certain about it because I no longer go to the bank every day. From time to time my husband takes money out, and I use cash from the till to buy from itinerant merchants. But I have a feeling there's something wrong. I daren't mention it to my husband, however.

My sister's vacation is coming to an end, and I've hardly seen her. On her last night we go to the disco with her and Edy. It's what she wants to do; she says she wants to get me out with other people. We leave Napirai with Priscilla. Lketinga and I sit at a table while Sabine and Edy dance together wildly. It's the first time in ages that I've had alcohol. My thoughts drift back to the time I came here with Marco and nearly fainted when Lketinga walked in the door. How much has happened since then. I try to keep back the tears; I don't want to spoil Sabine's last day, nor do I want a fight with my husband. He too was happier back then than he is now.

My sister comes back to the table and notices immediately that there's something wrong with me. I rush off to the toilet. I'm rinsing my face with cold water when I notice her standing next to me. She takes me in her arms and we simply stand there. Then she gives me a cigarette and tells me to keep it for later, it'll do me good—there's marijuana in it—and if I need more I should tell Edy.

We go back to the table, and Lketinga asks Sabine to dance. While they're on the floor Edy asks me if I'm having problems with Lketinga. "Sometimes," I reply briefly. Edy wants to dance too, but I say no. A little later Lketinga and I leave because it's the first time I've left Napirai with Priscilla and I'm a bit worried about her. I say my good-byes to Sabine and wish her a safe journey home.

We trudge back to the village in the dark. I can hear my little girl crying long before we get there, but Priscilla assures me she's just woken up and is looking for her familiar breast milk. I take her into our room, leaving Lketinga to talk to Priscilla. When Napirai's asleep again, I go back out and sit down in the muggy night air to light up my joint. I suck the smoke greedily into my lungs, and I've just finished and stubbed out the butt when Lketinga comes over. I hope he doesn't notice the smell.

I feel a bit better and give him a smile. My head's spinning a bit, so I go to lie down. Lketinga notices there's something up with me, but I tell him it's the alcohol, which I'm no longer used to. Tonight I have no problem fulfilling my conjugal duties, and even Lketinga is surprised how willing I am.

During the night I wake up with a weak bladder and creep out to do my business behind the hut because it's too far to go to the makeshift toilet and my head's still groggy. When I climb back into our big bed, my husband asks me in the dark where I've been. Shocked by this I tell him, and he takes the flashlight and demands I show him the spot on the ground. I'm still high enough to find it all funny, but Lketinga takes even my good humor to mean I've had an assignation. I can't take him seriously and show him the wet patch on the ground. Then we both go back to sleep in silence.

The next morning my head's throbbing, and all my misery comes flooding back. After breakfast we set off for the shop but for the first time can't find William. When we get there, however, he's already waiting for us. It's none of my business, so I don't ask him where he was. He's more nervous and restrained than normal. There's not much business today, but when the shop closes, I notice that there's money missing from my bag. What on earth am I to do? I watch William and my husband—when he's there—more closely after that, but I don't notice anything untoward and I don't believe the babysitter would be capable of such a thing.

When I come back after washing, Priscilla has come around and is sitting talking to Lketinga. She says William's been spending a lot of money in Ukunda every night. We should keep an eye out, she says, as she can't imagine where he's got so much money from. I'm uneasy at the idea I'm being robbed, but I say nothing and decide I'll have a quiet word with William myself. My husband would simply fire him, and then I'd have nobody to help with the work; up until now I've been very pleased with him.

The next day once again he comes to work directly from Ukunda. Lketinga tackles him direct, but he denies everything. When the first tourists come in, William goes about his work as normal. My husband drives off to Ukunda, where I imagine he's intending to find out what William's been up to.

When I'm on my own with William, I tell him straight up that I know he's been stealing money from me every day. I promise to say nothing to Lketinga if he promises he'll work properly and there'll be no more of it. I won't even fire him. The high season starts in two months and I'll even give him an increase. He refuses to look at me and says nothing. I'm certain that he's sorry and that he stole from us only to get revenge for the way my husband's treated him. When we were on our own, there was never a shilling missing.

Lketinga comes back, having found out that William spent the night in a disco. Once again he tackles him head-on, but this time I get involved and tell him I gave him an advance yesterday. Eventually things calm down, but the atmosphere remains tense.

After such a hard day I could do with another joint to calm me down and wonder where I might find Edy. I can't think of anything right now, but tomorrow I'll go to the Africana Sea Lodge to have my hair braided. That'll take three hours, and there's a good chance of bumping into Edy in the bar.

I set off for the hotel after lunch. Both hairdressers are busy, and I have to wait half an hour before they can start the painful business. My hair is braided together with strands of wool and little colored glass beads on the end of each strand. I want lots of fine strands, and the process takes over three hours. At five-thirty they're not quite finished.

No Exit

Suddenly my husband appears with Napirai. I don't understand what's going on because I've got the car and our shop is several miles away. He looks at his watch and starts asking me where I've been all this time. I tell him, as relaxed as possible, that he can see that they're only just finishing my hair. He dumps Napirai on my lap covered in sweat and with a full diaper. I ask him angrily what he's doing here and what happened to the babysitter. He's sent her and William home and closed the shop. He's not completely daft, he says: he knows that I've been seeing somebody or I'd have been back ages ago. Nothing I can say makes the slightest difference. Lketinga is sick with jealousy and convinced that I had a rendezvous with another warrior before I had my hair done.

I want to get away from the hotel as soon as possible, and we drive straight home. I don't feel like working anymore. I simply can't believe that it's not possible for me to spend three hours at the hairdresser's without my husband going nuts. It can't go on long like this. Angry and filled with hate, I tell my husband to go home and find himself a second wife. I'll support him financially, but he should get out of here and leave us all in peace. I don't have another lover and don't want one. I simply want to work and live in peace. He can come back in two or three months, and we'll see where we go from there.

But Lketinga isn't having any of it. He doesn't want another wife, he says; he loves only me. He wants things back the way they were before Napirai was born. He simply doesn't understand that it's his stupid jealousy that's ruining everything. I can only breathe freely when he's not here. We argue, and I end up in tears and can't see any way out of all this.

I'm feeling so sorry for myself that I don't even have the strength to console Napirai. I feel like a prisoner. I need to talk to somebody. Sophia will understand. Things can't get any worse than they are, so I climb into the car and leave my husband and child there. He tries to block my way, but I put my foot down and all I hear as I drive off is: "You are crazy, Corinne."

Sophia is completely taken aback when she sees the state I'm in. She thought everything was going swimmingly and that's why I hadn't been around for such a long time. She's shocked when I tell her how far things have gone. I tell her that I'm almost desperate enough to go back to Switzerland because I'm afraid something awful might happen. Sophia tells me I should pull myself together, now that I've got my work permit and the shop's doing so well. Perhaps Lketinga will go back to Barsaloi, she says, because he obviously doesn't feel at home in Mombasa. We go through all the possibilities, but I feel burned up inside. I ask her if she has any marijuana, and it turns out her boyfriend can give me some. I feel a bit better and go home ready to face the next argument. But instead my husband's lying on the ground playing with Napirai. He doesn't even ask where I've been. This is unprecedented.

I go into our room and hastily roll a joint and smoke it. Suddenly everything seems better and easier to handle. I sit down outside in a good mood and watch with amusement as my daughter keeps trying to climb a tree. When my head gets a bit clearer, I go and buy rice and potatoes for dinner. The joint has made me really hungry. Later I wash Napirai in the basin as usual before going off to the "bush shower" myself. As always, I steep the diapers overnight so I can wash them in the morning before going to work. Then I go to bed. My husband is driving a group of warriors to a dance performance.

The next few days drag by, and I find myself looking forward to a joint every evening. Our sex life is back on track, not because I enjoy it but because I couldn't care less. I go through the motions of opening the shop and working with William, though he turns up less and less regularly. On the other hand, Lketinga spends nearly the whole day in the shop now, and tourists turn up with their cameras and camcorders. My husband continues to ask for money to be photographed, which annoys me. He says he doesn't see why people want to take pictures of us: it's not as if we're monkeys. I can see his point.

Tourists keep asking where our daughter is because they think Napirai belongs to the babysitter. I have to explain to them that the child, who's now sixteen months old, is ours. The babysitter laughs along with us at their confusion until eventually Lketinga starts to wonder why they all make the same mistake. I tell him it doesn't matter in the slightest to us if they get things wrong. But he irritates our customers by going on at them about why they don't realize I'm her mother, until a few of them stalk out of the shop. He starts looking at the babysitter suspiciously too.

My sister has been back home for a month now. Edy turns up occasionally to ask if there have been any letters from her, but Lketinga starts to see even that in a different light. He's convinced Edy's coming to see me, and when one day he catches me buying marijuana from him, he starts to go on at me like I'm a major criminal and threatens to report me to the police.

My own husband—threatening to have me thrown in jail, even though he knows how awful conditions are! The laws against drugs in Kenya are very strict, and Edy has to work hard to persuade him not to go to the police in Ukunda. I'm standing there speechless, not even able to cry: at the end of the day I need the drugs to put up with him. Instead he makes me promise never to smoke marijuana again, saying he doesn't want to live with someone who breaks Kenyan law. *Miraa*, according to him, is legal, so it's not the same thing.

Then my husband goes through all my pockets and sniffs every cigarette I light up. Back home he tells the whole story to Priscilla and anyone else who's listening. They all act shocked and make me feel rotten. Every time I go to the toilet Lketinga comes with me. He won't even let me go to the shop in the village. All I do now is go to our shop, come home, and sit on the bed. The only thing that matters to me is my baby. Napirai seems to sense that I'm not happy. She won't leave my side and keeps saying "Mama, Mama" and a few other words I can't make out. Priscilla now keeps her distance from us; she doesn't want any trouble.

I don't even get any joy out of work anymore. Lketinga is there the whole time. He keeps an eye on me either in the shop or from the bar of the Chinese restaurant and empties my bag out up to three times a day. Once some Swiss tourists turn up, but I don't feel much like talking to them and say I'm not feeling well and have a stomachache. My husband turns up just as one of the Swiss women picks up Napirai and says how much she looks like the babysitter. Once again I'm telling her she's made a mistake when Lketinga butts in and says: "Corinne, why all people know, this child is not yours?" With that one sentence he wipes out my last hope and my final ounce of respect for him.

I stand up and, without answering any of the questions the others are putting to me, walk out as if in a trance and cross the road to the Chinese restaurant. I ask the owner if I can use his phone, ring the Swissair office in Nairobi, and book the next available flight to Zurich for myself and my sixteen-month-old child. It takes a while before they can tell me there are seats available in four days' time. I know that they don't take telephone bookings from individuals, but I beg the woman to keep the seats for me, telling her I can only pay for and pick up the tickets the day before departure, but it's extremely important and I will definitely be there. My heart skips a beat when she says the word "okay."

I walk back to the shop slowly and announce straight out that I'm going to Switzerland on vacation. At first Lketinga gives an uneasy laugh, then says I can go but without Napirai, so he can be sure I'll come back. I answer in a tired voice that my baby is coming with me. As always I'll be back, but after all the stress with the shop I need a break before the high season starts in December. Lketinga doesn't agree and refuses to sign a piece of paper allowing me to leave. Nonetheless, two days later I pack my bags. Priscilla and Sophia talk to him. They're all convinced I'll be back.

The Final Flight

On our last day I leave everything behind. My husband insists that I pack just a few things for Napirai. I hand over all the bank account cards to him to prove that I'll be back. Who would give away so much money, a car, and a fully stocked shop?

Torn this way and that and not knowing whether to believe me, he comes with Napirai and me as far as Mombasa. Right up until we're about to set off for Nairobi he still hasn't signed the piece of paper. I ask him one last time and tell him I'm going anyway. I'm so burned out internally, so emptied of all emotion, that there are no more tears left.

The driver starts up the engine. Lketinga is standing next to us in the bus and once again has one of the other passengers translate the letter I've written out which says that I have the permission of my husband, Lketinga Leparmorijo, to leave Kenya with our daughter, Napirai, for three weeks' vacation in Switzerland.

The bus driver beeps his horn for the third time. Lketinga scribbles his mark on the piece of paper and says: "I don't know if I see you and Napirai again!" and then he jumps off the bus, and we set off. It's only now that I burst into tears and I look through the window as we rush past the scenes I know and have loved and say good-bye to them.

Dear Lketinga,

I hope you can forgive what I am about to tell you: I am not coming back to Kenya.

I have been thinking a lot about us. For more than three and a half years I loved you so much that I was prepared to live with you in Barsaloi. I presented you with a daughter, but ever since the day you alleged that child was someone else's I could no longer think of you in the same way. You realized this too.

I have never wanted anyone else, and I never lied to you, but in all these years you never understood me, perhaps because I'm a mzungu. My world and yours are very different, but I thought that one day we could live together in the same world.

Now, however, after the last chance we had in Mombasa, I realize that you are unhappy and I certainly am. We are both still young and can't go on living the way we are. Right now you won't understand me, but in time you'll see that you will be happier with someone else. It's easy for you to find a new wife who lives in your world, but find a Samburu woman this time and not another white woman. We're too different. One day you'll have lots of children.

I have taken Napirai with me because she's all I have left. I also know that I will never have any other children. Without Napirai I couldn't survive. She is my life! Please, Lketinga, forgive me. I'm simply not strong enough anymore to continue living in Kenya. I always felt very alone there, had no friends, and you treated me like a criminal. You didn't even know you were doing it . . . that's just Africa. But I tell you once again: I never did anything wrong.

Now you have to make up your mind what to do with the shop. I'm writing to Sophia too. She can help you. I'm giving you the whole business, but if you want to sell it, you'll have to deal with Anil, the Indian.

I will help you from here as much as I can, and I won't leave you in the lurch. If you have problems, tell Sophia. The rent for the shop is paid up until the middle of December, and even if you don't want to work there anymore you must talk to Anil. I'm giving you the car too and am enclosing the signed paperwork for you. If you want to sell the car you should get at least 80,000 shillings. You will have to find someone reliable to help you. Then you will be a rich man.

Please don't be sad, Lketinga. You're young and good-looking, and you'll find a better wife. Napirai will always remind me happily of you. Please try to understand me! I would have died in Kenya, and I don't think that's what you wanted. My family don't think ill of you, they still like you but we are just too different.

Best wishes from Corinne and family

Dear James,

I hope you are okay. I am in Switzerland and very sad. I realize now that I can never come back to Kenya. I have written to Lketinga today to tell him. I no longer have the strength to live with your brother. I felt very alone there, just because I was white. You saw how things were with us. I gave him another chance in Mombasa, but things got worse instead of better. I loved him very much, you know. But the argument over Napirai ripped a huge hole in that love, and from that day on we only argued from morning to night. Every thought he had was negative. I don't think he really knows what love is, because if you love someone, you can't say things like that to her.

Mombasa was my final hope, but he didn't change. It was like a prison. We opened a good shop, but I don't think he's capable of working there on his own. Please go to Mombasa as soon as possible and talk to him! He has nobody left now and is all on his own. If he wants to sell the shop I can talk to Anil on the phone, but I have to know what he wants to do. He can keep the car too. Please, James, go to Mombasa as soon as you can because Lketinga will need you very much when he gets my letter.

I will help as much as I can from Switzerland. If he sells everything he will be rich, but he'll have to be careful or else your large family will simply use up all the money fast. . . .

Please explain everything to Mama. I love her and will never forget her. Unfortunately I can't speak to her. Tell her I tried everything to live with Lketinga, but his head was in another world. Please write back soon when you get this letter. I have a lot of problems myself and don't know if I can stay in Switzerland. If not, I will move to Germany. For the next three months I shall be living with my mother.

Best wishes and love,
Corinne

Dear Father Giuliani,

Since October 6, 1990, I have been back in Switzerland. I won't be coming back to Kenya. I no longer have the strength to live with my husband. I wrote to him two weeks ago to tell him this, and I'm now waiting for a reply. It will be a hard blow to him because I left him thinking I was only going to Switzerland on vacation. Otherwise he would never have allowed me to leave the country with Napirai.

As you know, we opened up a great shop on the south coast and did good business from the very first day. But relations between my husband and me did not improve. He was so jealous, even when I just talked to the tourists. In all those years he never trusted me. In Mombasa it was like living in prison. We spent the whole time arguing, which was no good for Napirai either.

My husband has a good heart, but there's something wrong with his head. It's hard for me to say that, but I'm not the only one who thinks so. All our friends abandoned us, and even some of the tourists were scared of him. It wasn't bad every day, but by the end it was almost every day. I have left him with everything: the shop, the car, etc. He can sell it all and go back to Barsaloi as a rich man. I would be happy if he were to find a good wife and have lots of children.

I am enclosing a few Kenyan shillings with this letter, which you might give to my husband's mother. I still have money in Barclays Bank, and perhaps you could see to it that this goes to Mama? I would be very grateful to you. Please let me know.

I have written this letter to you so that you will understand my side of the story if you hear what has happened from other people. You must believe I did my best, and I hope God will forgive me.

Best wishes,
Corinne and Napirai

Hi, Sophia!

I've just put the phone down after speaking to you and Lketinga. I'm really sad and can't stop crying. I've just told you that I'm not coming back and it's true. I knew that even before I got here. You know my husband a little. I loved him as I've never loved anyone in my life. I was prepared to live a proper Samburu life for him. I was ill so often in Barsaloi, but I stayed there because I loved him. But a lot of things changed after Napirai was born. One day he alleged she wasn't even his child. After that, my love for him was jaded. Our time together turned into an emotional roller coaster, and he regularly treated me badly.

Sophia, I swear to you on the Bible that I never had another man, not once! But I had to live with accusations from morning to night. I gave my husband one last chance in Mombasa, but I can't go on living like that. He didn't even notice he was doing it. I gave up everything for him, even my native country. Of course, I changed too but under the circumstances I think that's not surprising. I feel really sorry for him and for myself. I still don't know where I'm going to live now.

My biggest problem is Lketinga. He doesn't have anybody for the shop and can't run it himself. Please let me know if he intends to keep it. I would be happy if he could manage, but if not he should sell everything. The same goes for the car. Napirai is staying with me. I know she will be happier like that. Please, Sophia, look after Lketinga for a bit. He's going to have so many problems, and I'm afraid I can't help him much. If I came back to Kenya he would never let me return to Switzerland.

I hope his brother James will be coming down to Mombasa. I've written to him.

Help him deal with the business. I know you have problems of your own, and I hope for your sake that they sort themselves out. I wish you all the best and that you find another girlfriend. Napirai and I will never forget you.

All my very best,
Corinne

© AI Verlag, München

CORINNE HOFMANN has written three books based on her life story, including two sequels to *The White Masai—Back from Africa,* which is a bestseller in Germany, and *Reunion in Barsaloi,* which was released in 2005. She lives with her teenage daughter in Switzerland.